FAITH ALIVE

edited by
Father John Redford
and
Rowanne Pasco

Hodder & Stoughton
LONDON SYDNEY AUCKLAND TORONTO

"*FAITH ALIVE*": by The Reverend John Redford STL LSS

NIHIL OBSTAT: The Reverend James Tolhurst DD

IMPRIMATUR: The Right Reverend Monsignor John Hine
Ph.L

British Library Cataloguing in Publication Data

Redford, John
   Faith alive.
   1. Catholic church
   I. Title   II. Pasco, Rowanne
   282

   ISBN 0-340-49380-2 Hbk
   ISBN 0-340-48716-X Pbk

Contents

ACKNOWLEDGEMENTS

We cannot thank all of the people who have helped us in Faith Alive; the number would run into hundreds, if not thousands.

But some people deserve our very special thanks.

My thanks are first due to Rowanne Pasco, who, when Editor of The Universe, asked me to become General Editor of Faith Alive, thus beginning the inspiring idea.

Then, I would like to thank my own Archbishop, Michael Bowen, who released me from responsibility in the archdiocese of Southwark to work on Faith Alive, and supported us all the way.

Gerald McGuinness, Kieran Moore, and Kevin Grant also played important editorial and managerial roles in setting up and publicising the course, for which we are most grateful.

But most of all, our thanks are due to Anne White, editorial assistant of the Universe course, who laboured ceaselessly to subedit the weekly supplements, organised the hugely successful correspondence course, and ran the Faith Alive study days up and down the country using her own excellent slide presentation.

Helping us also to produce the original Universe supplements was a first-class editorial team, who spared time from their busy lives to look at the material before publication and to take an important share in writing for Faith Alive; Dom Henry Wansborough, Dr Francis Clarke, Fr Michael Prior, and Fr Austin Flannery. Our thanks are also due to Mgr. George Leonard for giving a great deal of his time and advice.

We would also like to thank Tim Anderson, David Rooke, and the staff at Hodder and Stoughton for all their patient work in helping us re-edit the material.

I would like personally to thank Bishop Gordon Wheeler, who received me into full communion with the Catholic Church in 1960, and who gave me many insights into the Faith, especially in my early years.

Finally, both Rowanne and I would like above all to thank our mothers, from whom we first learnt the Good News. This book would never have happened without them.

John Redford

Prefaces

Preface by Cardinal Hume
Archbishop of Westminster

I warmly commend 'Faith Alive' as an inspiring presentation of the Catholic faith for adults and congratulate the many people from all walks of life who have contributed to it.

I pray that it will lead many Catholics to a deeper understanding of the riches of our tradition and give many Christians of other denominations and people of other faiths enlightenment in their spiritual journey.

Preface by Cardinal Ó Fiaich
Archbishop of Armagh

I am delighted to learn that the 'Faith Alive' series of articles published recently in 'The Universe' is now finding its way into book form. I am sure that many of those who read the articles week by week will appreciate having them all together in one book and I am equally sure that those who come upon the book for the first time will find in it a well of inspiration for their faith.

The 'Faith Alive' series is a compendium of the teaching of the Church expressed in 20th century language and enriched by the teachings of the Second Vatican Council.

Preface by Cardinal Ward
Archbishop of Cardiff

I would like to congratulate and thank you and 'The Universe' for this valuable contribution to the life and witness of the Catholic faith in this country. I hope the book will become a best-seller within and beyond the Catholic community of Britain.

Preface by Cardinal Winning
Archbishop of Glasgow

The great need today for adult formation in the faith is rivalled only by the hunger in people for that very kind of formation. Both need and hunger can be satisfied in many different ways. One of these is by 'Faith Alive', and I am very happy to note the development of this Universe project. It is a sign of the times, not a sign of declining concern but a real wakening of the Christian conscience. I wish it every success.

Introduction

Who is this book for?

THIS BOOK originally appeared as a series of 48 weekly supplements in *The Universe*, the best-selling religious newspaper in Britain.

It was felt that there was a great need to 'update' the adult Catholic's understanding of the Church and its faith, particularly since the changes introduced by the Second Vatican Council, summoned by Pope John XXIII in 1962.

The course 'Faith Alive' was a great success. But, in re-editing 'Faith Alive' into the form of a book, we have a much wider readership in mind.

First, there is the person who is thinking of joining the Catholic Church. These days, since the introduction of the new Rite for Christian Initiation of Adults (RCIA), enquirers are encouraged to discuss and share their faith, and to follow a whole process of growth towards commitment. This book is intended to be a handbook for those following RCIA.

Then, there is the ecumenical dimension. No Christian today should be 'boxed off' into a private denomination. We are all learning about each other's vision of the Christian faith, with a view to eventual full unity. We trust that 'Faith Alive' will help every committed Christian, of whatever denomination, to grow in his or her faith, whether or not there is full agreement on every point of doctrine.

The same applies to those of other faiths than the Christian. The meeting called by Pope John Paul II at Assisi in 1987 was a great landmark in the mutual recognition by different religions of each others' good faith. 'Faith Alive', while not compromising on what we know to be essential points of the Catholic faith, tries to present that faith in a way which emphasises what we have in common, rather than that on which we disagree.

However, the last group to be mentioned, and for whom this book is intended, is perhaps the largest and the most important target. The twentieth century is distinctive to this extent, that for the first time in the history of the human race, large numbers of people profess to no religion at all.

It is our conviction that this state of affairs is simply unnatural. Man – a word used as a description of the human species – is a religious animal. 'Our heart is restless, O God', said St Augustine, 'until we find our rest in Thee'. And he ought to know, because he tried to avoid God for many years.

This book, therefore, is addressed most specially to a person who is not particularly committed to any religion, but whose mind is not closed to the possibility that there might be something in it all.

And, of course, the distinction between 'believers' and 'unbelievers' is perhaps not so great as we imagine. Many committed Christians of many years standing, pillars of their congregation, even clergy, will have doubts about their faith, even its most basic fundamentals. And many committed atheists and agnostics will sometimes wonder whether their anger about religious superstition is not after all the love of some infinite Unknown Being trying to get out.

I will never forget, as a young curate, visiting a house, and asking a man, 'What do you think about God?' I expected him to say something like 'Don't ask me about all that rubbish. You Christians are all hypocrites, anyway.'

Instead, his answer completely threw me out of balance. 'I just do not know what I think about God', he said. 'I'm really waiting for you people to give me some idea.'

Well, here is an attempt at least.

John Redford

Foreword

FAITH ALIVE came about partly because I did not go to university. Much to the dismay of my convent school headmistress I left school as soon as I could to become a reporter. In those days journalism was not desirable for convent girls.

For many years I regretted missing university life. It seemed I had made a wrong decision. But, as I later discovered, it is not always easy to judge whether what happens to us is for the best or not.

In 1971 the Open University started in England and at once I became a student. Suddenly anyone could go to university.

The Open University was far from just another correspondence course. With study groups, seminars, weekend lectures and summer schools it soon became a way of life.

During my nine years as editor of the Catholic newspaper *The Universe* I saw the great need for teaching of the Catholic faith and I found myself wondering whether the concept of the Open University, which had proved so successful, could be transferred to the Catholic faith.

The Vatican II documents on the media pointed out that it was almost impossible for the Church to carry out Christ's command to teach all nations without using the media, and Catholic newspapers are in a particularly strong position to do this. *The Universe* had one great advantage over the Open University. There was no postage. Why could we not simply add the education unit to the paper each week? The readers would get it totally free.

The need was there not because readers wanted a university degree but because they wanted to know more about their faith. They wanted to understand exactly what the Church had said at the Second Vatican Council and how it affected their lives.

Now those 48 newspaper units have been turned into this book. There has been much re-writing and re-thinking to produce something for a wider audience as Fr Redford has explained.

Many books have been written to help people understand Christianity. What makes Faith Alive different is that we have tried to present the teaching of the Catholic Church in the language and style most familiar to people, that of a popular newspaper. We have also tried to relate our text to everyday experience.

Faith Alive is also unique in that it has not been written by a single author, still less by a committee. It is a team effort, with people involved from all areas of church life – theologians, journalists, parish priests, nuns, teachers, lay people young and old and middle-aged. Representatives of the whole Church have been involved.

Looking at Christianity in this way has certainly helped me in my journey of faith. I hope it helps you.

Rowanne Pasco

I am delighted that the work begun by Rowanne Pasco and Father John Redford has come to fruition in the book 'Faith Alive'. I hope particularly that it will provide an important source book for the new Rite of Christian Initiation of Adults, which has such exciting possibilities for the renewal of Christians in the church today.

Michael Bowen
Archbishop of Southwark
(Course Patron of 'Faith Alive')

FAITH ALIVE

1-Faith

always needs to grow.
is a gift from the Holy Spirit.
is our 'yes' to God's revelation.
throws light on our life in the world.

'All of us need faith in something or someone . . .'

WHAT IS FAITH?

'Faith' is not easy to define. In fact, in the broadest meaning of the term, faith is not confined to what we call 'religious people' at all.

We talk of sports stars having faith in their own ability. We speak of politicians having faith in their party policies. We refer to people 'believing in themselves'.

We live in a 'scientific' age, when, we might think, we rely on hard facts rather than on faith. We are taught not to go beyond the evidence of our senses, or of our reason, but to verify everything scientifically before we accept it as true.

But real life is not like that. In our day-to-day decisions, we cannot be given copper-bottomed guarantees, firm evidence for everything. What businessman can be sure that the market will go in a certain direction? What computer will give absolute certainty that you are matched perfectly with your partner? What pop star can be absolutely sure that the new record will hit the charts?

All of us need faith in something or someone, in order to make our life worth while, even possible.

RELIGIOUS FAITH

'Faith is the assurance of things hoped for, the conviction of things not seen.' So says the Epistle to the Hebrews, an early Christian work (c. AD 70–90).

The essence of faith is that it relates to trust in something or someone in a matter which goes beyond the immediate evidence of our senses. This would be true, even if our faith was in our country winning the World Cup. Even more is it true of religious faith.

All the world religions promote faith

in a reality beyond our sight. Religious faith holds that such a reality exists; and, perhaps even more important, that this invisible reality can be kindly disposed towards us, if we begin to relate to It in some way or other, by offering It prayers, sacrifices and so on.

Religions differ as to the nature of this unseen reality. Primitive religions present visible objects of worship, such as trees or statues, which are believed to possess some kind of invisible power (polytheism, 'many gods'). Some religions, particularly in the East, do not make this unseen reality separate from the world, but make it in some way the totality of all things (pantheism, 'all (is) god').

But the religion with which most of us are familiar in the West relates to one God, whether we are Muslim, Jewish or Christian: that is to say, this one supreme deity is not part of the world, nor even identifiable with the whole of reality. Rather, this One True God exists 'above' everything but also 'in' everything, as infinite Mind or Spirit.

Something else is also common to Muslims, Jews and Christians, in their faith in the One God. They believe that God has 'revealed' himself and his will to those who accept him in faith.

The power and vitality of these three great monotheistic world religions is self-evident. Two thousand million people worldwide publicly profess their faith in this One God. It derives from an extraordinary kind of religious faith; belief that this Supreme Deity not only exists, but actually has our interests at heart. Muslims, Jews and Christians are all linked together by reference back to a nomadic wanderer, dated most likely about 1800 BC, called Abraham.

The book of Genesis tells us that this man Abraham, or Abram, was given a message by the Supreme God, telling him that 'I shall bless you and make your name famous' (*Gen 12:2*). God did not first tell Abraham what to do. God just promised him good fortune. And Abraham believed.

CHRISTIAN FAITH

Christian faith differs from Jewish and Muslim faith in one crucial respect.

Muslims and Jews see God's revelation as culminating in giving his 'will' or 'law' in a book, or collection of books. The Muslims venerate the Koran, a book laying down the way of life and faith which they believe was dictated by the Angel Gabriel to the prophet Mohammed by Allah, the One God. Jews believe that the same Supreme God Elohim or JHWH revealed his will

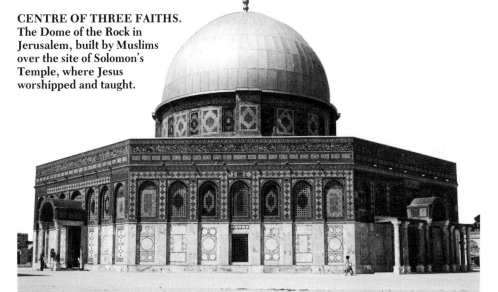

CENTRE OF THREE FAITHS.
The Dome of the Rock in Jerusalem, built by Muslims over the site of Solomon's Temple, where Jesus worshipped and taught.

most of all to Moses, the prophets and the wise men in the holy books of their tradition (Taanach), the most holy of these, which they keep in their Tabernacle, is the Torah, the five books of Moses.

Christians also have holy books, treated as the inspired word of God. What they call the 'Old Testament' is mostly identical with the Jewish Taanach; and, in addition, the 'New Testament' books which are seen as the fulfilment of the 'Old Testament'. All this, we shall explain later.

The difference is that, for the Christian, God's revelation, his 'Word', is first and foremost not in a book, but in a man, Jesus of Nazareth. He himself was and is (because Christians believe this Jesus to be ascended into heaven now) the revelation of God's will. His whole life was God's message to the whole of the human race. Jesus Christ was and is God become man.

What makes Christian faith distinctive is that, in the words of St John's Gospel, 'Jesus is the Christ, the Son of God'; and, 'believing this, you may have life in his name' (*John 20:31*).

CATHOLIC FAITH

Among the Christian denominations, the largest is the 'Catholic' or 'Roman Catholic' Church, with roughly eight hundred million members worldwide.

A distinctive feature of the Catholic Church is its belief that the 'Pope', the Bishop of Rome, is the successor of Peter the chief of Christ's apostles (see *Matt 16:13–20*), and is entrusted with Peter's authority given by Christ to lead the Church on earth.

Throughout this book, we will be referring to this Church as 'The Catholic Church' rather than 'The Roman Catholic Church'; and this particular choice of title may need explanation, above all in these days when Christians are making strenuous efforts to overcome differences, and work towards unity.

Some Christians would prefer us to call ourselves 'Roman Catholics', because they think of themselves, though Church of England or Lutheran, as equally 'Catholic' as ourselves. After all, they recite the same Creed as ourselves every Sunday, in which they say 'We believe in the Holy Catholic Church . . .' Is it not arrogant of us 'Roman Catholics' to use the term 'Catholics' of ourselves, thus excluding everyone else from that term?

St Peter's Basilica in Rome.

We deliberately decided to use the term 'Catholic', as distinct from 'Roman Catholic', because we do not wish to narrow the concept of what we believe. The word 'Catholic' means 'Universal', 'According to the Whole'; and we wish to emphasise the universality of our church, even though our Chief Pastor on earth lives in Rome.

The word 'Catholic' without any qualifying adjective also stakes a claim for our church. 'The Baptists' are called such because they place emphasis on Believers' Baptism (see Ch. 27). 'The Church of England' claims in a special way to be the national church in this country. 'Evangelicals' believe that they have returned to the pure 'evangel' or 'gospel' of Jesus Christ. The name of those Christian groups stakes a claim for their church, or group of churches.

The term 'Catholic Church' stakes out our claim that, in order to achieve full 'Catholicity', full universality, it is

necessary to be in visible communion with the Bishop of Rome. We intend, again, to explain this more fully later.

HOW DO I COME TO FAITH?

First of all, faith is a 'gift of God'. We cannot come to faith simply by our own intellectual efforts. This is because faith, of its essence, leads us to trust in the revelation of the Unseen God. To believe in God, we need God's help.

That is why it is most important to pray for the gift of faith, even if we are not even quite sure that God exists! In the Gospels, a father who wanted his boy cured was challenged by Jesus saying 'Everything is possible for one who has faith'; to which the man replied, 'I have faith. Help my lack of faith' (*Mark* 9:24). This paradox of belief and unbelief is in all of us to some extent.

But this does not mean that all that we can do to come to faith is to pray. We can, and must, work at it, like every other human 'gift' (a talent for music, courage under difficulties). Success in our quest for faith is, like success in show business, ten per cent inspiration, and ninety per cent perspiration.

QUESTIONS OF FAITH
1. What do you believe in?
2. Who has influenced your faith most?
3. How has your faith been tested?
4. Have you any particular expectations from reading this book?

WHAT THE PEOPLE SAY
'Faith is not just doctrine, though that is important. It is a personal thing, something that helps me every day. My faith has changed a lot since I was a child. Then it was a duty but now I go to Mass for myself. It has grown since I started work, meeting other people, and also by looking at the situation – the problems – in the world.'

LIGHT FROM THE COUNCIL
The Second Vatican Council was summoned by Pope John XXIII, and opened in 1962. Its declared aim was to renew the whole Catholic Church. Throughout this book, we will be quoting extensively from this Council, because it throws light on so many aspects of our faith.

'For faith throws a new light on everything, manifests God's design for man's total vocation, and thus directs the mind to solutions which are fully human.' (Pastoral Constitution on the Church in the Modern World, para 11.)

LIGHT FROM THE WORD
'I do have faith. Help the little faith I have' (*Mark* 9:24).

2-The Human Person

is made in God's image.
has infinite worth.
is part of a sinful human race.
is part of a race saved by Christ.

HOW MUCH ARE YOU WORTH?

Some people try to put a price on another human being in terms of how much that person can earn, or benefit other people. For the Christian, no limit can be set on the worth of any person.

God loves us, just as we are. He made us in his own image and likeness. Alone among living creatures, we can be aware of ourselves – to know that we know – and of a power which we call 'God' greater than ourselves, an infinite spirit.

God created us for a loving relationship with himself and with each other. But this image has been tarnished by what we call 'sin'.

One effect of this is that we tend to develop a low opinion of ourselves. When we do not experience the love of other people, we feel that God does not love us either. We think he can only love us if we are good and successful. This is particularly true when we experience misfortune.

But God the Father sent Jesus his Son to show us the way to become really ourselves again; to show us how to love with God's own love, and to realise to the full our human dignity.

The challenge for the Church and for each Christian is to find a way to proclaim this Good News; to love and not to be afraid to show it. This is how the early Christian community attracted so many people.

The One who created the galaxy created you and me.

GOD DOES NOT MAKE RUBBISH!

Christians believe that God created all human beings in love, and calls us to be his children, brothers and sisters in one human family. 'God saw everything he had made, and indeed it was very good' (*Gen 1:31*).

It is important to remember that we are essentially good, since God creates us, calls us by name, and makes us holy. God does not make rubbish. People can become so obsessed with their own sin and failure that they grow blind to the goodness of God which is in them.

Christian faith is meant to heal us and set us free. Faith gives us a profound knowledge and experience that 'God is love' (*1 John 4:8*). This reality is shown in our creation and our redemption. It makes us believe in ourselves no matter what happens. Every person has a value and a dignity, which makes them lovable.

'. . . since God has loved us so much, we too should love one another' (*1 John 4:11*).

Human dignity is not always easy to recognise; particularly among the outcasts of society. Mother Teresa is an outstanding example of a Christian who finds this dignity in the poorest of the poor in India. She started her homes for the dying people abandoned on the streets when she saw a woman lying on the roadside. 'She had been half eaten by rats and ants,' said Mother Teresa. 'I took her to the hospital, but they could not do anything for her. I went to the municipality, and asked them to give me a place where I could bring these people, because on the same day I had found many others dying in the streets.' She took them to a Hindu Temple, the only place available. Within twenty-four hours, she had started the home for the destitute, sick and dying. About a thousand people every year are brought to her, and half of them die.

'We want them to know there are people who really love them, who really want them, at least for the few hours they want to live; to know human and divine love; and that they are the children of God. The work is only the expression of the love we have for God. We do it to God, to Christ, and that's why we try to do it as beautifully as possible.'

HUMAN NATURE HAS A FLIP SIDE

God does not make rubbish. But good products can be spoiled. Christian faith teaches that the human race is tarnished by sin. From the beginning, we have disobeyed God revealing himself to us

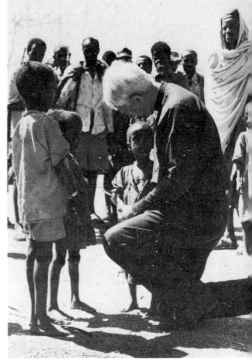

'We want them to know there are people who really love them'. Cardinal Hume visits famine victims.

in our conscience. This does not mean that the human person has less value; but it does mean that we are weak in our resistance to sin. We must always take this into account.

WHAT IS SIN?

Many people think of 'sin' as something 'naughty but nice'; God like a miserable father who cannot bear us enjoying ourselves, gives us rules just to make us unhappy. In reality, sin is a stunting of our human growth, a loss of our dignity as human beings. Adam and Eve, after eating of the forbidden fruit, are ashamed of their own bodies, and have to cover themselves up. They cannot bear to look at each other. This is a powerful image of the loss of dignity and pride in ourselves as made in God's image.

This story of the 'Fall of Man is recounted in Genesis 2,3. This is a popular story, and is not intended to be an accurate history of the creation of man in detail. But the Catholic Church teaches that the human race has disobeyed God from the beginning of its history; and that the effect of this has been passed on to the whole of the human race. Thereby, Man and Woman (Adam and Eve in the biblical story) lost their perfect happiness, which can only be with God.

What was this sin? In the book of Genesis, we are told that this was eating from the fruit of a tree which God told Adam and Eve not to touch. (Note that the Bible does not say that it was an 'apple', *Gen* 3:2.) Clearly, this element of the story is symbolic. We do not know what the 'original sin' actually was; except that this was a deliberate act of disobedience against God.

But the important thing about the story of Adam and Eve is that it is a parable of our own human story. We are constantly having choices, and often tend to make the wrong ones.

But, just as the Christian believes that Paradise was lost by the folly of one person, so we believe that it was regained for us by the perfect life and love, and sacrificial death of one Person, Jesus Christ, God's divine Son.

Through this, God has redeemed human nature, offering it forgiveness and a new life. But it is up to us to accept or reject this offer.

Being baptised into the Christian community signifies our acceptance of this offer, and frees us from Original Sin; but, like a sick patient who is cured from an illness, we are still weak. We need the daily strength of the Holy Spirit to conquer that weakness, and the support of each other. That is one important reason for the existence of the Church, the community of believers.

LIGHT FROM THE COUNCIL

'Believers and unbelievers agree almost unanimously that all things on earth should be ordained to man as to their centre and summit.'

'But what is man? . . . Sacred Scripture teaches that man was created "to the image of God", as able to know and love his creator, and as set by him over all earthly creatures . . . So God, as we read again in the Bible, saw "all the things that he had made, and they were very good"' (*Gen 1:31*). But 'when man looks into his own heart he finds that he is drawn towards what is wrong and sunk in many evils which cannot come from his good creator' . . . 'But the Lord himself came to free and strengthen man, renewing him inwardly . . .' (Pastoral Constitution on the Church in the Modern World, para 12–13).

The value of a human being?

SIN IS . . .
a rejection of God's love.
a turning in on self.
an offence against conscience.
hurting someone who loves me.
blocking the flow of God's love to me and
   through me to others.
being a hypocrite.
something like sand in a lovely cake or in
   the cogs of a machine.

PLACE FOR PRAYER
Lord, of your goodness give me
compassion for myself, and for others, and
never let me give up trying for the sake of
your Son, who genuinely loved and cared
about sinners and outcasts. (*Michael
Hollings and Etta Gullick.*)

LIGHT FROM THE WORD
*It was you who created my inmost
   self,
and put me together in my mother's
   womb;
for all these mysteries I thank you;
for the wonder of myself, for the
   wonder of your works.*
(*Psalm 139:13,14*)

QUESTIONS
1. Jesus said 'love your neighbour as
   yourself' (*Mark 12:31*). What does
   loving yourself mean in Christian
   terms?
2. Which people have been 'images of
   God' for you? (They could be people
   you know personally or people you
   know about.)

DON'T CHANGE
I was a neurotic for years. I was anxious
and depressed and selfish. Everyone
kept telling me to change.

I resented them, and I agreed with
them, and I wanted to change, but
simply couldn't, no matter how hard I
tried.

What hurt the most was that, like
the others, my best friend kept insisting
that I change. So I felt powerless and
trapped.

Then, one day, he said to me, 'Don't
change. Don't change. Don't change
. . . I love you as you are.'

I relaxed. I came alive. And suddenly
I changed!

Now I know that I couldn't really
change until I found someone who
would love me whether I changed or
not.

IS THAT HOW YOU LOVE ME,
GOD?

From: *The Song of the Bird*, Anthony de
Mello SJ (*Image Books*)

GOD'S IMAGE
We say, 'He's the image of his father'.
What we mean is that in his looks and in
his behaviour, that person is just like his
parent.

We are the 'image of God' (*Gen 1:27*)
because we have intelligence and so can
create, we are immortal, in that our
'soul' will never die, we can love others,
we have responsibility for creation.

We are not a perfect image of God. He
is infinite, we are limited. The perfect
image of God is Jesus Christ, the eternal
Son.

3-The World We Live In

is the home of human society.
is destined to become God's Kingdom.
will only be happy when human rights are respected.
needs to be enlightened by God's Word.

A COMMON criticism of religious people is that 'they are so heavenly minded that they are no earthly use'. This attitude springs from two mistaken attitudes to religion, which run deep in Western society.

First, religion is seen as a private affair, between ourselves and God. Our duty is to save our souls and go to heaven. Other people are seen as either a hindrance to our salvation; or simply there to be 'used' for our path to God.

Second, religion is seen as an escape from the world. The world is like a battlefield, which we have to go through in order to get to heaven. The things of this world are seen as either to help us get through this battlefield, or which might destroy us. Either way, they are essentially ugly.

There is a grain of truth in both positions. There is a secret area of life which is between ourselves and God, a 'space' which not even the closest loved one can enter. Often in scripture, the Christian life is referred to in military terms, as a 'fight of faith' (*1 Tim 6:12*); and Paul exhorts all Christians to 'put on the whole armour of God' (*Eph 6:11*).

But, alone, these attitudes spell the death of religion as an optimistic way of life which is one of the reasons why so many have abandoned the practice of religion.

Christian faith is essentially a Communion, sharing of the life of God in the spiritual family of the Church. Religious life in the Christian vision mirrors human life as it really is, 'man by his very nature stands completely in need of life in society' (Church in the Modern World, para 25).

The world is created by God as a sign of his love for us. It is not inherently evil.

There are so many of us. What are we all doing here?

Our task, as Christians, is to transform the world into the kingdom of God even though we know that this will never be complete until God finally brings it to perfection in his own way and in his own time.

HOW DO WE INTRODUCE THE KINGDOM OF GOD?

The whole life of Jesus was taken up with proclaiming the Kingdom of God in word and deed. This Kingdom has always been difficult to understand. Even when Jesus spoke about it people had problems in grasping its richness.

For this reason, Jesus spoke in parables about it. He likened it to treasure found in a field that changes one's whole outlook, or a net cast deep into the sea, or to a wedding feast.

The Kingdom proclaimed by Jesus is a new spiritual and social reality embracing all people through the love and mercy and justice of God, drawing them into one family. This new reality comes as a gift in this life when good news is brought to the poor, release to captives, liberty to the oppressed, sight to the blind, hearing to the deaf, healing to the sick, and life to the dead (*Luke 4:18; 7:22*). It is experienced as future promise when we realise that these present gifts have their true fulfilment in God.

The role of the Church is to continue this preaching and practice of Jesus. The Church is the sign and sacrament, the instrument and agent of the Kingdom of God in the world. This means that the Church like Christ is always signalling the power and presence of the reign of God: reaching out to the estranged, building bridges between the divided, healing broken lives, and gathering the scattered into the one new community of the Kingdom of God.

By Church we mean the community of women and men who profess 'Jesus Christ as Lord' (*Phil 2:11*), and actively commit themselves to his service.

Within this community, there

Healing.

Learning.

SIGNS OF THE KINGDOM

HEALING. Jesus cured 'all kinds of disease and sickness' (*Matt 4:23*). All kinds of healing are a sign of God's rule of love and power.

LEARNING. 'I have come into this world', said Jesus, 'so that those without sight may see . . .' (*John 9:39*). Jesus cured blindness, not only physical but also spiritual. Education is bringing about God's kingdom, in curing the blindness of ignorance.

FEEDING. 'I am the bread of life. No one who comes to me will ever hunger' (*John 6:35*). Christ also showed his concern with our material needs. When we feed the hungry, we are sharing in his ministry.

WORSHIPPING. 'The kingdom of God is among you' (*Luke 17:21*). The human race is called to 'converse with God'. (Pastoral Constitution on the Church in the Modern World, para 19.) Acknowledging God's rule, therefore, involves worshipping him.

SHARING. Jesus said to Zacchaeus, 'Hurry, because I am going to stay at your house today' (*Luke 19:5*). Communicating with each other is an essential part of being human. With modern technology and transport God's Kingdom COULD be brought much further forward.

are different callings and gifts:

'some should be apostles, some prophets, some evangelists, some pastors and teachers, for the work of the ministry' (*Eph 4:11–12*).

All Christians are responsible for bringing about the Kingdom of God – not just bishops, priests and sisters.

One of the great rediscoveries of Vatican II was that the Church's mission in the world is both religious and temporal, both spiritual and social. There had been a tendency to see this mission as mainly spiritual, concentrating on the salvation of souls for the next life. In contrast, the insight of Vatican II was taken up at the different Synods in Rome which spoke about the human development and liberation of the person in this life, referring to it as essential to the preaching of the Gospel of Christ (Justice in the World, 1971).

Paul VI pointed out that 'the Church has the duty to proclaim the liberation of millions of human beings . . . the duty of assisting the birth of this liberation, of giving witness to it, of ensuring that it is complete.' (Evangelisation in the Modern World, a.30 1975.)

This recognition of the social mission brings the Christian community into direct contact with the practical issues as something intrinsic to its mission. The Church, continuing the work of Christ on earth, must confront social problems. Thus, the Church is concerned to promote the dignity of the individual, to defend their rights, to fight discrimination, and to struggle for justice. More specifically, the Christian community must be involved in problems of poverty, unemployment, drug abuse, loneliness, divorce and homelessness.

Thus, the Church as People of God is

Feeding.

Sharing.

Worshipping.

Family and Friends.

Society.

Individual.

The Church.

WHERE IS THE KINGDOM?
THE INDIVIDUAL. God is present in each of us. He makes his home in us when we say 'yes' to him.
FAMILY AND FRIENDS. God's kingdom is in our relationships when we recognise him in each other.
SOCIETY. God rules in human institutions, national and international, when justice and human rights are respected.
THE CHURCH. God is present especially in the Church which is the sign of his kingdom on earth.

summoned to be a leaven in the world, an agent of social change.

This means the individual Christian is faced with new responsibilities. Being a member of the Christian community carries with it an explicit commitment to work to change society in the name of the coming reign of God set in motion by Christ.

APE OR ANGEL?

Are we worth saving?
Both instant creation and gradual evolution need an ultimate cause, an energy-source. Science can tell us what happened, but not why. God still remains the only convincing answer to the riddle of existence. Our human ability to think, choose and love, and our self-awareness are unique in the material world.

Natural selection does not explain the spiritual dimension of life. Man is more than 'the naked ape'. It is Christian teaching that each individual is made in the image of God. Even the fact that man is a social being bears this out. Human society reflects 'through a glass darkly' the life and love of the Trinity revealed in the New Testament.

New knowledge about the origins of life and of the universe emphasises the unity and wholeness of creation. This is entirely consistent with faith which tells us that creation expresses in different forms the outpouring of God's life and love. In the past, faith has focused on the relationship of the individual to God and of individuals to each other. Now there must also be a theology of nature; an understanding of our relationship to the created world.

God's Spirit always penetrated and gave meaning to all created things. After Christ became man, the material world takes on new significance bringing God closer to us. Flesh and blood, bread and wine, water, oil and the laying on of human hands make present his life and love. The Christian therefore approaches material things with respect and reverence. It is evil to exploit, pollute and squander resources. We are stewards, not overlords, of creation.

History also unfolds God's creative purpose. But God never invades our freedom and so the Holocaust and Hiroshima can happen, even in a world brought to life by a loving Father and in which all human beings are one people by birth and baptism, brothers and sisters of Christ. Faith in God and in life after death in no way absolves us from responsibility for this life and our world.

The achievements of the human race are a sign of God's greatness and the fulfilment of his loving design. The work to heal and restore the world continues until the end of time. 'After that will come the end, when Christ will hand over the Kingdom to God the Father' (*1 Cor 15:24*). Christianity believes in the final victory of God, which no power can stop.

SUMMARY – THE CHRISTIAN IN THE WORLD

*The world is good, created by
  God . . .*
But evil also exists in the world.
*Our vocation as human beings is to
  build up the world . . .*
*But we look beyond this world to a
  new heaven and a new earth.*
*Created things have their own
  laws . . .*
*But not independently from God their
  creator.*
*Evil in the world comes from our own
  free will . . .*
*But there is also a personal spirit of
  evil active in the world.*
Christ came to save the world . . .
*But he condemned the Prince of this
  World, Satan.*
*The human race constitutes one family
  under God . . .*
*But there is now a new family, the
  Church, being formed by Christ.*
*The whole world is destined for
  God . . .*
*But this can only happen through
  Christ and his Church.*

THE WORLD

The use of the word 'world' in the Bible carries two senses; one good, and the other bad.

In most texts, 'the world' has a good meaning. It refers to the universe, made and loved by God. This is the world which Christ came to live in and to save (*John 3:17*). Into this world we are all sent to preach the Gospel (*Matt 26:13*).

In other texts, however, 'the world' has a bad meaning. It refers to that dimension of the universe ruled over by the devil, or Satan. Thus the devil, in one of the temptations, shows our Lord all the kingdoms of the world, and offers them to him if he will do him homage (*Matt 4:9*). And, in the same sense, Jesus refers to the devil as 'The Prince of this World' (*John 14:30*).

Even in these texts, the omnipotent rule of God in his own world is not denied. It is only because the human race has given in to Satan that he has any rule, and only then because God allows it as a consequence of his creating us with free will.

Keep thoughts on things above; but watch below as well.

JUSTICE AND RIGHTS

The Ten Commandments look like a series of 'don'ts' but they are the basis of our society. Behind each of the negative statements, there is a positive principle. For instance, behind the commandment 'You shall not steal' lies a judgement of value: 'Respect your neighbour's property.'

Tradition has it that the Ten Commandments were given to Moses on Mount Sinai, but rather than being a sudden revelation they in fact developed in Israelite society, which remembered the famous escape from Egypt, and the 'forty years' wandering through the desert trying to find a land to settle. They were their 'bill of rights', the foundation of their way of life. Through them they were led to recognise their responsibilities to God and to each other. They also learned to value their dignity and rights as children of God. They had to survive in a rough world. But these ten rules – which could be remembered by counting on their fingers – ensured that violence was checked and true religion fostered.

Catholic theologians have always insisted that the Ten Commandments also spring from our own conscience.

They were written in our hearts as well as in Scripture.

The Ten Commandments

- YOU MUST HAVE NO OTHER GODS THAN ME
- YOU MUST NOT WORSHIP A GRAVEN IMAGE
- YOU MUST NOT MISUSE GOD'S NAME
- KEEP THE SABBATH DAY HOLY
- HONOUR YOUR FATHER AND YOUR MOTHER
- YOU MUST NOT KILL
- YOU MUST NOT COMMIT ADULTERY
- YOU MUST NOT STEAL
- YOU MUST NOT GIVE FALSE EVIDENCE
- YOU MUST NOT SET YOUR HEART ON WHAT BELONGS TO SOME-ONE ELSE

The Pastoral Constitution on the Church in the Modern World

– expressed at Vatican II. Note how these rights compare with and reflect the commandments themselves.

- FOOD, CLOTHING AND SHELTER
- THE RIGHT TO CHOOSE A STATE OF LIFE FREELY
- AND TO FOUND A FAMILY
- TO EDUCATION
- TO EMPLOYMENT
- TO A GOOD REPUTATION
- TO RESPECT
- TO APPROPRIATE INFORMATION
- TO ACTIVITY IN ACCORD WITH ONE'S OWN INFORMED CONSCIENCE
- TO PROTECTION OF PRIVACY
- AND TO RIGHTFUL FREEDOM IN MATTERS RELIGIOUS

QUESTIONS

1. We cannot fail to be aware of the power of sin in the world. Try to recall those occasions when you were convinced of the power of God, of his goodness, and of the certainty that good will win in the end.

2. 'Some Christians are so heavenly-minded that they are no earthly use.' What, in your opinion, are some of the practical contributions Christianity has made to the world?

4-God the Father

is the creator of the world.
is known as The Unknown.
is our loving heavenly Father.
calls us into relationship with himself, in this world and the next.

THE GOOD news for the human person, for society, and for the world is that there is Someone who loves us, cares for us and is able to provide for all our needs.

The Christian revelation names this Someone as God and goes on to say that God is Trinity. Another way of saying that is that God is community. The Father, the Son and the Holy Spirit are in a perfect communion of love. Their love initiates and empowers the faith of each individual. Their relationship is the model for the community of believers – the Church.

The Trinity (Latin for 'threefold unity') is a mystery. The revelation of God in Scripture and in the Church invites us to know God through our relationship with the Father, through the Son, in the power of the Spirit.

'You have made us for yourself, O God, and our heart is restless until it finds its rest in you' (St Augustine).

How do we experience God?

When Moses came down from the mountain, his face was shining from his personal encounter with God. God, for Moses, was not a boring Sunday chore. God inspired and enriched his life and also his relationships with others.

How can we come to, or regain, a sense of the transcendent Holy God?

EXPERIENCING GOD – IN PRAYER

The God of Christians is a hidden God. Though we can and should go a long way in seeking God through reason, God is 'beyond' reason. St Paul writes: 'Now we see in a mirror dimly' (1 Cor 13:12), and: 'we walk by faith, not by sight' (2 Cor 5:7).

Praying because we simply believe is essential. It does not deny but supplements the use of reason. For prayer experience we need scriptural study, the use of theological insights, shared experience of Christian living, practical involvement in loving God, self and neighbour.

In the Old Testament, God is so holy that his name is not to be used. Yahweh was substituted. God is distant, the smiter of enemies, the judge. People reading and even teaching the Old Testament can miss the trust shown by Abraham in prayer, the close contact of Jacob wrestling with the angel, the forgiveness of David, the immense patience of God as he reclaims Israel again and again from idolatry.

Yet God is also portrayed more gently; 'I have loved you with an everlasting love' (Jer 31:3): 'As one whom his mother comforts, so I will comfort you' (Isa 66:13). Patriarchs, prophets and writers of the psalms experienced his tenderness and closeness.

We share their experience when we read the Old Testament.

When Christ came, the heart of his good news was that every human being should come to address God as 'Father'. We are all included: 'Love your enemies and pray for those who persecute you, so that you may be sons of your Father who is in heaven; for he makes his sun rise on the evil and on the good' – 'pray then like this: Our Father,' (Matt 5, 6).

It seems a far cry from Yahweh to Father. But in the breakdown of distance between God in heaven and the men, women and children he has created in his world, Jesus is not satisfied with simply saying 'Father'; he uses the intimate, family name 'Abba' – daddy. This is his revelation of closeness and reality.

We know from our human experience that though we may be fortunate, it is not every child who is close enough to say 'daddy', let alone to live with the intimacy it means. Yet God offers this familiarity of his love. It is almost beyond belief . . . impossible.

Each one of us has access to the love of the Father through prayer and worship. This is the constant witness of millions of people, young and old, of all classes and colours and centuries. In prayer, events of life, the wonder of nature, and personal relationships, we experience the presence, power, compassion and love of Abba, who is the tenderness of mother and the strength of father.

NOTHING COMES FROM NOTHING

The arguments for God's existence have been presented by the greatest minds; Anselm, Kant, Newman, Berkeley, and above all in the Five Ways of St Thomas Aquinas. Philosophers dispute the validity of these proofs, and indeed no one can come to love God just as a result of logic. The gift of faith is needed. But all these proofs have their use in demonstrating that nothing comes from nothing. Either the world as we know it comes from nothing, and so everything is absurd, or there is an infinite creator, the cause of all things.

Thomas Aquinas puts it this way in his Argument from Causality:

In the observable world causes are found to be ordered in series; we never observe, nor ever could, something causing itself, for this would mean it

preceded itself, and this is not possible . . . One is therefore forced to suppose some first cause, to which everyone gives the name God. (Summa Theologiae, 1, q.2, a.3.)

Many people ask, 'If everything is caused by something, then who caused God?' The answer is almost as simple as the question. No one made God, because God, and God only, as the First Cause, is the Cause of all things that are made. We come into existence only when something causes us to exist, God simply is.

This is just the reply God gave to Moses, when Moses asked for God's name. God replied, 'I AM WHO I AM' (*Ex 3:14*).

St Thomas Aquinas, a rotund individual, loved English pickled herrings, and said at the end of his life that all he had written was straw. It is nice to know that a man with such a great mind was also human!

St Thomas Aquinas; called the 'Angelic Teacher'. But his frame, as well as his philosophy, also had body.

INTRODUCING CHILDREN TO GOD

It was a great moment when the little boy became aware of God for the first time. Gazing out of the window on a clear night he suddenly asked 'Mummy, who made the moon?' 'God made the moon, Pedro' she said. 'And he made the stars too. And he made them for you and for me.' His first reaction on hearing about God was a prayer of thanksgiving. 'Oh thank you, Mr God.'

WHY THREE TIMES

The disciples asked Jesus to teach them to pray 'as John taught his disciples' (*Luke 11:1*).

Jesus gave them a prayer that would sum up his deepest convictions, the Lord's Prayer: Our Father. And this was such a total prayer (an early African teacher called Tertullian said that it is a compendium of the entire Gospel) that Christianity felt it could replace the Jewish prayer texts entirely. So the

We call God our Father; with good reason.

early Christians said it three times daily – replacing the three times appointed for Jewish prayer.

Is the 'Our Father' a 'blank cheque' kind of prayer? Can anybody who feels that there is one creator and that the human race is one family pray it adequately? The Christian community has never thought like that. We do not deny that God is Father of all and loves all. He is and he does. But is this the Lord's Prayer? It can be prayed with full meaning only by those who live the life of Jesus and embody his attitudes.

Admittedly – and this is often a puzzle – there is no reference to the passion and resurrection of Jesus. But the passion and resurrection were possible because Jesus lived his prayer. His stance towards God and towards us is shown in it.

The secret is one word: Abba! Jesus called the awesome and omnipotent Lord by the baby's word for father. Christians were so stunned by this that they kept the word, even in other languages.

God is Abba. He is Jesus' full horizon and endless sustainer. He is to be hallowed and obeyed. He will give what is needed and preserve his loved ones in the evil hour. In Gethsemane Jesus was still saying Abba, and on Easter morning he told Mary that he was going 'to my Abba and your Abba'. The Lord's Prayer is the Lord's relationship with the Father. When we pray it we enter into this most sacred mystery.

When a person comes by grace to faith in Christ this faith is fostered and developed in the community by the Rite of Christian Initiation of Adults which we are using as the structure for this book. As this draws to a close the catechumen is solemnly entrusted with one of the Church's most precious treasures: the Lord's Prayer. This usually happens during the fifth week of Lent. The catechumen will undoubtedly have often read and pondered on this prayer – but from the outside, as it were. Now he or she is offered it as something to cherish, to love and to pray continually.

LIGHT FROM THE COUNCIL

'The eternal Father, in accordance with the utterly gratuitous and mysterious design of his wisdom and goodness, created the whole universe, and chose to raise up men and women to share in his own divine life; and when they had fallen in Adam, he did not abandon them, but at all times held out to them the means of salvation bestowed in consideration of Christ the Redeemer . . . He determined to call together in a Holy Church those who should believe in Christ.'
(Constitution on the Church No 2)

QUESTIONS

1. In the Old Testament, God is sometimes portrayed as being distant and remote and at other times he is seen as being very close to his people. How do you imagine God? Make a list of the qualities and characteristics you think he has.

2. Some people see the 'Our Father' as containing a list of all the elements we should include in prayer. Using the text of this greatest of all prayers, discuss how these essential elements are present in the 'Our Father'.

Holman Hunt's famous picture of Christ knocking on the door of the human heart. The door opens only from the inside . . .

5-Jesus the Son

is the Son of God.
is true God.
is true Man.
is One Person, come to save the world.

JESUS CHRIST is the starting-point, the centre and the goal of the Christian life. How we understand him affects the whole way we live.

The early Church wrestled with two problems. Since there is only one God, what is the relationship of Jesus to the Father? And how could they express the union of the human and divine in the one Christ?

Some saw Jesus only as God, just appearing to be human but not truly so.

Others saw him just as a man, adopted by God and filled with his Spirit.

The crisis came in the eastern region of the church, when a priest called Arius taught that the Word who became flesh was not truly God but a created being. Against him, the Council of Nicea (325) upheld Christ's divinity, proclaiming that the Son of God is 'God from God, light from light, true God from true God'. He is not made but rather be-gotten, coming from the being of the

Father himself. He is 'one in being with the Father'. This divine Son, 'true God', became flesh for our salvation.

Nicea established Christ's divinity, but how then could this true humanity be upheld? Some theologians so stressed Christ as God that he ceased to be fully human. This was rejected by the Council of Constantinople (381) which taught that Jesus did indeed have a human soul. Nicea taught Christ's divinity against Arius, Constantinople taught his humanity against Apollinarius. But how could these ideas be held together?

It was the Council of Chalcedon, in present day Turkey (451), that brought together the insights of the two main centres of Christian learning – Antioch's stress on the full humanity of Christ, and Alexandra's stress on the unity of Christ as the divine Word. The Council's definition has been the classical expression of orthodox Christian belief ever since. It taught that one and the same Son is truly God and truly man, and like us in all things except sin.

This is the heart of the Catholic understanding of Jesus. It is stressed so emphatically because if Jesus is not both true God and true man, we are not saved! Salvation means overcoming the gulf between God and us and we are saved only if God comes in person as one of us.

IN SCRIPTURE

Only gradually did Christians find ways of expressing their belief in Jesus as Lord.

It may come as a shock to find that Christ is actually called 'God' by Paul probably only once. It occurs in a thanksgiving 'Christ who is above all, God for ever blessed! Amen' (*Rom 9:5*).

Otherwise it is only at the end of the development of the New Testament, in the letter to the Hebrews, that he is freely called 'God'.

In the first three Gospels Jesus never claims the title 'God' and never states his divinity. He is called son of man,

messiah, prophet, son of God, but never 'God'. He himself seems to have preferred the title 'the son', speaking of God as 'the Father' with a staggering boldness and intimacy.

Jews at that time spoke of God often as father of Israel, and of Israel as God's son, but only in the collective sense. They would never claim God as father in an individual sense, as Jesus did.

But the titles given to Jesus in the New Testament are not the only evidence that he is God. Jesus acts in a way which is tantamount to a claim of divinity.

The Law was given by God and is his means of communicating himself to his people. BUT Jesus teaches with authority and completeness and manipulates the Law with a sovereignty which suggests that he has rights over the Law.

God can forgive sin, as the opponents of Jesus point out. He claims precisely this divine prerogative.

God has power over life and death. Jesus is seen raising the dead by his own authority.

Jesus, although Son of God, still wanted to be baptised by John.

After the resurrection, Christians were constantly being challenged to give an account of how they saw their Lord. Their immediate reaction was not to say that he was God.

In Jewish-Christian circles, they turned automatically to the Old Testament. Paul certainly does. He pictures the risen Christ in biblical imagery. He is the Lord who will come again on the clouds to judge the world and take his faithful followers with him in his triumphal procession (*1 Thess 4:16*).

Later he had to explain the contrast between the old and the new covenants. He describes Christ as the second Adam, the founder and leader of a renewed humanity. He is now the model and exemplar of humanity. He is the Son of God in whom all others can become adopted sons and call God intimately 'Father'.

At about the same time, confronted with the divisions within the Christian community at Corinth, Paul sees the Church as the body of Christ, the indivisible Christian community. Its members make up the total body of Christ and live with his life.

Paul expresses this faith of the early Christian community most strongly in his use of the word 'Lord' (Kyrios) – Jesus is the Lord. It also refers back to the Old Testament use of 'Yahweh' as the name for God. Jesus is given this title by the Father because he was the obedient son.

The final stage in the development of understanding was the vision in St John's Gospel of Christ as the 'Word made flesh'. This idea of the Word of God links back to the creation story in Genesis where God created all things by his word. Christ is revealed as the Son of God.

LIGHT FROM THE COUNCIL
'As an innocent lamb he merited life for us by his blood which he freely shed. In him God reconciled us to himself and to one another, freeing us from the bondage of the devil and of sin, so that each one of us could say with the apostle: the Son of Man "loved me and gave himself for me"' (Pastoral Constitution on the Church in the Modern World, para 22).

PLACE FOR PRAYER
If we look at Jesus in the Gospels, we find one outstanding fact about his relationship with his Father – he gives him lots of time!

The key factor in prayer is giving time regularly to God. I often speak of this as 'wasting time with God'. We decide to pray and immediately there are a hundred and one things claiming our attention – a person to see, a letter to write, the potatoes to be peeled. But unless we follow Jesus in making ourselves available for God, we will never know him more clearly, love him more dearly. Look at Jesus! No matter how busy he was, he went off to pray: 'Great multitudes gathered to hear him and to be healed by him in their infirmities. But he withdrew to the wilderness and prayed' (*Luke 5:15, 16*).

Prayer of St Richard of Chichester
Thanks be to you, my Lord Jesus Christ, for all the benefits and blessings which you have given me, for the pains and insults which you have borne for me. O most merciful Redeemer, Friend and Brother, may I know thee more clearly, love thee more dearly, and follow thee more nearly.

THE REAL IMAGE?

The Turin Shroud is a piece of cloth 14 feet by 3 feet, which some people believe to have been the winding sheet of Jesus Christ. It was discovered in the 14th century, but it was then lost, and only found again in 1898. A photograph of it was taken by an Italian; and to his astonishment the negative revealed a remarkable likeness to many early icons of Christ. There is evidence to support its authenticity. The cloth is from first-century Palestine, plant deposits on the cloth coming from the region of the Dead Sea. There is genuine blood on the Shroud. Scientists conclude that it may have been the winding-sheet of a man crucified in the first century AD. Research continues.

QUESTIONS

1. Make a list of stories, incidents or sayings from the life of Jesus which emphasise
   a) his humanity
   b) his divinity.
2. Choose three stories from the New Testament which show individuals coming to faith in Jesus as the Son of God. What do they have in common? What lessons do they teach us about how to help people in their search for God?

LITURGY THE SIGN OF THE CROSS

Have you ever wondered why the sign of the Cross on the forehead, breast and shoulders is coupled, not with a reference to Calvary, but to the Blessed Trinity? The cross is much more than an emblem of suffering – it is shorthand for the whole Christian reality of salvation.

We say 'In the Name of the Father, and of the Son and of the Holy Spirit.' We are calling on the power of the Trinity which has been manifested in history for us. We call on the creating love of the Father, the redeeming love of the Son, and the liberating love of the Spirit.

Catholics begin and end their prayers with this sign and these words.

JESUS CHRIST: WHO WAS HE?

HE WAS BORN IN AN OBSCURE VILLAGE, THE CHILD OF A PEASANT WOMAN.

HE WORKED IN A CARPENTER'S SHOP UNTIL HE WAS THIRTY, AND THEN FOR THREE YEARS HE WAS AN ITINERANT PREACHER.

HE NEVER WROTE A BOOK.

HE NEVER HELD AN OFFICE.

HE NEVER OWNED A HOME.

HE DID NONE OF THOSE THINGS WE USUALLY ASSOCIATE WITH GREATNESS.

HE HAD NO CREDENTIALS BUT HIMSELF.

WHILE HE WAS STILL A YOUNG MAN, THE TIDE OF PUBLIC OPINION TURNED AGAINST HIM.

HIS FRIENDS RAN AWAY.

HE WAS TURNED OVER TO HIS ENEMIES.

HE WENT THROUGH THE MOCKERY OF A TRIAL.

HE WAS NAILED TO A CROSS BETWEEN TWO THIEVES.

WHILE HE WAS DYING, HIS EXECUTIONERS GAMBLED FOR THE ONLY PIECE OF PROPERTY HE HAD ON EARTH, AND THAT WAS HIS COAT.

WHEN HE WAS DEAD, HE WAS LAID IN A BORROWED TOMB THROUGH THE PITY OF A FRIEND.

NINETEEN CENTURIES HAVE PASSED, AND TODAY HE IS THE CENTRAL FIGURE OF THE HUMAN RACE.

ALL THE ARMIES THAT EVER MARCHED, ALL THE NAVIES THAT EVER SAILED, ALL THE PARLIAMENTS THAT EVER SAT, ALL THE KINGS THAT EVER REIGNED, PUT TOGETHER, HAVE NOT AFFECTED THE LIFE OF MAN UPON THIS EARTH AS HAS THAT ONE SOLITARY LIFE.

WHY?

These candidates, having heard the Good
News of God's love in Christ, and having
signified their commitment to it, are
enrolled as 'catechumens', and are from
now on formally under instruction to
become members of the Church, helped by
the Holy Spirit and by the community of
God's people.

6-The Holy Spirit

**is the Third Person of the Trinity.
came upon the Church at Pentecost.
gives us faith to join the Church.
makes us members of the Church.**

THERE WOULD not be a Church without the Holy Spirit. He brings believers into the community – the Church, is the appointed means by which God saves the world, and continues the redemptive work of Christ.

The Holy Spirit works through particular gifts to build up the body of Christ's followers – the Church. These may be called 'charisms', a Greek word meaning gifts.

Some are permanent, called hierarchical as in the Sacrament of orders of bishop, priest and deacon.

Some are occasional, like prophecy and healing. Not everyone has these and indeed, the same person may not have a particular gift all the time.

Many people if you say 'church' think of a building. But if all the church buildings were destroyed there would still be a Church. It is the 'koinonia', the community of believers, which is the Church, the temple of the Holy Spirit and the sign of salvation for the world.

In the same way the body of bishops led by the Pope is the gift of the Holy Spirit to the Church. They continue the mission of the apostles. The Pope is the centre of visible unity of the universal (catholic) Church.

This unity of hierarchy and people is the new family, brought to life by the Holy Spirit. We are all brothers and sisters of Christ.

Within this family the Spirit's gifts are for everyone (*1 Cor 12:4*). To be 'charismatic' simply means to acknowledge our gifts come from God. And to use them.

The Spirit is at work even when we are not aware of it. Sometimes we can only discern his presence with hindsight. But we have Christ's promise that the Spirit will be with us always to guide us into the truth.

'For when we cannot choose words in order to pray properly, the Spirit himself expresses our plea in a way that could never be put into words . . .' (*Rom 8:26*).

At Pentecost the Church exploded into life in the wind and fire of the Spirit. Some of the crowd accused Peter and the other apostles of being drunk, but what they were seeing was the transforming effect of the Holy Spirit.

Just before the Ascension the apostles had asked 'Are you now going to restore the Kingdom to Israel?' They got not the answer they wanted, but a fairly clear hint about the real nature of the kingdom of God: 'You will receive power when the Holy Spirit comes upon you, then you will be my witnesses to the ends of the earth' (*Acts 1:6–8*).

During Christ's earthly life people had generally come to him as individuals. He called James and John from their boat, and Matthew from his counting-house. Andrew brought his brother Simon, and Philip fetched Nathaniel. But with the coming of the Spirit at Pentecost the call, and the effect, were now communal, showing us how 'God has willed to make men holy and save them not as individuals, without any bond or link between them, but as people' (Lumen Gentium 9).

There seem to have been two stages to that incorporation into the Church. In his sermon on Pentecost Peter said 'Repent and be baptised every one of you, in the name of Jesus Christ, for the forgiveness of your sins, and you will receive the gift of the Holy Spirit' (*Acts 2:38*). This double process, now crystallised for us in the two sacraments of baptism and confirmation, had a parallel in Christ's own life.

Just as the Spirit had brooded over the waters of chaos at creation, so he overshadowed Mary when Christ was conceived. Later, after John had baptised him in the River Jordan, Christ was led by the Spirit into the desert to begin his public life with a forty-day fast.

Just as the Spirit enlivened the human Christ, so too he is the life-principle of the Church. Indeed he has been called 'the soul of the Church'.

Christ promised his apostles that the Holy Spirit would bring back to their minds everything he himself had taught them. The same Holy Spirit inspires all authentic teaching in the Church, and all true development.

This same Holy Spirit is active in all aspects of the life of the Church. His gifts or charisms are varied. They include the grace and authority conferred on members of the hierarchy by the sacrament of ordination as well as the spiritual talents of great poets and preachers like St Francis of Assisi, or those of the great apostles of mercy like St Vincent de Paul or Dom Helda Camera. They include everyday gifts of faithful perseverance and love in family obligations and in unpublicised help for our neighbours.

As St Paul pointed out, 'there is a variety of gifts, but always the same Spirit' (*1 Cor 12:4*). The Spirit who transformed the crowd into a new community at Pentecost is the same Spirit who keeps the Church together in unity now.

Everyone baptised into the Church is baptised in the name of the Father and of the Son and of the Holy Spirit. The Holy Spirit is the mutual love uniting the Father and the Son. The Church is itself the means by which we are actually inserting into the life and love of God. God's love, revealed to us as the doctrine of the Trinity, leads him to create us so that we may share in that life and love. The movement is circular. Caught up in that love we respond to it by the same power of the Holy Spirit dwelling within us. Sometimes we are consciously aware of his presence, and are stirred to strong and courageous faith and true joy. More often we are not. Yet we believe that through our Baptism He is always with us.

SPREADING THE GOOD NEWS

No religion ever spread so rapidly. St Peter's preaching converted 3,000 people on Pentecost day itself. The faith, called at first 'The Way', spread like wildfire through the Jewish communities of Palestine, Samaria and Syria. Within 30 years of the death and resurrection of Christ it had spread right through the known world.

The key figure in the explosion of Christianity to the non-Jewish world was St Paul. Born in Tarsus, in modern-day Turkey, he was a Pharisee who studied in Jerusalem. He was fanatical in his persecution of Christians. After his dramatic conversion on the road to Damascus he went from city to city preaching the Good News and founding Christian communities.

The Holy Spirit was given to the Church on the morning of the first Pentecost to be with her until the end of time and to accomplish in her a unique mission: to make present for all generations and throughout the world, the redemption that Christ acquired once and for all. He comes as the one sent by the Son, as the one who prolongs and completes the task of the Father.

His mission, then, is not to add anything whatsoever to Our Lord's Revelation. Christ has merited everything for us by his Passion which saved the world, but it is through the Spirit that the fruits of the redemption are 'ripened'. The Holy Spirit – this Spirit of life who gives life – comes to us to clarify from within the Master's words, to guide us 'into all truth'.

The deposit of faith can be discovered only in Scripture and Tradition.

The Holy Spirit was given to the Church to guarantee her fidelity to the mission confided to her. But it is also the work of the Spirit to introduce her progressively into the fullness of the truth. A distinction has to be made between what belongs to authentic Tradition and what arises from traditions that are purely human. Much confusion comes from the fact that customs and usages, perhaps a century or less old, are confounded with true Tradition which goes back to the beginnings and which, in the course of time, has sometimes been obscured.

Often what seems revolutionary is simply a return to the sources.

The Lord did not wish to leave this process of discernment to the whim of individual interpretation or to the mercy of our prejudices. It is his Spirit who leads each phase of development. It is he who, as soon as new problems crop up, helps to bring the answer that is truly in keeping with Tradition.

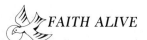
PLACE FOR PRAYER

The Holy Spirit has often been neglected in the prayer life of the average Catholic. Yet, St Paul tells us, 'you can only say the Lord Jesus by the power of the Holy Spirit' (*1 Cor 12:3*).

Today much more emphasis is given to the Spirit in our lives. There has been great development in prayer of the Spirit, charismatic prayer and gifts.

It is especially important in prayer to realise that the individual only contributes very little. The immense power of prayer in us comes from the Spirit. For this reason, it is necessary for us not simply to be tied to the use of words, but to open ourselves – be still and silent in God's presence, in our hearts asking for the Spirit to be with us – to speak with us 'when we do not know what to say' (*Rom 8:26*).

PRAYER

Come Holy Spirit
Fill the hearts of your faithful
and enkindle in them
the fire of your love.
Send forth your Spirit
and they shall be created
And you will renew
the face of the Earth.

QUESTIONS

1. In Ephesians 4:11, St Paul gives a list of the different ways the Spirit works. 'To some his gift was that they should be apostles; to some, prophets; to some, evangelists; to some, pastors and teachers . . . to build up the body of Christ.' What other gifts could be added to this list as we look at the parish today?
2. At the first Pentecost, described in Chapter 2 of the Acts of the Apostles, people looked at the disciples who had just received the Spirit and thought they were drunk. How do we recognise the Spirit working in people? What fears do we have of the work of the Spirit?

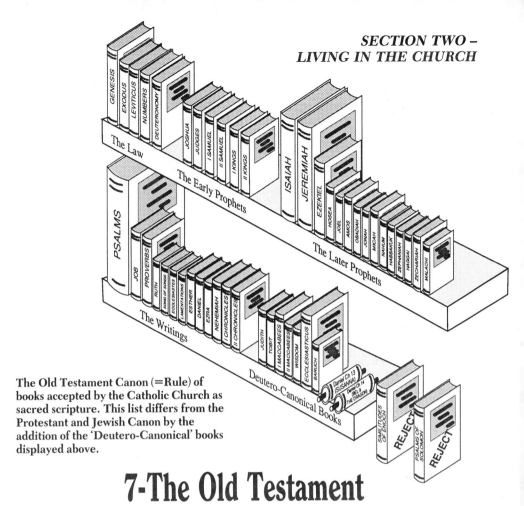

The Old Testament Canon (=Rule) of books accepted by the Catholic Church as sacred scripture. This list differs from the Protestant and Jewish Canon by the addition of the 'Deutero-Canonical' books displayed above.

7-The Old Testament

is the Word of God in words of human writers.
is a library of different books.
is the story of God's people before Christ.
looks towards Christ.

WE TREAT the Bible as one book but it is a library of works by different authors, written during many centuries. They write poetry, prose, prayers and songs, fact and fiction.

One thing binds them all together. They are the Word of God. God speaks His truth to us. We call this Revelation. He does so through human writers. We call this Inspiration.

The Old Testament is the foundation for God's self-revelation in the living Word made flesh, Jesus Christ.

The Bible is the world's best-selling book. It has been translated, in whole or part, into 1,745 languages and dialects.

How has it come to us?

The first 'books' of the Bible were scrolls, hand-written in Hebrew. In 1947, in a dry desert cave in Palestine, near the Dead Sea, a remarkable collection of scrolls was found. They were the records and writings of a religious sect called the Essenes. Among them was the complete text of the prophet Isaiah. It is, to date, the oldest surviving Old Testament manuscript.

The first complete translation of the Old Testament, into Greek, was begun in the third century BC. It was called the Septuagint because 70 scholars are supposed to have worked on it (Greek septuagint = 70).

The story goes that each was shut in a booth to do his work and at the end all of the translations were identical.

This version was the Bible of the early Christians.

The first Catholic translation from the Hebrew and Greek was done single-handed by St Jerome. It took him 15 years.

Born in northern Italy (about AD 345) he was baptised in Rome at the age of 19. He was a scholar and travelled through Europe and the Middle East.

Pope Damasus was so impressed by a letter from him that he made him his secretary. St Jerome was a great letter writer and several survive to his friend St Paula. She travelled with him in Egypt and Palestine and finally founded a community of nuns in Bethlehem. The cave where St Jerome lived is now a chapel under the Church of the Nativity in Bethlehem.

In Bethlehem St Jerome studied Hebrew with a rabbi and about AD 391 began his translation of the Bible. He wrote in Latin. Not the classical Latin of the scholars but the common speech of ordinary people. So his version was called 'the Vulgate' from the Latin word for common – 'vulgar'.

This became the official Bible of the Roman Catholic Church and for centuries all translations had to be made from this text. Unofficial translations were made. In England, St Aldhelm, St Bede and King Alfred the Great made translations into Anglo-Saxon but little survives.

The great contribution of the middle ages to the story of the Bible is in the illuminated manuscripts. They are works of art as well as evidence of the reverence for the Bible.

The first printed Bible was produced by Johann Guttenberg (in Germany) in 1455. Printing encouraged translations.

In the 14th and 15th centuries many reformers set to work. In England William Tyndale, Myles Coverdale and Matthew Rogers produced Bibles for the Protestant reformers. But there was no official Catholic translation.

In 1609, two years before the King James Authorised Version appeared in England, the first official English translation for Catholics was printed. This was the Douai Bible translated from the Latin Vulgate at the English College, Douai, in France.

It was a literal translation of the Latin. Bishop Challoner, vicar apostolic and bishop of London 1741–1764 made two revisions. The second in 1722, became the second official English version for Catholics.

THE 20th CENTURY

It was over 200 years before another official Catholic English translation of the Bible. This was the work of Mgr Ronald Knox. It was readable and stylish.

In 1966 the Jerusalem Bible appeared, edited by Fr Alexander Jones. The translators used the French translation La Bible de Jerusalem as well as the original Hebrew and Greek texts.

In 1973 the first version produced by Catholic and Protestant scholars together appeared. This was the Common Bible, a new edition of the Revised Standard Version first published in 1952.

In 1985 under the general editorship of Dom Henry Wansborough OSB, one of the 'Faith Alive' contributors, the New Jerusalem Bible was published.

ORIGINS: THE CRADLE OF HISTORY

The early chapters of Genesis tell us that God created the world. They also tell us how the human race alienated itself from God, in the stories of the Fall, the Tower of Babel, and the Flood. And how God promised eventually to save us.

There is no conflict between the biblical account of creation, and scientific attempts to date the origins of the

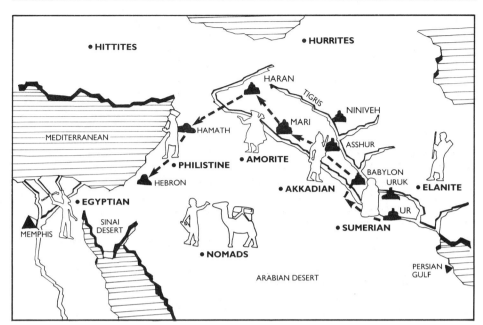

God's Theatre of Action, The Fertile Crescent.

universe millions of years ago. Scientific explanations only theorise about how and when the universe was created.

Augustine said 16 centuries ago, the scriptures do not tell us about the heavens, but rather how we can get to heaven.

Archaeology has also unearthed fascinating information about the beginnings of civilisation centred around the river Nile in Egypt, and Mesopotamia, the land etween the two rivers the Tigris and the Euphrates, in present day Syria, Iran, and Iraq.

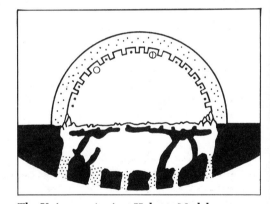

The Universe, Ancient Hebrew Model.

THE PATRIARCHS: OUR FATHER ABRAHAM

Abraham's people lived a nomadic life, wandering round the 'fertile crescent', rearing sheep and cattle, and trading in the cities. At God's command, Abraham settled in the land of Canaan, south of Jerusalem at Hebron.

Abraham's great-grandson Joseph went down to Egypt, sold into slavery by his brothers (*Gen 37*). In Egypt he prospered, becoming Prime Minister, and having charge of the Pharoah's grain-storage. Finally, Joseph's brothers came to Egypt seeking food during a time of famine, and settled there (*Gen 47:27*).

Archaeology provides some fascinating parallels to these ancient biblical stories.

The journey into Egypt, for instance, may have as its background migrations into Egypt after an invasion in the 18th century BC by the 'Hyksos' (Egyptian for 'rulers of foreign countries').

EXODUS AND CONQUEST

The Exodus was the most important event in the Old Testament. The miraculous escape from Egyptian slavery, followed by the wanderings in the desert and the giving of the Law on Mount Sinai, are still remembered and celebrated as the beginning under God of the nation.

The conquest of the Promised Land under Joshua and the Judges was also most important in the nation's memory. When they entered the land, Canaan (now Israel and Jordan) was a country of independent city-states, with their own gods. Joshua and his followers believed that they were commanded by God to destroy these gods, together with their people (*Josh 6:17*). Otherwise, they themselves would have been contaminated by idolatry. Such commands seem cruel, but we must remember that God's revelation was gradual and progressive.

KINGS AND PROPHETS

With Saul's anointing as king by the prophet Samuel, a new age began. God's people needed a stable government, to counter the threat from the Philistines, invaders from Crete, who were conquering and settling.

Then came David (see next chapter), the greatest king of Judah (1010–970 BC), who destroyed the Philistines. He conquered all the surrounding nations, and set up God's Ark of the Covenant in Jerusalem (*2 Sam 6*).

With David's son Solomon, prosperity continued, and a magnificent Temple was built in Jerusalem (966 BC). But the ten northern tribes rebelled against the cruelty of Solomon, setting up their own separate government. This kingdom became known as 'Samaria', from the name of its capital.

This northern kingdom at first grew very wealthy. But, in the 8th century, the prophets Amos and Hosea warned of God's coming punishment. 'They have sold the upright for silver, and the poor for a pair of sandals' (*Amos 2:6*).

In 721, the kingdom of Samaria was ravaged by the Assyrian armies, and the ten tribes were carried off into captivity (*2 Kings 17*). Then, in 597 and 587, the 'impossible' happened. Jerusalem was captured by the Babylonians and the Jews were carried off to exile. The warnings of the prophets Jeremiah and Ezekiel had been ignored. All seemed lost.

During this period, the book of Deuteronomy was completed, and the books of 1 and 2 Samuel, and 1 and 2 Kings.

EXILE AND RETURN

Man's extremity is God's opportunity. In Exile, far from the Temple, the Jews learnt to love reading the Law, and committing themselves to obey it as individuals. During that period, the Pentateuch was edited, and it was soon to be in its final form. Worship in the synagogue probably began in Exile.

But deliverance was at hand. Cyrus, the Persian, was the new star in the Middle East, and his armies walked into Babylon without a fight. Under Cyrus's new policy, the Jews returned rejoicing to the Holy Land, to rebuild the Temple and their nation.

PREPARING FOR THE MESSIAH

But it was not quite the same. Gone was the power that the Davidic kings enjoyed. From now on, the Jews were always to be an occupied nation.

During their time in Exile, an unknown prophet had sung strange songs, about a 'servant' who was a prophet and a Messiah. This servant would not be like the kings of old, ruling by the sword. He would be gentle, not breaking the bruised reed (*Isa 42:3*). He would call even the Gentiles to repentance. He would die for the sins of the people. Who was he?

The returning Jews built the Temple in 520–515 BC, strongly encouraged by the prophets Zechariah and Haggai. Now the idea of the Messiah came into full flower.

Before the Exile, the Messiah meant simply the anointed king of Judah in Jerusalem. He was called 'Messiah' (= anointed) because he was anointed king by a prophet, as David was by Samuel.

But after the Exile, the concept of messianic king of the future developed. Ezekiel said, this king would be a shepherd to God's people, who would live secure in their land (Eze 34:23–31).

Generation after generation passed, and this ideal Messiah did not come. In 333 BC the Persian empire finally collapsed, and the Jews had a new set of masters – the Greeks.

A Jewish colony was set up in Alexandria in Egypt, and the Torah and the Prophets, in their completed form, began to be translated into Greek. At this time the Old Testament as we know it today took shape, the community beginning to recognise the books of our Bible as sacred or 'canonical' (a word meaning 'measure'), that is, inspired by God.

The earliest manuscripts of the Old Testament date from this period. A scroll of the prophet Isaiah was found in a cave by the Dead Sea in 1947. Also, during this period, books such as the Wisdom of Solomon and Ben Sirach which spoke of Wisdom as co-existing with God, were written. All was set for the coming of Jesus of Nazareth.

QUESTIONS

1. The Exodus story is one of enormous significance in the Old Testament. Have you personally experienced an 'Exodus' in your life – where you have been liberated from some form of oppression, or led out from one way of life to another?

2. God sometimes chooses the most unlikely people to be the instruments of his plans for people. Which person/people do you consider have been most instrumental in helping you on your journey of faith?

LIGHT FROM THE COUNCIL

Thus, we can speak of the New Testament as having been 'hidden in the Old' and of the Old Testament as having been 'made manifest in the New'. We can assert that 'the books of the Old Testament, all of them caught up in to the Gospel message, attain and show forth their full meaning in the New Testament and, in their turn, shed light on it and explain it' (No 16).

However, even though taken on their own the books of the Old Testament 'contain matters imperfect and provisional', they 'nevertheless show us authentic divine teaching. Christians should accept with veneration these writings which give expression to a lively sense of God, which are a storehouse of sublime teaching on God and of sound wisdom on human life, as well as a wonderful treasury of prayers . . .' (No 15).

PLACE FOR PRAYER

Joseph, Mary and Jesus grew up and lived in the atmosphere and teaching of the Law and the Prophets. Basic to this was reading from the holy books.

There was no complete break from the old when Jesus began the New Covenant. He came to fulfil the Law and the Prophets. The Evangelists, St Paul, the early Fathers, the desert Fathers and developing tradition all draw upon the teaching, prayer and praise from the treasury of Israel.

Scripture is the lasting heritage of all Christians. There are many levels of meaning and appreciation if you give a little time often. Like Mary, keep these things and ponder them in your heart (Luke 2:51).

8-The Psalms

are God's own prayers.
reflect all aspects of human life.
were inspired by the life of David.
are a major source for the Church's worship.

SING TO THE LORD!

At the Last Supper Jesus as a Jew sang psalms with his apostles before he went to his death (*Matt 26:30*). He was brought up on the Psalms and sang them regularly in the synagogue.

The significance of the Psalms in Jewish life can be summed up in the words of a yiddish saying that applies to a time of danger or trouble: 'Don't wait for a miracle – zog tillim recite psalms!'

Virtually every religious service in the Jewish calendar, every life-cycle event, is marked by the recital of entire psalms or particular verses.

Christians and others have sung the Psalms because they find in them varied moods which relate to their needs at different times and of course our roots are in the Jewish tradition.

We seem to have become more aware of Psalms over the past few years. At one time they were just part of another book of the Old Testament. Now they are a feature of every Mass as the Responsorial Psalm and, indeed, of every full celebration of any of the sacraments. The Liturgy of the Hours, the Prayer of the Church, prayed daily by an increasing number of lay people, uses the Psalms as its basic form of prayer.

Psalms can also be used as Entrance Chants, at the Offertory and Communion. Psalms are often included in the celebration of other sacraments or as processional chants.

The Psalms are important to the liturgy because they are prayers inspired by the Holy Spirit. 'The Holy Spirit, is always present with his grace to those believing Christians who with good intention sing and recite these songs' (General Instruction on the Liturgy of the Hours No 102).

'We were born with this book in our very bones. A small book; 150 poems; 150 steps between death and life; 150 mirrors of our rebellions and our loyalties, of our agonies and our resurrections. More than a book, it is a living being who speaks, who suffers, groans and dies, who rises again and speaks on the threshold of eternity; who seizes one, bears one away, oneself and all the ages of time, from the beginning to the end.'

PRAYER LIFE OF A PEOPLE

When reading or praying the psalms we eavesdrop on the private prayer-life of a people. The soul of Israel is exposed with an honesty and frankness which, to the modern Christian, can be disconcerting.

At the root of Israel's spirituality is faith in God's steadfast love and faithfulness. It is based on a 'creed': the account of God's choice of Israel to be His special possession, and the history of the wonderful works that He performed in bringing the people out of Egypt and into the Promised Land (*Ps 105; 136*). Israel's destiny is to be the Kingdom of God on earth.

Three main types of psalms have been identified: Hymns, Petitions and Thanksgiving.

Hymns are songs of praise (*Ps 100*). They begin with an invitation or statement of intent to praise God, followed by the reasons for such praise. Two reasons predominate: God's wonderful

Trumpet of God. Jewish shofar.

works in creation (*Ps 104*), and God's wonderful works in salvation (*Ps 135*). These include God's continued care for creation and constant care of his people, especially the humble and afflicted (*Ps 113*). God is the centre of these psalms, and the person of the psalmist does not intrude or distract.

Petitions begin with a cry for help or with a statement of need (*Ps 5:2*). The plight of the petitioner forms the main interest. With frank simplicity the psalmist professes his own innocence and righteousness (*Ps 17*) while at the same time drawing attention to the malice and treachery of his enemy. He may suggest to God ways and means of dealing with his enemy (*Ps 109*). These are the 'cursing' psalms. God is even reminded that it is to His advantage that one of his worshippers should be saved and not lost (*Ps 6:4f; 58:10*).

These psalms often end on a note of confidence, almost as though the prayer had been answered.

Thanksgiving psalms result from petitions that have been answered. They focus on the need of the psalmist who relates how God came to his aid in answer to his prayer. The occasion is sometimes used as a lesson for others and to that extent these psalms could be termed 'didactic' or 'teaching' (*Ps 34*). The language is often strongly figurative (*Ps 18:88*), and seldom can the precise situation be identified. This gives them a universal application.

Themes may suggest when certain psalms were used. 'Royal' psalms celebrate the Kingship of God (*Ps 47; 96*). Others honour the human king and were probably used at his coronation (*Ps 110*), his wedding (*Ps 45*), his departure for war (*Ps 20*) and his return (*Ps 21*). The regal language of the ancient East makes these psalms exuberant. The king is God's son, 'begotten by God'. All the nations of the earth are to be subject to him (*Ps 2*). The reality was very different (*Ps 89*). This language allowed for a reinterpretation or 're-reading' of these psalms, to refer to the King of the future

(*Ps 72*), the Messiah. This is how they are quoted in the New Testament.

'Pilgrim' psalms recall the beginning (*Ps 112*), the journey and arrival at Jerusalem (*Ps 48; 84*). Jerusalem is the place of God's chosen dwelling (*Ps 46*). These psalms, too, take on a further meaning when given a messianic interpretation (*Ps 87*).

The spirituality of the Psalms is influenced by the writers' views of life and death. There is some sort of existence in Sheol but no life after death. Reward for goodness, punishment for evil and the realisation of God's kingdom are features of life on earth. Consequently, justice means the removal of those who cause injustice; peace means the end of war and the destruction of the enemy, who are also God's enemies.

There is also a strong sense of 'balance': the lowly cannot be lifted up without the mighty being brought low; the hungry fed without the rich being sent away empty. This gives rise to what seems to be a vindictive streak. The psalmist prays for the destruction of enemies, in the most forthright language (*Ps 109; 137:8*). He is frank in protesting his own innocence and honesty. He also admits his own sinfulness and the disloyalty of his people (*Ps 51; 106*). He expresses his anger at God for the way he is treated (*Ps 44; 88*). He even tells God to 'get up' and do something (*Ps 44:23*).

DAVID – THE MAN OF THE PSALMS

Saint, sinner, and super-star all rolled into one.

How many of the 150 psalms David wrote or sung, it is impossible to say. Even those 73 psalms which are entitled 'Of David' could have been dedicated 'to' him, or written 'for' him, rather than written 'by' him. The Hebrew word used, *le*, can have all those meanings.

But David still more than merits the

title 'man of the psalter'. He inspired the worship and the music of God's people through centuries.

A shepherd-boy in the fields of Bethlehem is summoned by the prophet Samuel, and is anointed future king. He slays a giant, Goliath, and enters the court of King Saul, a soldier, a court musician to soothe the king's frayed nerves.

Eventually, Saul is killed in battle, and David is crowned king. He captures Jerusalem and sets up his capital there, bringing in the Ark of the Covenant as the focus of regular worship, and celebrating the entry into the city with music and dancing. He destroys the Philistine armies.

David during his lifetime was already a national hero. But not all his actions were heroic, for example he sent one of his best soldiers, Uriah the Hittite, to certain death, in order to marry Uriah's beautiful wife Bathsheba, whom David has seen bathing.

And David was over-indulgent with his son Absalom, who rebelled against him. Absalom was killed hanging from his hair caught in a tree; but David was inconsolable.

David's spirituality, and rich personality, seem often to be reflected in the psalms. His strong faith in Yahweh. His penitence. The way in which he speaks of God personally, even in anger. His suffering. His joy. His passion and his love.

A note on numbering

The numbering of the psalms can be confusing. Older Catholic translations were one figure behind modern versions such as the Jerusalem Bible, for most of the psalter. That is because the older Catholic translations followed the Greek and Latin numbering making Psalms 9–10 one Psalm. The Douay joined 114 and 115 of the Hebrew Bible but divided both 116 and 147 into two. The Jerusalem Bible has gone back to the numbering of the Psalms in the official Hebrew texts.

WONDER:
*OW great is your name
O Lord our God,
through all the earth!*
Ps 8:1
*(All references Grail
translation)*

JOY:
*RY out with joy to the
Lord, all the earth
Serve the Lord with
gladness. Come
before him, singing
for joy.*
Ps 99:1–2

DESPERATION:
*Y God, my God, why
have you forsaken
me? You are far from
my plea and the cry of
my distress.*
Ps 21:1

FAITH:
*HE Lord is my shepherd
There is nothing I shall
want.*
Ps 22:1

IN OLD AGE:
*OW that I am old and
grey-headed do not
forsake me, God.*
Ps 70:18

**THANKS FOR
FORGIVENESS:**
*APPY the man whose
offence is forgiven,
whose sin is remitted.*
Ps 31:1

FRUSTRATION:
*WAKE, O Lord, why
do you sleep?
Arise, do not reject us
forever.*

Ps 43:24

SORROW FOR SIN:
*Y offences truly I know
them, my sin is always
before me. Against
you, you alone, have I
sinned. What is evil in
your sight, I have
done.*

Ps 50:5–6

BLESSING:
*AY he never allow you
to stumble. Let him
sleep not, your guard.
No, he sleeps not nor
slumbers, Israel's
guard.*

Ps 20:5–6

HALLELUIJAH!
'Hallelui-jah' means 'praise Yahweh!' There is praise of God in all the psalms. But the final twenty psalms have a particular emphasis on praise. Psalm 150 refers to praising God with a fanfare of trumpets, and with 'tambourines and dancing'. It is clear that praising Yahweh is the whole person.

QUESTIONS
1. David was Israel's greatest king. He was also an adulterer and an accomplice in murder, yet Jesus accepted the title 'son of David'. What do we learn about relationship with God from the life of David?
2. The 'cursing' psalms sometimes cause problems for Christians today. Study these examples: Ps 58: 6–11; 137:9; 139:19–20; 140:9–12 (numbering as in Jerusalem Bible).

   Have you ever felt the emotions these writers express?

   What advice can you offer to Christians trying to come to terms with them?

LIGHT FROM THE COUNCIL
As well as understanding something of the psalms and being responsive to their music (all the psalms have a musical quality – No 103), one ought to 'meditate on them verse by verse, with the heart always ready to respond in the way the Holy Spirit desires' (No 104). One ought also to open one's heart 'to the different attitudes they express . . . grief, trust, gratitude, etc' (No 106).

And one should be on the look-out for their significance for one's own life: 'Though the psalms originated very many centuries ago among an Eastern people, they express accurately the pain and hope, the unhappiness and trust of people of every age and country, and sing above all of faith in God, of revelation, and of redemption.' (No 107).

Tradition has it that Paul was a small man . . .

9-The Epistles

were written in the first century AD.
were written to encourage the early Christians.
give us apostolic teaching about Christ.
put us in touch with the first communities.

IT IS remarkable that the earliest Christian documents we possess are not theological treaties, or manuals of church discipline, or even words of Jesus. They are letters; the earliest written by Paul to the newly-founded church at Thessalonica, barely twenty years after the death and resurrection of Christ.

It seems that these letters would first have been read out in the Christian community to which they were addressed, much like letters that are read out in the family.

Paul and the Christian leaders who wrote these letters sometimes had serious messages. There is deep theology, pastoral counselling, and even serious admonition. But the personal element is never far away. Paul wants to know how Syntyche and Priscilla are getting on. He wants them to know that he will come and see them as soon as possible. And, above all, don't forget the collection!

There are 21 epistles, or letters, in the New Testament. Of these, 14 are attributed to St Paul; 3 to St John, 2 to St Peter, and 1 to St Jude and to St James respectively.

The second Reading at Mass is always either from one of the epistles of the New Testament; or from the Acts of the Apostles, or the Book of Revelation.

Paul's letters were written to Christian communities in towns such as Philippi or Corinth; or to individual Christians, such as Timothy, Titus or Philemon.

The other letters, from Peter, John, Jude and James, are usually called The Catholic Epistles, because they were written to all Christians (kath-holos is Greek for 'according to the whole'), rather than to specific local churches, or to individuals, as were the epistles of Paul.

All the letters in the New Testament come from the early Christian community. None is dated by scholars later than the first decade of the second century AD, well within a century after Pentecost.

When we consider the authorship of the epistles, or any New Testament book, we must remember that the ancient world had a different concept of authorship to us. Then, the apostle – Paul, Peter, John – could be called author, even if he had not actually written the work. If a disciple of Paul, for instance, had written one of his epistles, and Paul had directed the work, even from a distance, the finished product would have been attributed to Paul as its authority and inspiration.

PAUL – MAN AND MISSIONARY

Tradition has it that Paul was a small man, who possibly suffered from epilepsy. His letters give the impression of a quick-thinking, fiery individual, who did not suffer fools gladly. No place for faint hearts with Paul.

Paul was highly educated and intelligent. He was born in Tarsus, on the Mediterranean coast of present-day Turkey (then called Asia Minor). His father was a Jew, probably a very successful citizen of Tarsus, because Paul tells us that he was a Roman citizen, a status which carried privileges such as the legal right to appeal to Caesar, and not to be flogged without trial. Paul would have gone to the best schools, and studied Greek philosophy as well as the Jewish Scriptures.

As a young man, he went to Jerusalem to study the Law under Gamaliel, a

Peter meets Paul.

leading rabbi. Here he first met the new sect of Christians. This group was claiming that a man called Jesus of Nazareth, whom Paul had never met, but who had been crucified only a short time before, was risen from the dead.

For Paul, as a member of the Pharisaic party, this was blasphemy. He became a zealous persecutor of Christians. But was his very zeal against the Christians evidence of a secret desire to find out more about their founder? Some scholars doubt whether his conversion on the road to Damascus, when he was blinded by a flashing light and heard the voice of Christ calling him, was completely sudden.

Paul was an 'all-or-nothing' person. As a Pharisee, no-one was more committed than he was. As a Christian, he slept, ate, talked, and thought Christ and Christ alone. He was the archetypal celibate. There was no room in his life for another commitment. Everything in him was taken up by his ambition to spread the Good News of Christ.

A man with such dynamism – writing letters to churches, mending tents to earn his living, preaching in the market-place – was moving so fast that most of us would find it difficult to keep up with him.

He also made enemies with ease. Some Corinthian Christians questioned his apostolic authority. After all, he had never actually met Jesus of Nazareth so what right had he to boss everyone around? These opponents accused Paul of writing strong letters, but being a weak person when confronting them personally.

Paul was capable of enormous affection, and lasting friendships. Luke, the convert doctor, Silas, and Sosthenes (people we know little about apart from their names) accompanied him everywhere, through shipwreck, floggings, long dangerous journeys, sleepless nights in prison, and constant worries about the churches.

His letters mention friends, both men and women, with great affection. He might have had ideas about the place of women which we would describe as male chauvinist. But he could love very deeply people of both sexes – and he could be very deeply hurt.

What was the 'thorn in the flesh' he mentions, which worried him greatly? We can only guess. It might have been some form of epilepsy, some nagging sense of failure. It might seem strange, that a man who had spread the Christian faith from Jerusalem to Rome, and converted thousands by his preaching, should feel failure.

But he was torn apart by the thought that the Jews had not accepted Jesus as Messiah. Many had become Christians but the Jewish authorities in the cities of the Roman Empire officially rejected Paul's claim that Jesus was the Messiah. And some Jews who had become Christians found it difficult to accept Gentiles equally, trying to insist that they undergo the rite of circumcision.

Overall, Paul was a man radiant with the joy of Christ.

The best way of understanding the way Paul's letters worked is to read them – for example his two letters to the Corinthians.

Corinth was a rich and busy city built on a neck of land joining north and south Greece, so that most of the goods passing westwards or eastwards in the Mediterranean were unloaded, carried across the neck of land and re-loaded.

Sailors attract prostitutes and the morals of Corinth were relaxed, as we see in 1 Cor 5. Crowds of visitors flocked into the city every two years for the Isthmian Games, second in importance only to the Olympic Games. No doubt Paul the tent-maker helped from a little shop in the market-place to cater for their temporary housing during his stay there. Corinth also had its own exports, the artistic and expensive Corinthian bronzes, to which Paul alludes, 'a gong booming or a cymbal clashing'.

The city clustered round the market-place and its temples. The thriving Jewish community would have been only

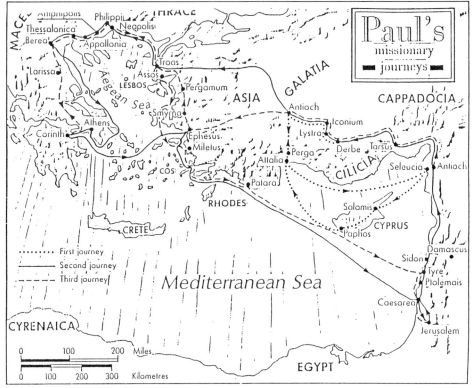

Paul's missionary journeys

First journey
Second journey
Third journey

Paul the incessant traveller; with a purpose.

too familiar with the pagan sacrifices and the moral problem of whether the faithful could buy left-over meat offered at bargain prices in the market (*1 Cor 8*). None of the houses discovered has rooms that could hold as many as 50 people for an act of worship, so there must have been several small groups in house-churches, which understandably led to the parties and factions which Paul condemns (*1 Cor 4*).

With this colourful community Paul had mixed relationships. Some time after he had first brought them the faith a delegation carried to him a list of problems which he settles in the second half of 1 Corinthians. But only after he had first dealt with other disorders the envoys mentioned by chance.

Among other distortions it seems that they had twisted his teaching, turning into slogans for anarchy sayings which he had intended quite otherwise: 'For me everything is possible', by which he

had meant that the restrictions of the Jewish Law were no more.

By the time of the second letter a whole series of exchanges had intervened: a painful visit by Paul, insults to his delegate and a stern letter of rebuke (now lost) written 'in agony of mind'. Only then were relations between apostle and his 'children' restored sufficiently to allow the still slightly wary 2 Corinthians to be written. With their vigorous individuality and their strong consciousness of the presence of the Spirit among them the Corinthians were hardly the perfect parish!

THE ACTS

Most of what we know of the first twenty years of the church is to be found in the book called 'The Acts of the Apostles'. This book together with the epistles and the book of Revelation is used for the second reading at Mass.

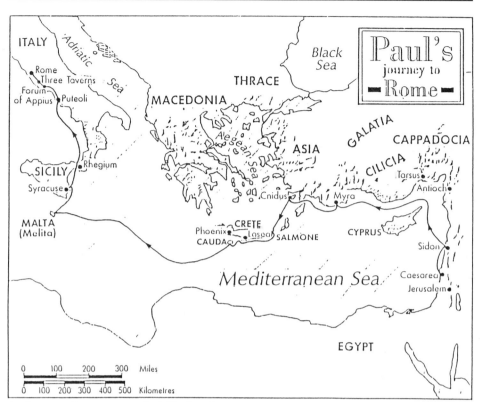

Paul's journey to Rome

And so on to Rome, to stand trial before Caesar . . .

Acts tells the wonderful story of how the Good News spread after the Day of Pentecost from Jerusalem, through Samaria, and then throughout the known world. It focuses on Peter, who founded the church in Jerusalem, and then on Paul, who took Christ's message to the Gentiles. The story ends with Paul's arrest in Jerusalem, his appeal to Caesar, and his eventful journey to Rome, on which he miraculously escaped shipwreck.

Acts reads like an exciting novel, but it must be taken seriously as history, even though that history has been reflected upon, just as have the Gospels, in the light of the Resurrection and the Gift of the Spirit.

The author of Acts is the same as the author of Luke's Gospel, and takes up the story where that Gospel leaves off, with the Ascension of Jesus. Tradition has it that the author of the Third Gospel and of the Acts was Luke the physician

and companion of Paul. There are good reasons advanced for this tradition – but it is difficult to prove. It is not a question central to faith. In any case, Acts is a very early Christian apostolic document, dated at the latest towards the close of the first century AD.

Although Acts finishes with Paul arriving safely in Rome, the story seems incomplete. What happened to Paul after he arrived in Rome? Acts does not tell us. Some scholars think that that is because Paul had only just arrived in Rome when Acts was written (AD 61), so there was no more to tell. But it may be also because the author of Acts wants us to realise that the story IS incomplete. The Acts of the Apostles is still being written, by the Church through the ages – and by you and me!

The Acts of the Apostles and the letters to the young churches (Epistles) give us many of the early hints and instructions on prayer.

PLACE FOR PRAYER

The work of the Spirit in prayer is a recurring theme with St Paul. Harking back to Christ's prayer he writes: 'When we cry, "Abba, Father!" it is the Spirit himself bearing witness with our spirit that we are children of God' (*Rom 8:15–16*).

A little further on, he gives great hope for those of us who find praying difficult: 'The Spirit helps us in our weakness; for we do not know how to pray as we ought, but the Spirit himself intercedes for us with sighs too deep for words. And he who searches the hearts of men knows what is the mind of the Spirit, because the Spirit intercedes for the saints according to the will of God' (*Rom 8:26–27*).

If you want to know when to pray, turn to Paul again: 'Rejoice always, pray constantly, give thanks in all circumstances; for this is the will of God in Christ Jesus for you' (*1 Thess 5:16–18*).

We must also realise that in our prayer we are praying for others, not just ourselves: 'I urge that supplications, prayers, intercessions and thanksgivings be made for all men, for kings and all who are in high positions, that we may lead a quiet and peaceable life, godly and respectful in every way' (*1 Tim 2:1–2*).

Finally, as a reassurance from St John: 'This is the confidence which we have in him, that if we ask anything according to his will he hears us. And if we know that he hears us in whatever we ask, we know that we have obtained the requests made of him' (*1 John 5:14–15*).

PRAYER

I bow my knees before the Father, from whom every family in heaven and on earth is named, that according to the riches of his glory he may grant you to be strengthened with might through his Spirit in the inner man, and that Christ may dwell in your hearts through faith; that you, being rooted and grounded in love, may have power to comprehend with all the saints what is the breadth and length and height and depth, and to know the love of Christ which surpasses knowledge, that you may be filled with all the fullness of God' (*Eph 3:14–19*).

LIGHT FROM THE COUNCIL

Besides the four Gospels, the New Testament also contains the Epistles of St Paul and other apostolic writings composed under the inspiration of the Holy Spirit. In accordance with the wise design of God these writings firmly establish those matters which concern Christ the Lord, formulate more and more precisely his authentic teaching, preach the saving power of Christ's divine work and foretell its glorious consummation. (Constitution on Divine Revelation No 20.)

QUESTIONS

1. Take any epistle and show how the writer relates doctrine to Christian living.
2. Is there anything in St Paul's life or character which strikes a chord with you?

The Lindisfarne Gospel.

10-The Gospels

are the Good News of Christ.
are based upon the apostles' teaching.
grew up within the Christian community.
are our main source for the life of Jesus.

WHAT IS A GOSPEL?

The word 'Gospel' means 'Good News' –
from the Anglo-Saxon God-Spell. When
the Church started, there were no Gospels written, and the word 'Gospel' referred to the preaching of the Good
News that Jesus Christ had risen from
the dead and had appeared to his
disciples and to his friends. The Good
News was the message, not the books.

However, very likely, from the

earliest times the sayings of Jesus, and
stories about him, were memorised, and
handed down to the first Christians by
Peter and the other apostles in their
teaching (see *Acts 2:42*). Jesus was acknowledged in his day as a Rabbi. He
would often sum up a lengthy instruction in a sentence which could be easily
memorised, such as 'many are called,
but few are chosen', or as in the 'Our
Father'.

In the first ten or twenty years after the Church began, the words of Jesus were handed on mostly if not entirely by word of mouth. These sayings were treated with great reverence, because Jesus himself was 'the Lord', governing his people on earth from his place in heaven 'at the right hand of the Father'.

Christians then began to collect the sayings of 'the Lord' and to write them down. Many scholars think that the teachings of Jesus were put into collections, some time before the Gospels as we know them were written. Some have even thought that these collections can be identified, from a scientific examination of the Gospel text. They have called one of these early collections 'Q' (from the German Quelle, 'Source'). This Source Q contained Jesus' sermons, such as the 'Sermon on the Mount' (*Matt 5; Luke 6:20ff*), and many of his parables.

Finally, the scholars considered that, from AD 60 to the close of the first century, the Gospels of Matthew, Mark, Luke, and John were put together in the form we know them today. Most experts consider that Mark's Gospel was first, then Matthew, Luke and John. They were eventually called 'Gospels' because they recount the Good News of Jesus' birth, life, death, and Resurrection.

The Four Gospel Makers.

THE WRITING OF THE GOSPELS
The Dates of the New Testament Books

30	Death and Resurrection of Christ. The Christians preach the Good News.
30–50	The sayings of Jesus handed on mainly by word of mouth.
50–64	Collections of the sayings of Jesus.
64	Gospel of Mark.
70	Gospels of Matthew and Luke.
90	Gospel of John.

Christian tradition has associated the four Gospels with the names of Matthew, one of the Twelve chosen by Jesus (*Matt 10:3*), a tax collector.

Mark, the John Mark mentioned in the Acts of the Apostles, a companion of Paul (*Acts 12:12*). He may have been the young man who fled naked at the arrest of Jesus (*Mark 14:51–52*). Mark according to tradition, used Peter the apostle as his main source of his Gospel.

Luke, the friend and physician of Paul the apostle (*Col 4:14, 2 Tim 4:11, Phil 24*).

John, son of Zebedee, with his brother James, and Simon Peter, one of the three closest to Jesus among the Twelve (*Matt 17:1*). John was also the 'beloved disciple' who at the Last Supper reclined on his master's breast (*John 13:23*).

The Catholic Church does not commit us to believing that the four Gospels were written by these authors. That is a matter of debate. But the Second Vatican Council does commit us to affirming the 'apostolic origin of the four Gospels' (Dogmatic Constitution on Divine Revelation, para 18). This means that there is a real link between the four Gospels and the original apostolic witnesses of Christ.

This link is affirmed most clearly at the beginning of Luke's Gospel:

'Seeing that many others have undertaken to draw up accounts of the events that have taken place among us, exactly as these were handed down to us by those who from the outset were eye-

witnesses and ministers of the word, I in my turn, after carefully going over the whole story from the beginning, have decided to write an ordered account for you . . .' (1:1–3).

The link with eyewitnesses is confirmed by modern scholarship. The four Gospels were all written before the close of the first century AD, within the possible lifetime of eyewitnesses, and certainly within the lifetime of those who knew those first apostles.

Although the Gospels are not a verbatim account of what Jesus said, they are an accurate record of the sense of what Jesus said. To guarantee this, we have the inspiration of the Holy Spirit, which, Jesus said, would teach his

disciples everything, and remind them of what he had said (*John 14:26*).

The writers are believers. They have not just been won over by this man's personality. They believe he is the Son of God and write so that others might come to faith.

In the 19th century, some critical scholars thought that St John's Gospel was written at about 180 AD, a century and a half after the events narrated. The discovery of this fragment of St John's Gospel has completely discredited this extreme scepticism. This fragment has been dated reliably at the latest about AD 150. Since it is most unlikely to have been the first edition of St John's Gospel, scholars now will not date this Gospel later than the end of the first century AD; within the possible lifetime of the apostles, and certainly within the lifetime of those who knew them. And St John's Gospel, in the majority opinion, was the last Gospel written.

Symbols

The symbols associated with the four gospel writers are based on the vision of the four living figures in Ezekiel's vision (*Eze 1:5–12*). Each had four faces, a human, a lion, a calf and an eagle. In the book of Revelation four similar figures appear (*Rev 4:6–8*).

The early Church found these figures, who 'went where the Spirit urged them', a good symbol for the writers who produced the Gospels under the guidance of the Spirit.

Matthew is the human face because his Gospel begins with the family tree of Jesus, the man. Written for Jews it stresses Jesus the Messiah.

Mark's Gospel which is based on the teaching of the apostle Peter begins in the desert, the home of wild beasts, so his symbol is the lion. Jesus, in Mark, overcomes the devil who in early Christian symbolism figures as a lion. For example, 'your enemy the devil is on the prowl like a roaring lion' (*1 Pet 5:8*).

Luke wrote for Gentile Christians. His emblem is the calf, a symbol of

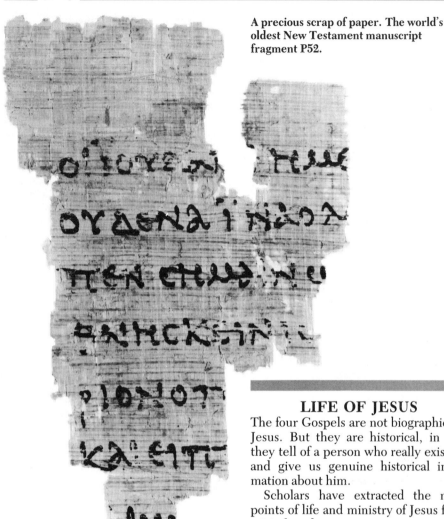

A precious scrap of paper. The world's oldest New Testament manuscript fragment P52.

sacrifice. His Gospel opens with the story of Zechariah taking his turn to offer sacrifice in the temple. Jesus, in Luke, is the Good Samaritan and Healer, laying down his life for all people.

The eagle fits John's Gospel which begins in the highest heaven with the Word who was in the beginning. Jesus in this Gospel is Christ the King, Son of God and Lord of all. John had written to deepen the faith of Christians when the first witnesses were dying and to make them realise that Christ had sent his Spirit to be with them at all times.

LIFE OF JESUS

The four Gospels are not biographies of Jesus. But they are historical, in that they tell of a person who really existed, and give us genuine historical information about him.

Scholars have extracted the main points of life and ministry of Jesus from critical study.

1. Jesus came from Nazareth in Galilee, and was born some time between 4 BC and AD 5. His mother was Mary, who was married to a man called Joseph.
2. At about the age of thirty (*Luke 3:23*), around AD 27 Jesus met the celebrated John the Baptist, who was teaching in the wilderness of Judaea, and was baptised by him.
3. Jesus began his ministry, being renowned for miracles of healing and exorcism, and becoming very popular (*Mark 1–3*). The place of his early ministry was in Galilee, modern northern Israel, and Jordan.

4. The main theme of his preaching was the kingdom of God, which was fulfilled in himself. He taught the people mainly in parables, and drew large audiences particularly around the shores of Tiberias.
5. He called disciples, and had many followers, being called 'Rabbi', a mark of respect, and 'prophet'. But he also had enemies, in particular scribes and pharisees, who saw him as a dangerous innovator (*Matt 15:3*).
6. A short time after the beginning of the ministry of Jesus, John the Baptist was beheaded by Herod the Tetrarch, son of Herod the Great (*Matt 14:1–12*). From that time onwards focus of interest shifted to Jesus, who became more and more aware of his impending death (*Matt 16:21–23*).
7. Jesus went to Jerusalem more than once in his public ministry (*John 2:13, 5:1, 7:10*), where he taught in the Temple area as did the Rabbis (*Mark 14:49; John 7–10*).
8. His final visit to Jerusalem took place at about AD 30. Jesus was arrested and put to death by crucifixion by order of Pontius Pilate, the Roman Procurator.

PRAYER

Prayer was defined by what is known as the 'Penny Catechism': 'The raising of the mind and heart to God'.

There is no better way of doing this than by reading about and meditating on Jesus in the Gospels.

That way you give time, patience, thought, openness, listening – and you will come much further in the knowledge of God and Jesus Christ.

You must learn to 'pray the Gospel'!

When 'praying the Gospel' you are not actually doing a textual criticism or especially seeking the original meaning of a word. You are asking the Spirit to lead you through the text, so that God really becomes Father and Jesus Christ is not a cardboard figure but your acquaintance, your friend and finally someone you love who loves you.

From the Gospel you can learn the story of Jesus' birth, life, preaching, miracles, teaching, death and resurrection. Reading his direct teaching and his parables you can learn his mind. Reading the miracles you can ponder God's power in him and in the world. Watching him with individuals – Peter, John, Judas, the woman of Samaria, the widow of Nain – you can know his compassion, forgiveness, tenderness and love.

Try these passages:

'God sent his Son into the world not to condemn the world, but that the world might be saved through him' (*John 3:17*).

'He who eats my flesh and drinks my blood has eternal life, and I will raise him up at the last day' (*John 6:54*).

'Blessed are they who hear the word of God and keep it' (*Luke 11:28*).

LIGHT FROM THE COUNCIL

The Church has always been concerned that 'reverence should attend the reading of the Gospel' at Mass (introduction to Lectionary 17). The Book of the Gospel was most carefully produced, was more highly embellished and was shown greater respect than was any other book of readings' (Ibid. 36).

The reason for such reverence and care is that 'among all the inspired writings, even among those of the New Testament, the Gospels have a special place, and rightly so, because they are our principal source for the life and teaching of the Incarnate Word, Our Saviour'. (Constitution on Divine Revelation No 18.)

QUESTIONS

1. Jesus most likely wrote nothing down. Has this been good or bad for Christianity?
2. Choose one of the parables and re-tell it in a modern setting.

11-Divine Life in Us

Christian Life is God's Life in Us.
God through Jesus His Son makes His Home in Us.
The Holy Spirit helps Us grow in Holiness.
Through God's help we are able to choose virtue.

Murillo's 'The Two Trinities'.

GOD IS always present to us. Sometimes we experience that presence and sometimes He seems to be far away. But he is always with us.

Many religions agree with this but disagree about how God is present. Christian faith is that we actually share in the inner life of God, the Father, the Son, and the Spirit. Jesus taught his disciples to call God 'Abba' – Daddy. Jesus taught us this, because through his coming we really have been made the children of God.

St Paul expresses this beautifully in the letter to the Romans. 'Everyone moved by the Spirit is a son of God. The spirit you received is not the spirit of slaves bringing fear into your lives again; it is the spirit of sons, and it makes us cry out "Abba, Father". The Spirit himself and our spirit bear united witness that we are children of God' (*Rom 8:14–16*).

It is the Holy Spirit who brings about this change. When Jesus was leaving his disciples he promised that he would come with the Father and that they would make their home in us. In the Gospel of John we find this promise fulfilled when Jesus is raised from the dead. He stands among his disciples and he says to them: 'Peace be with you'. Then he breathes on them and says 'Receive the Holy Spirit. For those whose sins you forgive, they are forgiven' (*John 20:22–23*).

We live by the Spirit of Jesus. 'I live now not with my own life but with the life of Christ who lives in me' (*Gal 2:20*). We are so identified with Christ that the love the Father has for us is the love he has for Christ. So it is, that we can pray in the name of Jesus. 'Anything you ask for from the Father he will grant in my name' (*John 16:23*).

Our Christian faith is founded in our relationship with God – the Father who created us out of love and to whom we are infinitely lovable – the Son who made that love visible in his life and death; the Spirit, the love of Father and Son who confirms us in the power to live in faith and love. The Trinity is not an abstract mystery up in the clouds somewhere. God comes to dwell in us and in Him we live and move and exist (*Acts 17:28*).

Our natural life is a mystery to us. We know it but we cannot grasp it. How much more true is it of God's life in us. God is known by us in the way someone who is loved knows the one who loves. When we love we enter into the world of the one we love. God, in Jesus, enters into our world and our lives because he loves us.

'Knowing' God means entering into a personal relationship founded in His totally unconditional love for us. But we are challenged also, to do our utmost to remain in and develop this relationship. Without it I cannot be fully myself.

PILGRIM PEOPLE

Christian faith is a journey through this world to the promised land of eternal happiness with God in heaven. None of us is perfect. We are on the way to perfection. The experience of the Church – the people of God – identifies three stages.

Every human being is a child of God by the fact of creation. Christians believe that because of original sin, our relationship with God is damaged. Baptism restores that relationship and through the gift of the Holy Spirit given to us in the death and resurrection of Christ we share the divine life.

But each of us must make our own response in faith. This is conversion. We commit ourselves to live in right relationship with God, following the example of His Son, Jesus Christ. We acknowledge the gift which enables us to do this, the Spirit of God. The theological term is justification (making righteous). We are set free to be what we are.

Our commitment brings us into the community of the Church, but there always remains a tension between the Holy Spirit in us and the old Adam, the inherent tendency towards sin.

The work of the Holy Spirit is to form Christ in us and us in Christ. Gradually and sometimes painfully his grace defeats the tendency to evil in us. This, in theological language, is sanctification – making us holy.

Holiness means not just freedom from sin, and good in the religious sense of the word, but whole and integrated human beings in a relationship of love with God. We are becoming what we are.

Not until we die will this tension between the tendency to sin and the divine life in us be resolved. Faith will give way to the sight of God and we will become perfectly what God wants us to be, in communion with Him and with each other.

It is impossible to imagine what this will be like except that it will be marvellous.

Theologians name this 'glorification'. Finally we are what we are.

There are two opposing forces in the human person. Some, the virtues, bring us closer to God – others, vices, keep us from him. The Spirit given at baptism, and the desires which spring from 'the flesh', that is from our disordered nature. In his letter to the Galatians (5:16–26), St Paul lists the virtues and vices.

'This is the time for the marriage of the Lamb' (Revelation 19:7).

FRUITS OF THE SPIRIT
love. John 13:35; 1 John 2:5
joy, delight. Rom 15:13
perseverance, patience,
   long-suffering. Rom 2:4
goodness of heart, kindness. Rom 2:4;
   2 Cor 6:6
goodness. Rom 15:14; 2 Thess 1:11
faithfulness. Matt 23:23
gentleness. 1 Cor 4:21
mastery, self-control. Acts 24:25;
   2 Pet 1:6

VIRTUE & VICE

Virtue (virtus in Latin) means 'everything that is excellent in the physical and moral constitution of a person'. The Romans in particular saw virtue in military terms, as courage and perseverance in battle. A virtue is a formed habit in us whereby we are able to translate good ideals into practical everyday living.

Vice (from the Latin vitium) means 'fault, blemish, deformity, depravity'. A vice, therefore, is any defect in us which prevents the growth of virtue.

The three theological virtues are faith, hope and love; called theological because they are particularly related to the life of God in us. (theos – Greek = God.)

But in reality, faith, hope and love

POISONS OF THE FLESH
sexual promiscuity. 1 Cor 5:1
idolatry. 1 Pet 4:3; 1 Cor 10:14
sorcery, witchcraft. Rev 9:21
hatred, enmity. Rom 8:7
jealousy. Rom 13:13
ambition, self-seeking, rivalry. 2 Cor
   12:20
heresy, factions. 1 Cor 11:19
drunkenness. Luke 21:34; Rom 13:13

God wants to marry us, too.

cannot grow in isolation from what are called the moral virtues, such as courage, perseverance, self-control. They are human qualities recognised as virtuous by everyone of whatever faith, or none.

Christian faith teaches that these human virtues have a new dynamism and direction given to them by the Holy Spirit in us. The power of the Spirit also strengthens virtue, and purifies from vice, it brings us to wholeness, that is, holiness, although usually this is a slow and gradual process. We need patience above all with ourselves.

QUESTIONS

1. What do I believe about God's relationship towards me?
2. What am I hoping for?
3. Do I believe God loves me unconditionally?
4. How do I express love for God?
5. How much have faith, hope and love brought me to adore God?
6. How do I express my adoration?

PLACE FOR PRAYER

God is always with us, but we need to find ways to make the divine life in us real to ourselves, hour by hour.

Different traditions have developed different methods. Brother Lawrence, a Carmelite lay brother (17th century) used the practice of the Presence of God – recalling God's presence all through the day. He was a soldier and court official for 20 years. Then for 30 years he was cook for the community. Prayer is rooted in daily life.

In the East, the 'mantra' or single word has often been used. It is used today by teachers of Christian meditation for individuals or groups. For instance there is one word 'maranatha' (1 Cor 16:22), and the phrase 'Come Lord Jesus' (Rev 22:30). The method is to take the word or phrase, use it in rhythm with your breathing or your heart beat, and repeat it gently over and over until it becomes a habit, almost a part of your existence.

Orthodox Eastern Prayer has for centuries used the Jesus Prayer in the same way. 'Lord Jesus Christ, Son of God, have mercy on me a sinner.'

The Cloud of Unknowing, the 14th century classic on mysticism, suggests using the one word 'Love'.

PRAYER

Lord Jesus Christ, help me to be still and know you are with me, in me. Help me to realise your presence at any time of day or night. Do not let me be so busy that I cannot remember you are with me.
Maranatha!
Come, Lord Jesus! Amen.

LIGHT FROM THE COUNCIL

There is one vocation, and one only, which is imperative for everyone: popes, bishops, priests, religious, lay people, married and single. That is the vocation to holiness: 'It is quite clear that all Christians in every walk or state of life are called to the fullness of Christian life and to the perfection of love' (Church 40).

'The Lord Jesus, divine teacher and model of all perfection, preached holiness of life (of which he is the author and maker) to each and every one of his disciples without distinction. "You therefore must be perfect, as your heavenly Father is perfect." For he sent the Holy Spirit to move them interiorly to love God with their whole heart, with their whole soul, with their whole understanding, and with their whole strength, and to love one another as Christ loved them'.

'The followers of Christ . . . have been made sons and daughters of God in the baptism of faith and partakers of the divine nature, and so are truly sanctified.' This holiness they must 'hold on to', putting on 'as God's chosen ones, holy and beloved, compassion, kindness, lowliness, meekness and patience'. When they sin – 'we all offend in many ways' – they must needs seek God's mercy 'and must pray every day: "And forgive us our debts"' (Church 40).

Infinitely varied the states and walks of life of Christians may be, but the holiness to which they all aspire is one. They 'act under God's Spirit and, obeying the Father's voice and adoring God the Father in spirit and in truth, follow Christ, poor, humble and cross-bearing, that they may deserve to be partakers of his glory. Each one according to his own gifts and duties, must steadfastly advance along the way of a living faith, which arouses hope and works through love' (Church 41).

12-Moral Teaching

The Church Teaches Right Conduct.
Sometimes, the Church clearly knows what is right.
But Moral Understanding grows in the Church.
All of us share in this growth.

WHY SHOULD the Church tell me what to do? First, because her teaching is not based purely on human reason. It has its foundations in the Word of God in Scripture and tradition. The Spirit of God who came upon the apostles at Pentecost continues to guide the Church into moral truth.

At no time in history have we been so effectively manipulated by 'the hidden persuaders'. The media, advertising and big business all conspire to make us do what 'they' want and what will make money for them. Should not the Church, founded by Christ, the Son of God, have the right to be equally energetic? It is not only a case of the Church telling me what to do. It is a case of the individual member of the Church, growing in faith, hope and love, and making his or her contribution.

At the same time, none of us is the whole Church. There is a tradition of moral teaching going back two thousand years that is part of the Church's life. There is also the official teaching mechanism of the Church, the magisterium, consisting of the pope and bishops, in consultation with theologians and experts.

Becoming a Catholic does not mean handing over our conscience to 'the Church', but recognising that the one Spirit is in the body of Christ, and in me.

The Church does not have all the answers. Some are clear and can be given with the full authority of the word of God. Sometimes the Church, like a body, is growing in its own awareness of the right way. And we are all called upon, as members of the body, to contribute to that growth.

THE CHURCH AND CONSCIENCE

'Conscience is the most secret core and sanctuary of a man. There he is alone with God, whose voice echoes in his depths'. This awesome description of conscience by Vatican II in the Constitution on the Church in the Modern World (p. 16) reflects a long tradition.

The word 'conscience' itself does not appear in the Hebrew scriptures or in the Gospels. St Paul took a Greek word (syneidesis) and applied it to the relationship between God and ourselves. This covenant is made first with the whole human race through Adam and then after the Fall through Noah, and then with Abram, renamed by God as Abraham, then with Moses and the people of Israel and finally in the new covenant with Jesus.

What can I do, Lord?

GROWING TOGETHER?

The Christian needs the community, especially the Church, to grow morally. The interaction between person and community is not simple. All members have a contribution to make to the shared understanding of Christian faith and morality. Each member has to develop his or her own understanding and convictions within the community, using its resources and the wisdom and experience of other members, especially leaders.

The responsibility of leaders is to promote personal convictions based on the established truths of the community. This requires respect for the integrity of the person and fidelity to acknowledged truth. Vatican II attempts to describe the delicacy of this task when it says: 'The truth cannot impose itself except by virtue of its own truth, as it makes its entrance into the mind at once quietly and with power' (Declaration on Religious Liberty).

FAITH AND ACTION

In discharging this two-fold responsibility every church member must have regard for the way people develop in their understanding of moral truth. What is accessible to an adult is not always accessible to a child. Many people remain childish in certain areas of moral behaviour. They must be helped to grow in understanding.

Moral development depends as much on good behaviour as it does on good instruction. The witness and example of a life of love remains the most forceful form of instruction in Christian living. Good practice also leads to fuller understanding.

MORAL TRUTH DEVELOPS

This has been recognised more in the last hundred years in the social teaching of the Church. From Pope Leo XIII's Rerum Novarum (1891) new dimensions of the moral life of the Christian disciple in society have been opened up. The 'social love' described by John Paul II goes far beyond the individual love of neighbour which was emphasised by earlier teaching.

Sometimes, the Church sets out her moral and social teaching as clear principles. Other times, particularly with new problems, church documents are a stimulus to discussion and reflection, rather than dogmatic statements.

A tension can exist between individual conscience and teaching authority, between respect for persons and commitment to truth. Jesus' disciples need to take seriously the way people grow, how truth is more fully understood, and the personal responsibility before God which no person can assume for another or pass to another.

What I decide to do concerns other people as well.

GROWTH OF CONSCIENCE

The foundations of Catholic morality are laid in the home and developed in school but must continue in adult life on a personal level and in the parish and community. It is contact with God in prayer, and the sacraments, which develops the mature Christian. From faith in God's love for me comes genuine appreciation of my value as a person. Self-respect enables me to appreciate others and their dignity and rights.

'Rules' must grow out of a loving relationship. If not they can appear as insensitive restrictions made by someone or some group who want to control and dominate.

MORAL AUTHORITY

The Church acts as teacher and mother. As teacher, she must set before us clearly the demands of the Gospel. She must equally show the individual the concern and compassion of Christ. This concern as mother involves an appreciation of the circumstances of each person's life.

To discover the true moral teaching the Church first looks to the life and teaching of Jesus; and then reflects on the experience of twenty centuries of Christian living. We can also learn a great deal about God's plan for us, and the natural law, by looking at His world, and at ourselves. In this way, we can often discover values and moral principles that we share not only with our fellow Christians but with many other people who are trying to do what is right.

There is great danger of seeing 'the Church' as Church authorities, but we all have our contribution to make to the Church's understanding of the Christian life; and this is being increasingly recognised. For example, public statements by bishops very often have lengthy consultation. There is, however, a history and a tradition of accumulated wisdom which is not of purely human origin, but is a gift of the Spirit. Catholics believe that the bishops are successors of the apostles, forming a 'college' in union with the Pope, the successor of Peter. These have the authority, given them by Christ, to represent the mind of the whole Church.

Our Lord promised that he would be with his church until the end of time, and that he would send the Holy Spirit to lead us into all truth. Thus a Catholic will always start from wanting to know the mind of Christ as the Christian community has come to understand it. The teaching of the Church is not just an ideal, but a real demand of Christ. Our Lord is always understanding and compassionate in the face of human failure and weakness, but he is always calling us to perfection.

Theologians disagree whether there are any infallible moral definitions in Church teaching. But there is a substantial amount of teaching which a Catholic must accept as part of the Church's magisterium.

One strand of clear moral teaching is the absolute sanctity of human life. In other words, it is always wrong deliberately to take the life of an innocent person such as in the case of abortion, murder or euthanasia.

This also means that a nuclear attack where millions of human beings are indiscriminately killed could never be justified, but this does not settle the question of the morality of nuclear weapons as a deterrent.

The Church's teaching authority clearly regards certain acts as being 'intrinsically disordered' or 'objectively wrong'. This does not necessarily indicate the moral guilt of this or that individual involved. The Church has great experience of human nature, and knows too well that mortal sin, that is, breaking off our relationship with God, is possible. However, it does not happen easily. Rather, it involves a free and deliberate decision with full knowledge, to turn away from God and his commandment. This must be in a grave or serious matter. But Christian life is not merely a matter of avoiding mortal sin, but rather a conscious desire to live as Christ would have us live each day. We must also remember that no sin is too great for forgiveness. To assure us of this, and to set us back on the road to renewal, Christ left us the sacrament of reconciliation (often called 'Confession').

MORTAL SIN

Many moral theologians are concerned that people should be aware how radical a decision sin must be in order to be 'mortal' (deadly): that is, to destroy the relationship of love with God.

The full decision of mind and heart must be involved. For instance, it is the tradition of the church that masturbation is objectively a grave sin. But, in order that an act of impurity would be sufficiently serious to destroy one's relationship with God, it would have to be much more than spontaneously giving in to a bad habit. It must be deliberate.

For a sin to be serious and deliberate, however, we do not necessarily need t make a conscious reference 'against God'. For instance, in the parable of the Last Judgement, Jesus condemns those who neglect to feed the hungry and clothe the naked (*Matt 25.45*). We must also remember that people are made in the image of God, and to ill-treat our neighbour is to ill-treat God.

However, even with the worst human actions, as Thomas Moore said, we do not have a window on a man's conscience. We never can know a person's motives. We can always say, 'There but for the grace of God go I'. And we can always say, as Jesus did, 'Father, forgive them, they do not know what they are doing'.

QUESTIONS
1. How can we help each other to develop morally?
2. Do you think that a moral life is perfectly possible without Christian faith?

LIGHT FROM THE COUNCIL
'It is therefore perfectly clear that all Christians in any state or walk of life are called to the fullness of Christian life and to the perfection of love, and by this holiness a more human manner of life is fostered also in earthly society. In order to reach this perfection the faithful should use the strength dealt out to them by Christ's gift, so that following in his footsteps and conforming to his image, doing the will of God in everything, they may wholeheartedly devote themselves to the glory of God and to the service of their neighbour' (from the Dogmatic Constitution of the Church).

'The Christian who shirks his temporal duties and shirks his duties towards his neighbour, neglects God himself and endangers his eternal salvation' (ibid).

LIGHT OF THE WORD
St Paul is clear that 'the law is holy' (*Rom 7:12*). But, a Christian who is filled with the Spirit of the risen Christ has taken on a greater commitment than that demanded by the Law. Such a follower of Christ is ruled by one law of the Spirit of love. If we love, says St Paul, we shall not commit adultery, kill or steal. 'Love can cause no harm to your neighbour, and so love is the fulfilment of the Law' (*Rom 13:8–10*).

PLACE FOR PRAYER
If we are serious about wanting to follow Christ, we will want to do his will, which includes prayer. Prayer does not solve all moral problems but the discipline of regular prayer helps widen self-discipline.

Openness to God inevitably casts light on my inner state, my sinfulness, my selfishness, my lack of love for God and others. It is difficult for anyone to live up to the high standard Jesus asks. But prayer can move mountains. 'If you love me, you will keep my commandments' (*John 14:15–17*).

True Love brings Happiness.

13-Love

has no legal limits.
comes from God.
acts in accordance with Natural Law.
is service to neighbour.

LOVE IS the most abused word in the English language. It is used to mean anything from self-sacrificing devotion to selfish lust.

C. S. Lewis, one of the greatest Christian communicators this century, speaks of four loves: Affection, Friendship, Eros and Charity.

Affection is the tender love of parent for child, or of an old age pensioner for his dog. Friendship is what Lewis calls companionship in common activities. Eros is a passionate love between the sexes. Charity is the love which is God himself, and which is poured into our hearts by the gift of the Holy Spirit.

For C. S. Lewis, all these loves are genuine. They spring from the fact that human beings have a physical and a spiritual dimension. We are related to the animals below, and to the angels above. Act according to these genuine loves, and we are acting morally. 'Love', said St Augustine, 'and do what you will'.

But these four loves can also go

wrong, due to our disordered nature as fallen creatures. Affection can become possessiveness. Friendship can be for what we can get out of the other person. Eros can simply be desire for pleasure, rather than desire for the other human being. And even charity can be perverted by using God to further our own ego.

The Christian life is a journey in which we purify our human loves, with God's help, to make them genuine; and learn day by day to relate affection, friendship and eros to charity, the highest love.

ALL YOU NEED IS LOVE?

Christian theology is clear that love is the greatest of the virtues. 'The greatest of them all is love', says St Paul (*1 Cor 13:13*). Paul also says that without love, none of the other virtues has any value in the sight of God. 'And though I have all the faith necessary to move mountains –

if I am without love, I am nothing' (*1 Cor 13:2*).

The problem about living is that we want to have a clear map of where we are going. We want rules and regulations which will guarantee a ticket to heaven.

This is not possible, precisely because the Catholic Church teaches the primacy of love among the virtues. If duty or hard work were the principle virtues, it would be easier. We could produce a list of duties to perform within a certain time span.

Generations of people seem to have got this message. Go to church on Sunday, say daily prayers, help a blind person across the street, and you will go to heaven. All these things are vitally important; and not to do them might put us in grave spiritual danger. 'Not everyone who says to me, "Lord, Lord", will enter the kingdom of heaven' said Jesus, 'But the one who does the will of my Father in heaven'. What we do is important. But that is not the whole story.

God made people to love each other.

That is that love has no limits. We can never say, 'I have kept all the rules, I am home and dry'. Always, we hear that command, 'Love God with ALL your heart . . . and your neighbour as yourself'. And we never know what the next demand of love will be.

Love is not afraid to make demands. If I love someone I want the best for them. This always includes discipline on my part and on theirs. If we love someone there are some things we will not do. The same applies to our relationship to God. In the Scriptures God's love is expressed first of all in the covenant, the bond between God and his people. 'You shall be my people and I shall be your God.'

Learning what true love is takes a life-time.

We discover what should be done by means of the Natural Law, the Word of God in Scriptures and the teaching of the Church. Conscience then judges whether the choices before us are right or wrong in the light of that knowledge.

THE NATURAL LAW

The Catholic Church has always taught that the basic principles of right and wrong are known to every human being even if those principles are partly obscured by our sinfulness.

This 'natural law', in all human beings is expressed in the Ten Commandments.

It is not like English law, it does not consist of clear written formulations. It is a principle of conduct within us, motivating us to do good, and to avoid evil.

It is not natural in the same sense as the laws which govern our physical life. These, the heart for example, operate whether I will them or not. But the natural law challenges our free will constantly. We are free to accept or to reject our conscience.

The law is 'natural' insofar as it springs from our very nature as human beings. To murder another human being is against the natural law because destroying human life made in God's image is against human nature.

The Natural Law as Christians understand it has no meaning without God. Because God is the author of life, we have an ultimate value, and have the 'right' to everything which furthers life – food, shelter, friendship, etc. The natural law is the law of God. It ensures that morality is not just a case of what we feel is right. There is truly an order, a law within us, which we ignore at our peril.

The supreme law of our nature is that of love. But again, that must be correctly understood. The Church has always resisted what are called 'situation ethics', which teach that there are no absolutes in moral teachings.

The Church needs rules. It teaches that love implies negatives, and sometimes absolute negatives. If I love my parents, I will not neglect them in their old age. If I respect the dignity of my neighbour, I will not degrade him in public. If I truly love my wife, I will not sleep with my secretary. These negatives are expressed in the Ten Commandments and are positive values of love.

Christian revelation is unique in saying that 'God is love' (*1 John 4:8*). The New Testament writers could make this statement because they had seen God's love in action in the life, death, and resurrection of Jesus. Jesus was and is God's love in this world.

To find out what love is, we look at Jesus. Not that this will immediately solve all our moral problems. Jesus lived at a specific place and time. He did not face the problem of nuclear weapons, or even have to drive a car.

That is why the presence of the Holy Spirit in the people of God is so important. We do not look back to Jesus as one who is dead. Rather, we possess his Spirit, who helps us to discern true love. He is the Spirit of Love.

Knowing that 'God loves me' I in turn bring that good news to others. In this way the face of the earth is renewed.

LOVING YOURSELF?

Love is at its most Christian when the recipient is not appreciative, takes it for granted, exploits or even rejects it, and yet we go on loving and serving, accepting in this the folly of the cross. It is this which makes people say: 'See these Christians, how they love one another'.

Jesus also commanded us equally to love ourselves.

This can be very difficult, as we are often plagued with a low opinion of ourselves.

We can become self-centred and distracted by this which stops us from giving and receiving love, and experiencing life fully.

We cannot love ourselves, if we are struggling with problems of worthlessness, unless we are loved by someone first. We need to have another person reflect to us that we are loving and lovable.

Therefore, loving myself in Christian terms means loving myself as Christ would love me. Seeing myself as Christ would see me. Of one thing I am certain. Jesus loved me so much. He laid down His life in sacrifice for me. He sees me with eyes of infinite love and compassion. It is obvious that I am very special to Him. One of the ways He expresses His love and how He sees me is through the eyes of someone who loves me. This is the closest I can get to an experience of how He is looking at me.

Loving oneself also involves a decision to surrendering our poor self-image and to have faith in the image presented by the One who loves us. There may be hesitation and doubt about surrendering that poor self-image. Would self-appreciation and evaluating my goodness amount to conceit? How should we behave towards someone complimenting us? It might be easier to brush it off, more comfortable to cling to the poor self-image as we may, at least, have learned to cope with it.

However, there should be no room for vanity when we remember that all the goodness we have, our talents and faculties are a gift from the Creator, and not of our own making. That faces us squarely with who we are – a creature belonging to God, and not a god in our own right. Loving oneself can be tough, but unless we do we cannot love anyone else.

PRACTICAL LOVING

When we hear of people whose needs are desperate, we immediately wonder what governments or charities could do to help. Our thoughts turn to money which seems a cure-all. Do we think of our own responsibility to show love to those in difficulty?

CONSIDER

Reconciliation in families could reduce the tally of 80,000 young people who did not have a roof over their heads last year.
A visit to one of the nation's 46,000 prisoners could mend their relationship with society.
A hand offered in friendship to one of Britain's AIDS victims could lessen their loneliness and fear.
A kind word, a smile, a gesture of affection might relieve the despair of someone on the edge of suicide.

ASK YOURSELF

Who are the 'poor' of my area? Do 'labels' prevent me from seeing a neighbour in need among 'the lapsed, the divorced, addicts, gays, ex-cons, AIDS victims, drop-outs, punks, vandals'?
Do I have a secret feeling that God is interested only in nice, intelligent, respectable, well-behaved people?
Who is the stranger in my neighbourhood?
Does 'custom, prejudice, fear or even law' build a barrier to my Christian love?
Does protesting help?
Have I failed to love enough?

Let us offer each other the sign of peace; and let peace be not only in church.

LOVE AND SERVICE

God does not call us in some rare mystical experience, or merely indirectly in the commands of conscience, but first and foremost in the needs of our neighbours. Indeed love of neighbour is not only an expression of my love for Him, but a test of that love. St John is quite explicit about this: a person 'cannot love God, whom he has not seen, if he does not love his brother, whom he has seen' (*1 John 4:20*).

But the connection was already made by Jesus himself in his description of the final judgement. Listing the works of mercy done to the hungry, the thirsty, the naked, the sick, the stranger, the imprisoned, he said: 'Whenever you did this for one of the least important of these brothers of mine, you did it for me'. Christian love of neighbour is not simply an act of obedience to God who commands it, but a recognition in action that those in need are brothers and sisters of Jesus. To be one with him and with his Father we must build up a community where people are truly brothers and sisters.

What does it mean in practice? First, that love is not mere talk or sentiment, but service. It is fine to feel sympathy for the starving in Ethiopia or the oppressed in South Africa, and I must do what I can to help them, but in daily living my neighbour is the person who turns up needing my help. His need is God's call to me.

Jesus gave no definition of 'neighbour' that would enable us to pick and choose, to exclude any. Judaism in his time considered hatred of enemies permissible, but Jesus said: 'Do good to those who hate you, bless those who curse you, pray for those who treat you with contempt'.

Christian forgiveness does not mean pardoning the enemy after he has apologised. Even the pagans do that. Our model is the prodigal father who rushes to welcome the erring son before he confesses, and pours out his love in a way that restores the son's confidence and self-respect.

Jesus is uncompromising in his demands as to how often we must forgive our neighbour. 'Not just seven times, but seventy times seven', without counting the times or the cost, because that is how our heavenly father forgives us.

The love of God poured into our hearts which invites and enables us to love our enemies should make us particularly sensitive to the plight of the poor, the weak, the sick, the neglected or shunned. We have only to look at the company Jesus kept to see that Christian love should break through all barriers that keep people apart.

PLACE FOR PRAYER

Prayer is about our loving relationship with God. Love is not simply an emotion, a falling in love. Love has to be worked at.

The mirror of this love is God's love in sending his Son. Jesus says: 'My food is to do the will of Him who sent me' (*John 4:34*). He had to work hard at this as he brought his human will into line with God's will. The cost, we can see at the Garden of Gethsemane.

This means in your daily life Jesus expects you to work out your salvation. You need to take on some form of discipline which can help you to centre on God in the midst of your ordinary busyness and distractions. So, for instance, you must exert your will out of your love for God, regularly each day, whether you feel like praying or not. It is the test of the seriousness of your love that you set aside time daily.

Morning and night prayers are an obvious example. Ejaculatory prayers during the day or a mantra are also excellent.

It is also important not only to 'say' prayers, but to follow Jesus' word and shut yourself in 'your private room' praying to God in secret. As an expression of love – stop – think – love. Only regularity, perseverance, and generosity will deepen your relationship of love. If you are doing your part, God will show you his everlasting love in return.

PRAYER

We wish you joy; try to grow perfect; encourage one another; have a common mind and live in peace, and the God of love and peace will be with you.

The grace of the Lord Jesus Christ, the love of God and the fellowship of the Holy Spirit be with you all (2 Cor 13:11,13).

LIGHT FROM THE COUNCIL

Our love for one another must be modelled on the limitless and everlasting love of the Father, Son and Holy Spirit.

There is a further and most challenging implication, that 'people can fully discover their true selves only in a sincere giving of themselves'.

'Today there is an inescapable duty to make ourselves the neighbour of everybody, no matter who they are and if we meet them to go to their aid, whether it be an aged person abandoned by all, a foreign worker held in low esteem, a refugee, an illegitimate child wrongly suffering for a sin he or she did not commit, or a starving human being who awakens our conscience by calling to mind the words of Christ: "As often as you did it to one of the least of my brethren, you did it to me"'.

(Church in the Modern World No 27.)

MONSIEUR VINCENT

All Saints are wonderful examples of loving God and other people. One particularly popular man throughout the world known for this is St Vincent de Paul.

He was a friend to all, prisoners, monarchs and bishops alike. He inspired people to care for each other, he spurred the church to feed the spiritually starved. His life spoke of God's love. It spoke to 17th-century France and it has inspired millions in the 300 years since his death. He is the patron saint of works of charity – Vincent de Paul.

But he was not born a saint. This man who has become an example of love and

**Some Christians have loved outstandingly,
like St Vincent de Paul.**

compassion admitted that by nature he was 'rough and cross'. It was the grace of God that made him tender, loving and always concerned for the needs of others.

At 20 he was a priest, with his eye on settling down in a comfortable, well-paid living in a country parish. For another 20 years he searched for fulfil-ment in travel, study, work as a chaplain in wealthy households; and all the time he was looking for a spiritual direction. Among those who helped him were Ss Francis de Sales and Jane Frances Chantal.

According to some accounts it was at the deathbed of a peasant that he be-came aware of the spiritual needs of the working poor of France. From then his life began to change. He inspired others to join him and he began with lay people. They went into the streets and into the homes of the poor. They found shelter for the sick, comfort for prisoners, food and clothing for those in need.

By the time he died at the age of eighty in 1660, he had also founded a community of priests to evangelise and a network of Confraternities of Charity. Together with Louise de Marillac he established the Daughters of Charity to serve the poor wherever they might be, battlefields, prisons, streets, hospitals, foundling homes.

His spiritual children in the Vincen-tians, the Daughters of Charity and the Society of St Vincent de Paul (SVP) con-tinue his work today.

He allowed God to touch his life, and learned to express God's love in loving others. Today there are 750,000 SVP members in 112 countries.

QUESTIONS
1. Use both Old and New Testament sources to show that God is love. How effectively, in your own experience, is this message being preached in the Church today? Are there any improvements you would suggest?
2. How do you understand the natural law? In your view is it possible to come to a knowledge of the natural law without Christianity?

14-Justice

was preached by the prophets.
was expressed in the
Ten Commandments.
was lived out completely by Jesus.
is yearning for 'right order'
in God's Kingdom.

Scales of Justice. The Old Bailey
Criminal Court, London.

JUSTICE IS the virtue by which we adjust. We try to reach a morally acceptable way of living in common, making way for love and friendship. To act justly is to have proper regard for others and what is due to them. It is unjust to take grapes from someone's vineyard and it is also unjust to buy grapes cheaply knowing someone else (perhaps an international company or a government) has appropriated them from a person too weak to claim their due.

Distance can blind our moral judgement. To be just we need to be well informed, weigh things up correctly; and investigate if we are suspicious.

We must take care to be involved in political and social life, and not just feather our own nest and opt for private affluence ignoring poverty around us.

Closely related to justice is this sense in the notion of distributive justice. This means that whoever has power or authority over common possessions must act justly in distributing them. The most obvious examples concern the State and governments. We need to examine how advantages, profits and resources are shared, taking trouble to avoid unjust accumulation, class interests and greed that deprive others of what should be theirs.

Distributive justice should be extended to cover relationships on a smaller scale too – in school, place of work or family. Justice does not only deal with money and possessions. Its purpose is to relate people to each other and each is due a basic and fundamental dignity and respect.

The Second Vatican Council taught that every person ought to have ready access to all that is necessary for a genuinely human life: food, clothing, housing, the right freely to choose a state of life and set up a family, the right to education, work, to a good name, to respect, to proper knowledge, to follow his conscience and safeguard privacy, and rightful freedom in matters of religion.

As individuals we need to keep the commitments we have made. In our home life we need to ask if we treat the others justly. Is each person getting their due; or are we using each other? Pope after pope has taught the importance of the social responsibility that goes with private possession, stewardship and trust. It is one thing to have a right to the possession of money and another to have a right to use the money as one pleases. We might be implicated in more injustice than we care to admit.

The Great Chart (Magna Carta) of British Justice, signed at Runnymede by King John.

Paul VI asked each individual to consider: am I prepared to support, at my own expense, projects designed to help the needy? Am I prepared to pay higher taxes so that public authorities can expand development work? Am I prepared to pay more for imported goods, so that the foreign producer may make a fairer profit? Am I prepared to emigrate in order to help the emerging nations?

Our society is rightly haunted by the centuries-old maxim, repeated at Vatican II:

'Feed the man dying of hunger, because if you do not feed him you are killing him.'

IS GOD JUST?

Horrors such as the Nazi concentration camps, the death of children and incurable diseases make many people ask how could a just God allow such terrible things to happen.

God is just. He has created a good world, but he has created human beings with free will and we can be violent, unjust and cruel. But he always promises that we will never suffer the ultimate misfortune – eternal death – if we follow his way.

God is just because he promises us the reward of justice – eternal happiness with him. He never allows any evil to happen to us without giving us the grace to endure it and without promising an even greater good to come out of it, although at the time we might not be able to see this.

We are aware as Christians that many who do not share our faith are examples of love, justice, and caring. One notable example is Gandhi, one of the greatest and holiest men of our time. But all of us know people who never go to Church, but who nevertheless sometimes put us to shame by their living-out of the command of love.

It is Catholic Faith that God is present in each individual, presenting opportunities for love and service. Vatican II's Pastoral Constitution on the Church in the Modern World is quite clear on this:

'For since Christ died for all, and since all men are in fact called to one and the same destiny, which is divine, we must hold that the Holy Spirit offers to all the possibility of being made partners, in a way known to God, in the paschal mystery' (para. 22).

But if non-Christians are doing good, then what is the point of being a Christian?

Our faith is that the Church is not the only place on earth where good happens but that the Church is the sign of the ultimate triumph of good. Being within the community of the Church identifies our commitment as God's own people, and gives us the most powerful moti-

vation for loving our neighbour. In the Church, we find that grace to love our neighbour, and we find unique opportunities for service.

As Christians, we beat our breasts and say that we need reformation. We think of the crusades, the Inquisition, the Borgias, when the Church has identified itself with oppression and even scandal. People who never go to Church have behaved much better than this.

But we must remember that the Church has a social record second to none. The caring institutions in European universities, schools, hospitals, relief organisations – all began with the Church.

If we criticise the Church for not doing enough – what am I doing? I am Church too!

One of the greatest fighters, for instance, in the modern Church was Archbishop Oscar Romero from San Salvador. He lived a simple and frugal life in a small room attached to the cancer hospital where he was looked after by the Carmelite Sisters. He had a small stereo and his special treat was to relax and listen to classical music.

He received all visitors, whether high officials from the State Department in Washington or illiterate peasants, with the same unfailing courtesy.

His ability to communicate was legendary.

Archbishop Romero was a model 'evangeliser'. He preached the Gospel clearly in all circumstances. He brought the Good News to the poor. But he also endeavoured at every stage to make the Word of God real and effective in El Salvador. The Gospel was Good News and it was for the poor. It became a light with which to make a critical judgement on everything which is contrary to God's plan.

The Good News for the poor became bad news for the wealthy and powerful. He denounced with the ferocity of the prophets of old the sinful structures which brought death; torture and killing, the exploitation on the plantations and in the factories, and the unjust land system which brought a slower but equally certain death through hunger and disease.

He called for conversion. It was a challenge to the interests of the powerful and an invitation to a change of heart. It was seen as a threat and was largely rejected.

He told the truth about the oppression of the poor and the atrocities they suffered. He put himself alongside them and offered them all the services of the Archdiocese. He gave them hope.

Archbishop Romero, like Martin Luther King, was a great evangeliser and like King he was persecuted and defamed for his preaching and his action: like him he was killed for it.

For the Church to remember Archbishop Romero means to continue his work.

He shows us that the social teaching of the Gospel and of the Churches is not just something to be admired but to be acted on.

All too frequently the Gospel is not being preached in its wholeness, it is not being shown as a challenge to the rich, but as routine, bland and anodyne. If the Churches take the Gospel seriously

they must get involved in trade with the Third World, unemployment and dignity of workers, the arms race and the nuclear question, and many other social questions. Authentic evangelisation is bringing Gospel values to bear on our world and its struggles.

CHRISTIAN LIFE MEANS DOING WHAT IS 'RIGHT' AND RESPECTING RIGHTS

John the Baptist was a martyr for justice. Fearlessly, he told King Herod that it was sinful for him to marry his brother Philip's wife (*Mark 6:18*). In fact, Herod Antipas had divorced his own wife in order to marry Herodias; and Herodias divorced Phillip.

The story of John the Baptist's beheading, at the request of the dancing Salome, is well known (*Mark 6:17–29*). At a time of sexual licence such as our own, John the Baptist stands up fearlessly against our society as well. Fidelity in marriage is also justice. Was John the Baptist, and not Stephen (*Acts 7:55–60*), the first Christian martyr?

Justice: living in a place like this? Britain's Dark Satanic Mills.

PLACE FOR PRAYER

There is a danger of becoming self-centred in prayer. Jesus illustrates this in the story of the publican and pharisee (*Luke 18:10–13*). If prayer is just you talking to God, it can become a cosy, private experience, leaving out the problems of the world.

The force of the great commandments is to love your neighbour as well as God and yourself. There must be balance. You can see balance in Jesus who is utterly given to people, yet always manages to slip away to pray. He links his work for others – miracles, preaching, calling apostles – with gaining renewed power through that time spent in prayer.

One yardstick for judging development in prayer is the depth of concern you have for the state of the world, for such issues as justice and peace.

This does not mean dashing out to join every group, never having a moment to yourself.

What it does mean is drawing closer to God in prayer, so that 'the mind is in you which is in Jesus Christ'. His concern is for all the world; yours becomes as wide. This concern shows in your life as your generosity and self-giving grow from your prayer. It is not easy to stand, sit or kneel before God humbly and openly, and to ignore the 'cries of the prisoners'.

PRAYER

Lord, make me an instrument of your peace.
Where there is hatred let me sow love,
where there is injury let me sow pardon,
where there is doubt let me sow faith,
where there is despair let me give hope,
where there is darkness let me give light,
where there is sadness let me give joy.
O, Divine Master grant that I may
not try to be comforted but to comfort
not try to be understood but to understand,
not try to be loved but to love.
Because it is in giving that we receive,
it is in forgiving that we are forgiven,
it is in dying that we are born to eternal life.

QUESTIONS

1. List some examples of prophets in the twentieth century. Which of these does each member of the group most admire and why?
2. It can sometimes seem impossible to reconcile the duty to love and forgive with the demands of justice. Using a real or imaginary situation (for example parole for someone serving a life sentence), suggest ways of dealing with the problem.

The eternal covenant. (See Genesis 9:12–17).

15-Hope

is an essential part of being a Christian.
is for the future.
is building a better world now.
is looking forward to the son of man.

IF ANYONE loses the will to live, death is never far away. We need a future that we can hope in, for ourselves and those we care about. An age which is obsessed with this world and sees nothing beyond is easy prey to despair and death.

When the bishops at Vatican II wanted to talk about the Church in today's world they began with the words 'Joy and hope' (gaudium et spes).

It is important to note the link be-tween hope and joy and to relate both to the future promised us by God. St Paul (*1 Cor 13:13*) brackets hope with faith and love as virtues of fundamental value.

Hope relates to the future good which is certain and attainable, but not auto-matic. The Christian hopes for everlast-ing happiness and finds strength to battle on despite failures and falls.

The celebrated German theologian, Karl Rahner, once wrote: 'We only know who God is and who man is when we hope'. He meant that hope gives impetus to our lives, enables us to commit ourselves to God and find peace in doing His will. The most radical act of hope was when Jesus gave himself to death on the Calvary cross. When all seemed lost, and he was apparently forsaken by his Father, the trusting hope of his prayer remained that the promise of salvation was being fulfilled.

Here we touch upon another essential element of hope, trusting acceptance of God's faithfulness. Hope means that we trust that God will keep his promises to me and to the world, and that we are all journeying towards a full experience of His love.

Christian hope is not only individual but also collective. We hope because we belong to the people of God, and are members of the Church, the body of Christ. We are a community of hope. We long for a world of peace, justice, love and truth.

Christian hope is far from passive. It must engage the individual and the whole Church in responsible action for a better world. It involves each of us in seeking our God's will. That is something we do by meditating on the revelation of God in Scripture and by participating in the Church's liturgy.

MARANATHA – COME LORD!

Christian waiting is not passive, but is eager expectation. When we say, with the early Christians, 'Come, Lord' we mean much more than 'Come, Lord, when you like. I will try to be ready for you'.

The early Christians said this together in their liturgy. They spoke it in Aramaic, the language Jesus and the first disciples spoke. And they meant 'Come, Lord, soon. We are ready for you and we will live our lives day by day as if you are coming immediately.'

The Christian vision of hope is breathtaking. It sees life as a shared pilgrimage from the city of man – where the powers of good and evil struggle for mastery – to the heavenly and eternal city of which we have been made citizens by our baptism.

In this world the people of God have a mission to reconcile and renew. We are called to restore to God the whole of our world. This gives us a task to be achieved in practical and political terms here and now. Hope enables us to commit ourselves to this task and not give up. But the hope which is 'stored up for us in heaven' is the promise of an eternal city, a new Jerusalem. There 'He will wipe away all tears from their eyes; there will be no more death, and no more mourning or sadness. The world of the past has gone' (Rev 21:4).

MORALS AND THE AFTER LIFE

It is easy to make our religion an insurance policy. Our thinking can go, 'If I behave myself on this earth, the Lord will reward me with eternal happiness when I die'.

This is a travesty of true religion. We should act well, not because we have eternal life as a reward, but because we know it is good to do what is right here and now, and to please God.

On the other hand because we are human we do not always live up to these pure motives. Then it helps to remember that what I do matters because I and my neighbour are made in God's image and I will have to answer for all I do before the judgement seat of God.

'When the Son of man comes in his glory . . . All nations will be assembled before him and he will separate people one from another as the shepherd separates sheep from goats . . .' (Matt 25:31–32). It matters whether we feed the hungry, visit the prisoners, and speak kindly to outcasts, because the Lord is in them.

'In so far as you did this to one of the least of these brothers of mine, you did it to me' (Matt 25:40). And we will be

We have an anchor that keeps the soul
Steadfast and sure while the billows roll,
Fastened on the rock which cannot move,
Grounded firm and deep in the Saviour's
love.

called upon to render an account of our stewardship, and the use we have made of our talents.

This brings us to the fiery question of hell. The New Testament word is 'gehenna', the name of the old rubbish tip outside Jerusalem which was often set alight by internal combustion – the 'fires of gehenna'. Does the place of eternal punishment which we called hell exist?

The Church has never defined that any particular individual has gone or will go to hell. She assures us that certain outstanding Christians – Mary the mother of Jesus, St Paul, St Thomas Aquinas, and many others – are in heaven. But the Church is not in the business of defining 'anti-saints'.

Some theologians, therefore, have conjectured that ultimately everyone will be saved, even the devil himself. God's mercy and love will eventually triumph in every individual. No-one, in this view, will suffer eternal punishment.

The Church has never formally rejected this idea. But we must realise that this is only conjecture. The warnings in the New Testament, and particularly the words of Jesus, are stern. He says

that the 'goats' on the left, who did not feed the hungry and clothe the naked 'will go to eternal punishment, and the upright to eternal life' (*Matt 25:46*).

In this life we can choose to reject God's love; and the Gospel tells us that such a rejection may have eternal consequences.

Hell is the state in which I become fixed in a position of being unable to accept God's love. I come to this state through the choices by which in situation after situation I form a habit of rejecting God's love.

The Good News is that no one need come to this state.

The Catholic Church teaches that the whole world will be transformed in Christ at the end of time. When and how this will happen we do not know. The transformation will include the resurrection of each person with their body. The Risen Christ had a body (*Luke 24:39*). He was recognised by those who knew him but clearly was also in some way different (*John 20:19*).

How will this happen? Paul, in 1 Corinthians 15, is struggling for words to explain it. He uses the analogy of a seed becoming a plant. The seed is the same 'being' as the plant, but the plant has become unrecognisable from its tiny seed when it is full-grown. So it will be, says Paul, at the Resurrection of the Body, in which the whole of the human race will share.

In this context, we can understand a little more when we say 'Christ will come again'. At this moment of transformation, Christ will be what he has always been, King of the Universe. But at that moment, we will not need faith to realise that. We shall see him, not only as our individual judge, but as the judge of the whole world. We need to recover some of the sense of urgency which the early Christians had for the second coming. Their image of the glorious Son of Man (*Daniel 7*) coming on the clouds of heaven might at least have kept them spiritually awake. They were also eager to see him again. When they said 'Christ

will come again', they did not only believe it; they were looking forward to it,
and committing themselves to bringing
that day forward.

What was it about Jesus which led
some Jews to recognise him as the
Messiah, while others remained un-
convinced?

HOPE – AT THE TIME
OF JESUS

Jewish people at the time of Jesus were
skilled at remembering the past, and
longing for a better future. The prophets
kept this hope alive.

The wolf shall dwell with the lamb,
and the leopard shall lie down with
the kid,
and the calf and the lion and the
fatling together,
and a little child shall lead them.
(*Isa 11:6*)
(See also *Jer 33:15; Eze 37:24*)

Up to the time of Jesus Jews had these
promises chiselled in their memories.
They experienced the joys and short-
comings of life. Their liturgy reminded
them that they were living between
Paradise Lost and Paradise Regained.

In the century before Jesus things
could hardly have been worse. The
glorious period of David was in the dim
past, and the more recent brief surge of
national pride had ended with the defeat of the Hasmoneans, and Pompey's
capture of Jerusalem in 63 BC.

Faithful Jews could hardly believe
that God would abandon them in their
hour of need. But what would he do?
Would some leader, a powerful politician, a soldier, prophet or holy man act
in his name?

Different groups had different expectations. In the Old Testament the
title 'Messiah' referred to any legitimately appointed priest or king. But in
later Jewish writings many of the ideals

The Jewish Community on the Dead Sea were also waiting for God to come.

and hopes of the people were focused on a specific anointed person, the Messiah, who would set things right.

According to the Psalms of Solomon, one of the most detailed accounts of some Jewish expectations in the immediate pre-Christian period, the Messiah would be a son of David, who would establish an everlasting kingdom of God.

> *See, Lord, and raise up for them*
>   *their king,*
> *the son of David, to rule over your*
>   *servant Israel . . .*
> *And he will be a righteous king*
>   *over them, taught by God.*
> *There will be no unrighteousness*
>   *among them in his days,*
> *for all shall be holy,*
> *and their king shall be the*
>   *'Christ-Lord' . . .*
>   *(Psalms of Solomon 17)*

With the odds stacked heavily against liberation by political or military means, the notion that God would act favourably within history appeared less than likely to some religious thinkers. History would have to be dramatically interrupted by God's intervention.

The New Testament documents come from people who believed that God's promises and Jewish expectations had been fulfilled in the mighty deeds and words of Jesus of Nazareth.

Luke presents Simeon and Anna as model Jews awaiting the Messiah (*Luke 2:25–28*). But Peter found it hard to reconcile suffering with his idea of the Messiah (*Matt 16:23*). The Eleven had to have their minds opened to understand the Scriptures that the Christ would suffer and be raised from the dead on the third day (*Luke 24:45*). The disciples on the way to Emmaus likewise found it hard to believe that the Christ should suffer and enter into his glory (*Luke 24:19–26*). And the last words of the Apostles to the departing Jesus were, 'Lord, will you at this time restore the kingdom to Israel?' It was not for them to know God's times or seasons (*Acts 1:6*).

THE LORD'S ANOINTED

For almost a thousand years after Abraham there had been no idea of a personal Messiah. God would bless his people and give them a land.

The Messiah King. *1 Kings 1:28–40*
The king was God's representative, being given God's spirit to enable him to fulfil this task. 'The Anointed One' (Hebrew, hamashiach, The Messiah). 1 Kings 21:1–29 and 2 Kings 16:1–4. But the kings of Israel and Judah were not good Messiahs. Most, according to the prophets, were a disaster. They did not reign in justice and worshipped false gods.

The Remnant. *Jeremiah 42:15,19*
All seemed lost. But the prophet saw hope for a purified people left behind after the disaster. The future lay with this remnant, provided that they obeyed the will of God.

The Good Shepherd. *Ezekiel 34*
The other prophet of the Exile saw coming an ideal shepherd of Israel, who would replace the 'wicked shepherds'. The people returned home from Exile rejoicing (538 BC), to rebuild their country. But their messianic hopes were not fulfilled. The political Messiah never came.

Elijah Coming Back. *2 Kings 2:12 and Malachi 3:2,3*
But by no means all Messianic hopes were political. Tradition had it that the prophet Elijah would return, coming down from heaven from whence he had ascended. The terrible day of the Lord would come.

The Anawim
The faithful Jews like Simeon (*Luke 2*) and Anna the prophetess were waiting for a Messiah to come who would be more like the Servant of Jahweh in Isaiah 42:1–5. This Messiah would bring justice to the land; he would not break the bruised reed, or quench the smoking flax. He would be good news for Gentiles as well as Jews.

JEWISH BELIEF

In Judaism religious practice is defined, belief is not, so the messianic hopes of former generations continue to live alongside each other, in addition to, or in place of, each other. All are a shorthand form for the future (it is no accident that the title of Israel's national anthem is 'The Hope'). All of them by implication compare the world as it is with the world as it ought to be, and the messianic task is the difference between them.

From this it is obvious that Jewish hopes have been various. The Messiah has been thought of as a man, an anointed king of the Davidic dynasty (Messiah means anointed), a general (bar Kochba), a statesman, a future or past king (rather than a priest or prophet), an age of peace and justice, someone who comes when all is lost, someone who comes when all is well, a suffering servant, the Jewish people, the redemptive element in every human being, a catastrophic event, and an act of love.

The messianic work has been thought of as including some or any of the following – the return from the exile, an independent Jewish state, peace in the Middle East, world peace, a change in human psychology, a change in the natural order ('the lion shall lie down with the lamb'), supernatural events, only natural ones, political utopias (liberation, socialist or Zionist), the restoration of the Temple with or without sacrifice, no restoration of the Temple but Jerusalem as a spiritual centre, the removal of restrictions in the Law, internal revelation to supplement the external one, the vindication of Judaism, the spread of its beliefs to all peoples, the union to all believers from all backgrounds and much else besides.

The Jewish messianic hope, so hidden in its origins, and so late to emerge has been the most potent of all its teachings. Christianity is built on it, and in a secular form it is a vital ingredient in the idea of 'progress'. In some form or other, it has conquered the world.

Jewish expectations have, in the main, concentrated on the establishment of God's kingdom on earth, and the Messiah or messianic age, as the agency of its reform. Some wait for it and some work for it. For some it is imminent, for others almost as remote as myth. Some have wondered if it is perhaps akin to the Christian second coming . . . perhaps.

PLACE FOR PRAYER

The discipline of prayer is simply that you should be there. Often nothing will seem to happen when you are there except distractions. You just have to wait. After waiting, waiting and waiting again – you wait! Believe the Lord is there with you – unseen, unfelt.

This faithfulness is essential to your relationship with our timeless and ever present God.

One of the best known commands to wait is the last message of Jesus to his friends: 'He charged them not to depart from Jerusalem, but to wait for the promise of the Father' (*Acts 1:4*). This they did: 'All these with one accord devoted themselves to prayer' (*Acts 1:14*). This was the first nine days of prayer recorded and from this grew a long-standing way of prayer called the 'Novena'.

PRAYER

Lord, you said ask and you will receive. Often we seem to ask and nothing happens. Help us to keep asking. Help us to praise and love you with patience and trust, day by day. Amen.

THE CLOCKMAKER'S DAUGHTER

Corrie ten Boom grew up in Holland in a shop full of clocks. Her father was a watchmaker and she was the first woman in Holland officially licensed to follow the same trade.

From her father, a preacher in the Dutch Reformed Church, she learned her Christian faith in homely everyday situations. The family was arrested for helping Jews. Her father died in prison and Corrie was with her sister when she died in Auschwitz. After the war Corrie became an evangelist and encourager. Her gift as a speaker was to relate the gospel to everyday life. Here she tells a Dutch parable:

A newly-made clock was put on a shelf between two old clocks. One of the old clocks said to the newcomer: 'I am sorry for you. If you'll just think ahead and see how many ticks it takes to tick through one year, you will never make it. It would have been better had the maker never wound you up'.

The new clock began to count the ticks.

'Each second requires two ticks, which means 120 ticks per minute.'

'That's 7,200 ticks an hour: 172,800 ticks a day, 1,209,600 ticks a week for 52 weeks which makes a total of 62,899,200 ticks a year. Horrors!'

He immediately had a nervous breakdown and stopped ticking!

But the wise old clock on the other side said 'Pay no attention to him. Just think. How many ticks do you have to tick at one time?'

'Why, only one, I guess', the new clock answered.

'There, now. That's not so hard is it? Try it along with me. Just one tick at a time.'

'Seventy-five years later the clock was still ticking perfectly one tick at a time!'

Moral: No man sinks under the burden of the day. It is only when yesterday's guilt is added to tomorrow's anxiety that our legs buckle.

QUESTION
1. 'We can justly consider that the future of humanity lies in the hands of those who are strong enough to provide coming generations with reasons for living and hoping' (Church in the Modern World, para 31). What reasons for living and hoping would you offer to coming generations?

Oh, please God, come on.

16-Incarnation

**Jesus is the Word become Flesh.
He was born of the Virgin Mary.
He shared our human nature completely.
He was and is God with us.**

CHRISTIAN FAITH is founded in an historical fact: Jesus of Nazareth lived and died and rose again in Palestine in the first thirty years of the first century AD.

He is the centre of our religion. The world has never been the same. The first Christians, who were all loyal Jews, had a powerful faith in the One God Yahweh. But, if Jesus was truly Lord, one with his Father in Heaven, then how could faith in the One God be preserved? Were there not two Gods now, Father and Son? And what about the Spirit, who came upon Jesus at his baptism, and upon the disciples at Pentecost? Were there three Gods? Or perhaps was there one God, with three different ways of showing himself?

After six centuries of controversy, the fully developed doctrine of the Trinity emerged. The Trinity (Tri-Unity) is the Christian faith that the One God is Father, Son and Spirit. Not three Gods, but One. And Father, Son and Spirit are not three aspects of God, but three persons in one God. It is because Christian faith is in Jesus as God made man, who sent his Spirit upon all believers, that the question of the Trinity emerged.

There was a second question, equally important. If Jesus was God, then how could he be human? The Greeks could understand that the gods walked the earth. It was often described in their own mythologies. But they could not understand how God could so lower himself to become a man, and immerse himself in the material universe (*Phil 2:1*).

The earliest heresy was not the denial of Jesus as God, but the denial that he was really human.

We find evidence of this before the

**Glory to God in the highest
And peace to his people on earth . . .**

close of the first century AD. Those who denied the humanity of Christ were called 'Docetists', because they believed that Jesus only seemed (Greek dokeo, appears) to be human. God could not die, they supposed. Therefore, Jesus could not have died on the cross. Simon of Cyrene, whom the Gospel of Luke tells us was made to carry Jesus' cross (*Luke* 23:26) in reality was put to death in his place, said some Docetists.

That is why we find such a strong affirmation of the true humanity of Christ in the Gospel and Epistles of John, written towards the close of the first century AD. 'The word was made flesh', says the Gospel of John, 'and lived among us' (*John* 1:14). And the First Epistle of John is even stronger, making belief in the humanity of Jesus a touchstone of faith (*1 John* 3:2–3).

The belief became known as the doctrine of the Incarnation – that in Jesus, God the Son has become flesh (incarnatus), that is human.

It became important for early Christians to provide a balance between the divinity and humanity of Christ, and to express both.

The human mind of Jesus was finite, created. Nevertheless, in the Middle Ages it was insisted that the human mind of Christ 'knew all things in the Word' (Thomas Aquinas).

But what do we mean by 'all things'? Do we mean that the infant Jesus, in his mother's arms, was aware of Einstein's mathematics and the Second World War?

This seems to make incredible the real humanity of Jesus. Modern theologians, therefore, have interpreted 'all things' as being 'all things relevant to his divine mission'; and known by Jesus in a human way. This knowledge came from his unique awareness of God as his Father.

There is an opposite danger in modern theology, that the divinity of Christ will be underplayed. This radical view is linked very much with the rise of modern biblical criticism, and the question of the 'historical Jesus'.

If Christ is to be our Saviour, he must not merely be God for us, but God with us, the true Emmanuel (*Isa* 7:14). This is the teaching of the New Testament, expressing the basic meaning of Christian worship. In the letter to the Ephesians (2:18) it is stated 'In him we both (Jew and Gentile) have access to the Father in the one Spirit'.

Unless we believe that Jesus the man is also truly God, we cannot expect him to be our Saviour and lead us to God.

INCARNATION AND LIFE

Through the Incarnation God has become one of mankind, he has become flesh and has forever 'hallowed the flesh'. The flesh, that is all human reality, all material things, has been made holy by the mystery of God's descent into matter.

All matter, through the power of the Holy Spirit, has become for us the principle whereby God's presence in the world is revealed to us. All reality is incarnational; all creation can disclose to us the love of God. This means that in the midst of the affairs of our daily life we can encounter God. Indeed the Second Vatican Council says:

'The laity, by their very vocation, seek the kingdom of God by engaging in temporal affairs and by ordering them according to the plan of God' (*Lumen gentium* 31).

To foster and maintain this vision we need an 'incarnational spirituality', which enables us to seek and find the kingdom of God in the midst of the business and the tasks of each day. Because of the Incarnation there can be no split between religion and life, between faith and work, between social life and spiritual life. Such a split, as the Council says, must be 'counted among the more serious errors of our age' (*GS* 43).

So often this split between religion and life occurs because religion remains in the intellectual realms and does not touch on experience.

Incarnational spirituality is experiential because it seeks, in the words of St Ignatius, 'to find God in all things'. It is experiential on a threefold level. On a personal level it is becoming aware of 'Christ in us, our hope of glory'

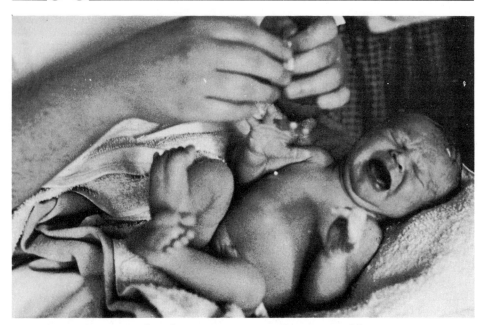

He shared our sorrows; even at five minutes old.

(*Col 1:27*); on a social level it is awareness that 'by his Incarnation the Son of
God in a certain way united himself
with each man' (*Gaudium et spes 22*);
on a political and economic level it is
realisation that we seek the kingdom of
God 'by engaging in temporal affairs'
(*LG 31*).

The Incarnation sheds a completely
new light on the whole of human existence and thus 'fully reveals man to himself'. As the Council says 'the truth is
that only in the mystery of the Incarnate
Word does the mystery of man take on
light' (*GS 22*) – the mystery is, Christ in
us, Christ in our neighbour, Christ's
Kingdom in the world.

But we must not confuse thinking
about the spiritual life with the life itself.
No one ever got intoxicated by thinking
about wine! Because Mary was open to
the Holy Spirit, Jesus became incarnate
in her womb. As we open our whole
lives to that same Holy Spirit, Christ is
formed in us and, in the most encouraging word of St Paul 'Christ becomes
our wisdom, and our virtue, and our
holiness and our freedom' (*1 Cor 1:30*).

Because of the Incarnation the whole

of creation discloses to us the glory and
love of God. We live out this great mystery in our own lives when we praise
God for the wonders of his creation and,
most of all, when we praise him for the
wonder of ourselves. As the Holy Spirit
teaches us to pray, 'For all these mysteries I thank you, for the wonder of
myself, for the wonder of your work'
(*Ps 139:14*).

As we pray in this way, thanking God
for the wonder of our being, we become
aware of that Original Blessing of creation and we hear again the words 'God
saw that it was very good' (*Gen 1:31*).

JESUS – THE EVIDENCE

Christians believe that Jesus is God and
Man. This is first and foremost a matter
of faith, and cannot be answered entirely by examining the historical evidence. But it is important for us to
demonstrate that Jesus really existed,
and that we have historical evidence
about his life on earth. Otherwise, our
faith that he was the most important
person who lived on this planet would
be unreasonable. Also, we would be
contradicting what we have already

claimed; that in Jesus, God actually became man. If he did, then it is essential to try to know something about Jesus, and the historical situation in which he lived.

Most of our historical information about Jesus is in the four Gospels, of Matthew, Mark, Luke and John. But is this information, written by believing Christians, confirmed by other sources?

The most reliable evidence outside the Gospels is that of Tacitus, the Roman historian, writing in AD 115. He is no friend of Christianity. But he writes of Jesus as a man who existed. Referring to the Great Fire of Rome in AD 64, and to the Emperor Nero fixing the blame on Christians, Tacitus traces the name 'Christian' back to 'Christus': 'who was executed by sentence of the procurator Pontius Pilate when Tiberius was emperor. That checked the pernicious superstition for a short time, but it broke out afresh – not only in Judaea, where the plague first arose, but in Rome itself, where all the horrible and shameful things in the world collect and find a home' (*Annals, xv, 44*).

The younger Pliny, while governor of Bithynia in Asia Minor, wrote to the Emperor Trajan about AD 112, asking what to do about the problems caused by the remarkable spread of Christianity in the province. The defence put forward by those who denied they were Christians throws light on early Christian customs. Pliny writes: 'they would meet on a fixed day before dawn and sing responsively a hymn to Christ as to a god, and to bind themselves by oath, not to some crime, but not to commit fraud, theft, or adultery, not to falsify their trust, nor to refuse to return a trust when called upon to do so. When this was over, it was their custom to depart and to assemble again to partake of food – but ordinary and innocent food. Even this, they affirmed, they had ceased to do after my edict by which, in accordance with your instructions, I had forbidden political associations. Accordingly, I judged it all the more necessary to find out what the truth was by torturing two female slaves who were called deaconesses. But I discovered nothing else but depraved, excessive superstition.'

Josephus, the Jewish historian, who completed his Antiquities of the Jews in Rome during the reign of Domitian (AD 81–91), twice mentions Jesus. In the first text (XX 9.1) he refers to the stoning of James, 'the brother of Jesus the so-called Christ', in AD 62. The second (XXVIII.3.3), mentions Jesus, who 'drew to himself many Jews and many of the Greek race . . . Pilate at the instance of the foremost men among us sentenced him to be crucified . . . and even now the tribe of Christians named after him is not extinct.'

In an earlier document, The Jewish War (about AD 77), there is the following description:

'It was at that time that a man appeared – if "man" is the right word – who had all the attributes of a man but seemed to be something greater. His actions, certainly, were superhuman, for he worked such wonderful and amazing miracles that I for one cannot regard him as a man; yet in view of his likeness to ourselves I cannot regard him as an angel either. Everything that some hidden power enabled him to do he did by an authoritative word.

'Many of the common people flocked after him and followed his teaching. There was a wave of excited expectation that he would enable the Jewish tribes to throw off the Roman yoke. As a rule he was to be found opposite the City on the Mount of Olives, where also he healed the sick. He gathered round him 150 assistants and masses of followers. When they saw his ability to do whatever he wished by a word, they told him that they wanted him to enter the City, destroy the Roman troops, and make himself King; but he took no notice.'

Some historians question the authenticity of this passage as it is found only in the Slavonic manuscript of the Jewish Wars.

But Jewish tradition accepts the existence of Jesus as historical fact. This
tradition, collected in the body of writings known as the Talmud, taught that
Jesus was a practiser of magic (referring
to his controversies with the Rabbis of
his day), and was hanged on Passover
Eve for heresy and for misleading the
people.

If Jesus had in fact never existed,
Jewish tradition would soon have spread
the story with glee.

The fact that the enemies of Christianity accept the fact of the existence of
Jesus is a most powerful argument for its
being an indisputable truth of history.

The system of dating by the birth of
Christ is only one of the many dating-
systems; others number from the Jewish
calculation of the day of creation, now
(1987) in the year 5747, or the prophet
Muhammad, the Muslim calendar is in
the year 1407. At the time of Jesus himself many systems were in operation
round the Mediterranean, of which
Luke (3:1–2) mentions a selection, still
not including, for instance, the Greek
system based on four-yearly Olympiads.
It was not for over 500 years that anyone
thought of using the birth of Christ as
the starting-point of a new era. And then
the monk who worked it out, Dionysius

Exiguus, got it wrong. He interpreted
the 'about 30 years old' of Jesus in Luke
3:23 as though it meant exactly 30 years
old.

If we are to take the historical data of
the infancy stories seriously, Jesus must
have been born before 5 BC. King
Herod died in 4 BC, and Jesus must
surely have been a year old if Herod
ordered the boy children up to the age of
two to be killed. Other data of the
infancy stories give little help: the cen-
sus of Luke probably took nine years to
complete.

But why 25th December? Nobody
knew the day or the season of Jesus'
birth. But a couple of days after the
winter solstice, the longest night and
shortest day of the year, the Romans had
a feast of the birth of the new sun. As the
symbolism of Christ as 'the rising Sun
come from on high to visit us' (*Luke 1:78*)
became more popular – and there is a
memorable wall-painting of it in the
catacombs below St Peter's – this feast
day seemed an eminently suitable day.
In the Eastern Church the Epiphany
receives more prominence than the day
of the Nativity, and this seems to date
from the fourth century, when the feast
spread to counter the still lively Alexan-
drian festival of the birth of the divine
'Eternity' on 6th January.

THE GOSPEL ACCOUNTS

Matthew and Luke present the birth of
Jesus from different perspectives.
Matthew recounts the annunciation to
Joseph (*Matt 1:18–25*); whereas Luke
recounts the annunciation of the angel
Gabriel to Mary (*Luke 1:26–38*).

Clearly, different traditions are at
work. It is all the more remarkable that
Matthew and Luke both record the following facts:

1. The principal characters were Jesus,
   Mary and Joseph.
2. These events happened in the days of
   Herod the King (*Matt 2:1; Luke 1:5*).
3. Mary, a virgin, was betrothed – a

formal engagement – to Joseph (*Matt
1:18; Luke 1:27, 2:5*).
4. Joseph was descended from David
   (*Matt 1:16; Luke 1:27, 2:4*).
5. Jesus was conceived in Mary's womb
   without intercourse with a male
   (*Matt 1:18,20; Luke 2:7*).
6. Jesus was born of Mary in Bethlehem
   (*Matt 1:25; Luke 2:7*).
7. The name Jesus was given prior to his
   birth (*Matt 1:21; Luke 1:31*).
8. Jesus was descended from David
   (*Matt 1:1; Luke 1:32*).
9. The family settled finally in Nazareth
   (*Matt 2:23; Luke 2:51*).

Come and join the Holy Family.

BORN OF THE VIRGIN MARY

Matthew and Luke both testify that Mary did not have intercourse with her husband Joseph, or with any other man, before Jesus was born (*Luke 1:34–36; Matt 1:18–25*).

This belief has always been part of Catholic Faith. Ignatius of Antioch (AD 117) and Irenaeus of Lyons (AD 180) are early witnesses among the Fathers of the Church. And the Perpetual Virginity of Mary was defined by the General Council of the Lateran (AD 649).

From early on, the doctrine of the virginal conception of Jesus was ridiculed.

But Christian faith refused to be put off. Ignatius argued that the virginity of

Mary was a sign of the new beginning in Christ. Adam and Eve communicated sin and death to the human race, said Irenaeus. The virginity of Mary, the new Eve, was a sign of this new beginning.

The virginal conception of Jesus is a sign, not only of this new beginning but also of the fact that Jesus is both God – because only God is his Father – and Man, because he shared in the flesh of Mary his mother. The Virginal Conception is one of the greatest safeguards of the true doctrine of Christ, as God and Man.

The miracle of the Virginal Conception does not mean that Jesus did not share our human condition. He learnt, worked, slept, prayed, suffered, and died as we all do. The way of his coming into the world is extraordinary simply because God becoming man was extraordinary.

LIGHT FROM THE COUNCIL

The word 'incarnation' comes from the Latin 'caro', which means flesh. 'The Word was made flesh' is a way of saying that God became man. The expression draws attention to the visibility which the Second Person of the Blessed Trinity, the Word, acquired when he became man. He was seen in the flesh. Being visible in the flesh he showed men and women what God was like. He revealed God to them and that is how the Constitution on Divine Revelation (No 2) presents the Incarnation: 'The most intimate truth . . . about God . . . shines forth in Christ, who is himself both the mediator and the sum total of Revelation'. The same Constitution offers a fuller exposition a little later. 'After God had spoken many times and in various ways through the prophets, "in these last days he has spoken to us by a Son." For he sent his Son, the eternal Word who enlightens all men, to dwell among men and to tell them about the inner life of God. Hence, Jesus Christ, sent as "a man among men", "speaks the words of God" and accomplishes the saving work which the Father gave him to do.'

(Constitution on Divine Revelation No 4.)

PRAYER

'The Word became flesh and dwelt among us' (John 1:14). This reality of Emmanuel – God-with-us – is central to all Christian growth in prayer relationship with God.

God has proved that he is not 'out there' but is here now.

As a sacrament – a sign of God's presence, Christ lived among us. Jesus Christ has made it possible for the human mind and imagination to focus on what he said and did while he lived.

The New Testament is an excellent help to prayer and meditation. St Ignatius Loyola and others introduced a pattern which can be followed, it is like this: Choose your passage – say the angel coming to Mary in Luke 1:26–38. Read it through twice slowly. Then set the scene – picture it in any way you like with Mary, Joseph, Jesus, the Shepherds etc.

Imagine yourself there as one of the characters – a shepherd, Joseph, Mary. Live in the scene, and experiencing it, see what comes into your mind and heart to which you can respond. This may be a very simple thought coming up from inside – 'Thank you' – or being filled with wonder – or feeling very humble in the presence of God made man.

This example you can extend to any passage relating to the life of Christ. Making a practice of such meditation works wonders in our growth in prayer.

How rich and deep are the wisdom and knowledge of God! We cannot reach the root of his decisions or his ways. Who has ever known the mind of the Lord? Who has ever been his adviser? Who has given anything to him, so that his presents come only as a debt returned? Everything there is comes from him and is caused by him and exists for him. To him be glory for ever! Amen (Rom 11:33–36).

QUESTIONS

1. Can a Christian legitimately seek for success, fame, promotion and leadership in worldly affairs?
2. 'Christian understanding of the Incarnation must hold a proper balance between the humanity and divinity of Christ.' Why is this so important? What dangers can you see of moving to either extreme?

NO ROOM AT THE INN

Christmas is more popular than Easter. All sorts of people who never normally go near a Church will be there. Why? The reasons will be mixed – nostalgia? curiosity? memories of lost innocence? feeling on the fringes but still wanting to be there?

And what Good News will they hear? It is tempting for preachers to call for 'Christ to be put back into Christmas' and challenge the 'hardy annuals' to be more regular in joining the worshipping community.

What is the challenge to the regular worshippers? Gandhi's comment, 'I love your Christ but not your Christians' makes quite a good start. The Church is called to become as caring and forgiving as Christ. It would be great if people could look at us as a Church and say 'Now we know what Christ is like'.

Charity begins at home and we might well begin by looking at those within the Church whom we call the 'Marginalised'. These include homosexuals, divorced and remarried, laicised priests and others who may feel that they exist on the fringes of the Church's life.

They need a welcome and an invitation to feel more at home. Or is there still no room at the inn?

17-Ministry of Jesus

Jesus preached the Good News of the Kingdom.
He called disciples.
He understood that he had to die and rise again.
He calls us to follow his Way – the way to God.

THE CONTEMPORARIES of Jesus knew him as one who healed the sick, opened the eyes of the blind, preached the good news to the poor, and challenged the establishment (*Luke 4:16–19*).

That was the difference between Jesus and any prophet before him. The prophets were excellent at telling people what they must, and must not, do, in the name of the Lord. What made Jesus different was that as God and Saviour Jesus brought salvation. He was not just a bearer of the message.

He came to die in a way no one else could, to save the whole of humanity. He came to show us, in word and action, that God loves us. He also showed us what God is like. 'Anyone who has seen me has seen the father' (*John 14:9*). Jesus is the Way to God.

Jesus' mission was one of love and forgiveness. But it was also a challenge to the faith of his hearers. His claims for himself were simply too much for many; and some who flocked to hear him and see him perform miracles went away when they heard what seemed to be blasphemy (*John 6:66*). But Peter in the name of the twelve expressed faith in Jesus: 'Lord, to whom shall we go? You have the message of eternal life, and we believe, we have come to know that you are the Holy One of God' (*John 6:67–69*).

The Christian faith affirms that in Jesus of Nazareth the eternal Word of God became man for our salvation. His incarnation, as we have just seen in the previous chapter, means that he was born at a particular time, in a particular place, into a particular family and nation, and lived in a particular historical situation. He became a figure of national significance during his lifetime but his ministry was limited to his own people, the Jews. His international significance increased phenomenally after his death and resurrection. Within a few years his followers began to proclaim him as Lord and Saviour throughout the Gentile world.

Hints of the mission to non-Jews appear earlier. St John tells us, for example, that the inscription placed above Jesus on the cross, announcing his identity and the charge on which he was sentenced to death, was written in Hebrew, Latin and Greek. The Hebrew needs no explanation; he lived and died in the land of Israel.

But why Latin? Because the land of Israel was at that time under Roman domination; the judge who pronounced the death sentence was the Roman governor of Judaea. And why Greek? Because Greek was the lingua franca of the Near and Middle East at that time. The empire which Alexander the Great had conquered for himself over three centuries before did not long outlast his death as a political unit, but as a cultural unit it endured for a thousand years.

To this cultural unit Jewish Palestine belonged, sharing its Greek language and (in some degree) its Greek way of life, although some of its population, following the precedent of the Maccabees, resisted these alien influences vigorously. It was to these latter elements in the population that Jesus belonged; he shared the traditional Jewish language and Jewish heritage. He spoke and taught, for the most part, in Aramaic, but the Gospels were written in Greek, because they were intended not for one nation only, but for all.

It is important to view Jesus in his

In the Steps of Jesus. Archaeology has uncovered the steps to the Temple at the time of Christ.

Capernaum, where Jesus taught in the synagogue.

historical situation, if we wish to apply his example and teaching to our lives. Even if our situation does not seem to have much in common with his, to see how he responded helps us to relate his response to our situation, making appropriate adjustments and adaptations.

Nothing anchors Jesus more securely in history than the fact of his death. Nothing makes him more truly the Christ of faith than the fact of his resurrection. It is because of this that we know him as the risen Lord, the Saviour of the world, the Builder of his Church, the coming King.

Apart from the historical Jesus, the Christ of faith might be a figment of our imagination; as it is, we know who we believe in because he lived on earth, he shared our human lot, he died and rose again, he is always present when we need him.

THE GOOD NEWS OF THE KINGDOM

All four Gospels link the beginning of Jesus' ministry to that of John the Baptist. Jesus' message was very similar to John's, and possibly was even inspired by him. They both called for repentance because the kingdom of heaven is close at hand (*Matt 3:2, 4:17*). John's personal appearance, asceticism and preaching all proclaimed an inevitable, imminent judgement that men and women would escape if they underwent a baptism of repentance and radically changed their lives. But Jesus' prophetic message proclaimed that the kingdom had arrived.

The reign of God is not so much God's violent intervention, but the revelation of God's identity in all its fullness. Jesus' ministry is one of making this good news known. His parables express this from several different angles. The parables of the sower (*Matt 13:4–9*), the mustard

Come down, Zacchaeus. I am going to have dinner with you today.

seed and the leaven (*Matt 13:31–33*) speak about the inevitability of God's full and final manifestation. The parable of the unmerciful servant (*Matt 18:23–35*) speaks dramatically of the human response of forgiving others – not as a condition of God's love but as a consequence of it. The parable of the good Samaritan, besides answering the question 'who is my neighbour', is another lesson in undeserved, even extravagant response to someone in need. These and other parables point to the God whom Jesus describes with a special word: 'abba'. And this is a term of endearment for a father, similar to our word 'papa' or 'daddy'.

Jesus' message of God's nearness in mercy was offered to all of Israel; not just an elect few. And Jesus did not only say God was merciful. His actions showed this.

Some religious groups in Jesus' day tended to separate themselves from ordinary people and especially from those considered 'unclean' or sinners. Anyone suffering from a disease, for instance, or from what was considered a demonic possession, was considered unworthy of the coming deliverance of Israel. Anyone who collaborated with the Roman occupation forces, and in particular the tax collectors or 'publicans', were without hope. Women of easy virtue were also excluded, as well as other marginalised individuals in Jewish culture like half-Jewish Samaritans, non-Jews or the poor.

But Jesus offered the gift of God's graciousness to all – and this was a large part of his Good News. Only those who stubbornly refused to accept this offer – or who refused to accept that it was offered to all – would go unforgiven and unreconciled. In Matthew 12:31 Jesus is reported to have said that any sin could be forgiven except this refusal, which was 'blasphemy against the Spirit'.

It was this indiscriminate generosity and reconciling love that was seen in all Jesus' healings. It was God's fatherly/motherly care that was revealed in Jesus' association – particularly in the intimate gesture of sharing meals – with outcasts and sinners, rich and poor, male and female, religious elite, or religiously excluded, with men like Zacchaeus the tax collector and Simon the pharisee and women like Mary of Magdala.

Jesus' parables of the wicked tenants (*Mark 12:1–12*), of the wedding feast (*Matt 22:1–10*) and the great parable of the final judgement (*Matt 25:31–46*) all illustrate Jesus' conviction that God's reign is intended for all, and that now is the time for a joyful but radical change of heart.

As a Church our task is to continue Jesus' ministry of proclaiming the reign of God. We do this in our faithful teaching of the message of God's indiscriminate, lavish love, and in our own actions on behalf of men and women of all nationalities, all races, and all degrees of brokenness.

WHO DO YOU SAY I AM?

From the beginning of the public ministry of Jesus people were saying 'Who is this man? He gives orders to unclean spirits and they obey him' (*Mark 1:27*).

Jesus was reluctant at first to encourage too much speculation as to his true identity (*Mark 3:12*). This may have been either because the people would have followed him for sensationalist reasons rather than for his message; or because they would have expected him to lead a revolt against the Romans if he gained the reputation of being the Messiah (*John 6:15*).

He wanted to be known as the one who brought the kingdom of God (*Luke 11:20*), conquering the power of the kingdom of Satan by his healing miracles and by his exorcisms, the healing power of God in action.

But he could not stop people wondering. He challenged his own disciples to answer, 'Who do you say I am?' (*Matt 16:14*). Peter's response of faith, 'You are the Christ . . .' drew the answer from Jesus that human beings had not revealed this to him, but God the Father.

As time went on, Jesus began to make statements which seemed to be blasphemous to his Jewish hearers. 'Who can forgive sins but God?', said the bystanders angrily after Jesus had said to a sick man, 'Your sins are forgiven you' (*Mark 2:1–12*).

But it was when he went to Jerusalem that the real 'offence' occurred, as the Gospel of John recounts (chapters 7–10). Jesus became more forthcoming about his own identity. 'Before Abraham was, I AM' (*John 8:58*), he said, linking his identity back to the Yahweh God of the Old Testament (*Ex 3:14*). The Gospel tells us that the Jews took up stones then to stone him for blasphemy, but Jesus escaped and left the Temple (*John 8:59*).

FOLLOWING JESUS

What was expected of the first disciples? In the first place, renunciation. Theirs

I taught . . . in the Temple. (John 18:20)
The outer wall of the Temple in Jerusalem.

would be no easy road: 'Foxes have holes and the birds of the air have nests, but the Son of Man has nowhere to lay his head' (*Luke 9:58*). Jesus may not have been technically a vagrant, but after the beginning of his public ministry there is no mention of his having a home to which he returned. His disciples were expected to take the barest necessities as they set out to preach the Good News.

Alongside this capacity for renunciation, and forming part of it, was singleness of purpose: 'You cannot have two masters; either you will love one and

to be persecuted simply because they acted like the master and in his name: 'Blessed are you when men persecute you and speak ill of you on account of my name' (*Matt 5:11*).

On the other hand Jesus expected different types of commitment from different people. He did not require everyone to take the road and follow him literally. For instance, the man who had been cured of a legion of devils begged to stay with Jesus, but the Master said No. 'Go home to your people and tell them all that the Lord in his mercy has done for you' (*Mark 5:19*). This man, like so many of us, was to follow his vocation at home.

The disciples also played different roles within the Jesus group. He chose the Twelve, who were to be the leaders of his community; and one of those, Peter, was to be the leader. Christ called Simon 'Peter' (Rock), 'and on this rock I will build my Church' (*Matt 16:18*).

Christ did not expect his disciples to be only in a movement which would finish when he died, but to build a church (Hebrew qahal, assembly), which would last until the end of time. During Christ's own life, this was to be the leaven within Israel.

Much of what applied to those disciples can be applied to us. We can expect persecution if we truly follow Christ, and especially if we renounce materialistic values. We can expect ridicule if we accept the faith of Christ, not least if we affirm faith in the Real Presence of his body and blood. In Jesus' own day, we are told, many of Jesus' followers could not take this teaching.

hate the other or respect the one and despise the other' (*Matt 6:24*).

Springing from this are such harsh sayings as, 'Leave the dead to bury the dead'. Burying the dead has always been a sacred duty for the Jews, for which they are willing to expose themselves to mortal danger, as the Book of Tobit shows. Yet in his whole-hearted commitment to his Master, the disciple of Jesus was required to surrender even this sacred duty for which generations of his countrymen had risked their lives.

Even without taking such deliberate risks, the disciples of Jesus had to expect

Above all, we are called to be disciples of Christ by loving one another. 'By this love you have for one another,' said Christ, 'everyone will know that you are my disciples' (*John 13:35*). The fields are white with an abundant harvest. An army of disciples is urgently needed to go out and gather it in.

We can be disciples in any situation.

'His goodness embraced all, the just and sinner, the poor and the rich, fellow-citizens and foreigners. If he loved any people more than the rest, it was the sick, the poor and the lowly. He showed a reverence and a solicitude for the human person which nobody had ever shown before' (53).

Jesus kept his ministry strictly to the Jews. Indeed, on one occasion he seemed positively rude to a Syro-Phoenician woman (present-day Lebanon), when he was passing through that region. She wanted Jesus to cure her daughter, but the Lord replied, 'The children should be fed first, because it is not fair to take the children's food and throw it to the house-dogs' (*Mark 7:27*). Perhaps he was being sharply humorous, because she replied in kind; 'Ah yes sir', she said, 'but the house-dogs under the table can eat the children's scraps'. And he cured her daughter! That Jesus could not refuse to cure Gentiles was a sign that his message was eventually to reach the whole world.

QUESTIONS

1. The Gospels portray Jesus as sometimes going against the customs of his day: against the traditions of the elders, against the current interpretation of the Law, and in being the friend of outcasts and sinners. How far should we oppose the trends of today in following him?
2. How is the ministry of Jesus continued in the Church?

Raising of Lazarus.

18-Miracles of Jesus

Jesus performed many miracles.
He healed the sick, and cast out demons.
His miracles were signs of his power to save.
Miracles still happen.

JESUS – MIRACLE WORKER

'When the Messiah comes, will he perform more miracles than this man?' (*John 7:31*).

In his time, Jesus was renowned as a miracle-worker. His healing the sick, raising the dead, casting out demons, made the crowds wonder whether he was the Messiah, the chosen one of God who was to come and save his people.

Even his enemies had to acknowledge that Jesus had extraordinary power. He could not do the wonderful things that he did unless something supernatural was working through him.

His enemies explained this power as being the Devil in Jesus, or 'Beelze-bub' as the devil was then called, the Babylonian evil deity 'The Lord of the Flies' (*Matt 12:24*). Jesus retorted that this idea was completely absurd. How could the Prince of the Devils be casting out his own army?

Through the centuries, people have tried to explain the miracles of Jesus. Since the age of science, the tendency has been to become highly suspicious of the miraculous. We tend to want rational and natural explanations for everything.

Many people, even some Christians, prefer to play down the miraculous element in the life of Jesus. Perhaps the 'devils' he cast out were psychological illnesses which his peaceful presence cured? Perhaps the girl he raised from the dead was not dead (*Mark 5:41*), but only asleep? Perhaps he did not walk on the water, but only on the shore, the mist on the sea of Galilee at the time causing the disciples to make a mistake?

Two thousand years after the events, it is impossible to verify whether individual miraculous events associated with the life of Jesus occurred. It is difficult enough when a miracle occurs in our own time to get at 'the facts'. It is impossible when the witnesses are not to hand to interrogate.

What we can do is to discuss whether miracles are possible; in what conditions they occur; and how they can help us come to faith.

THE TEACHING OF THE CHURCH

The First Vatican Council, which was called by Pope Pius IX in 1870, dealt specifically with one question of the miraculous, in the light of attacks on the Christian faith by rationalists. The Council states both that miracles are possible, and that they are a sure sign of divine revelation.

'In order that our faith might amount to a "submission in accordance with reason" (*Rom 12:1*), God wished to link external arguments of his revelations to the internal helps of the Holy Spirit.' These external arguments are divine happenings, and especially miracles and prophecies which, since they clearly demonstrate God's omnipotence and infinite knowledge, are certain signs of Divine Revelation, and suited to every intelligence'.

'We read of the apostles: "and they went forth and preached everywhere, while the Lord worked with them and confirmed the message by the signs that attended it" (*Mark 16:20*) and again it was written: "and we have the prophetic word made sure. You will do well to pay attention to it as to a lamp shining in a dark place" (*2 Pet 1:19*). (Session III Ch 3: Faith).

The Council put what it had to say on the subject in more forceful language, in one of the 'canons' (No 4).

'If anyone asserts that miracles cannot happen and that consequently all accounts of them, even those contained in the sacred Scriptures, belong to the realm of fable and myth: or that it is never possible to establish with certainty that a miracle has taken place; and if anyone asserts that miracles do not prove the Divine origin of the Christian Religion, let him or her be anathema. (That is, excommunicated.)'

These strong words of Vatican I are confirmed by the effect the miracles of Jesus had in his own day. Many people saw Jesus just as a superstar, and did not grasp the deeper meaning of his miracles; yet others, like the man born blind who was cured by the Lord, were helped to come to faith by the extraordinary healing power of Jesus. As the Vatican Council says, these miracles were signs 'accommodated to the intelligence of all'.

But were these miracles only effective because Jesus lived at a time when people did not have the benefit of a scientific education? Can miracles today help to lead us to faith? We now have to look more deeply at what we mean by 'miracles'.

WHAT IS A MIRACLE?

The word 'miracle' (Latin *miraculum*) means 'to marvel at, to wonder'. A miracle, therefore, is a happening which amazes us, and arouses wonder.

We sometimes refer to miracles in a non-religious sense, such as an 'economic miracle'. But usually, we mean by a 'miracle' an event which is so mysterious that we cannot explain it from natural causes. God has had a special hand in it.

As Christian thinking has developed, more emphasis has been placed upon the idea that a miracle demands a supernatural explanation. But this emphasis has not always been there; and, when we analyse the meaning of 'miracle', we find that there are three ideas:

a) an amazing event has happened.

b) an event has occurred which we cannot explain. Believers say only God himself could cause it.

c) something important has occurred. God has given us a sign, he has used this extraordinary event to teach us something.

All three elements are present in the scriptural presentation of the idea of 'miracle'. But the most important idea in St John's Gospel is the idea of 'sign' (*John 20:30*). A miracle is a sign of the presence and power of God.

Everyday events can be miracles in the sense that they are wonders, or that they are signs of the presence and power of God. Saint Gregory the Great speaks of daily miracles which escape our notice because of their frequency:

'The birth of human beings who did not previously exist, is more wonderful than the resurrection of a dead person who has previously been alive, and the multiplication of the loaves is less wonderful than a grain of wheat which is sown in the earth, dies and then produces a harvest. It is only their familiarity which has caused these daily marvels to pale, for what happens daily, however wonderful it is, is weakened by its regular occurrence . . . "Familiarity breeds contempt".'

But there still are unusual events, which are in a special sense signs of God's activity; miracles of healing, etc. St Thomas Aquinas picked out three elements in this kind of special miracle; it is unusual, it is above and outside (not against) the laws of nature, and it can only be brought about by God.

THE CHURCH AND MIRACLES OF HEALING

It is very difficult to verify a miracle. In the 19th and 20th centuries, the Church developed stringent systems to do this.

At Lourdes, for instance, a medical bureau was set up, for specialists of all faiths and of none to attempt to authenticate the many miracles which were submitted to have occurred.

The problem is not that wonderful cures do not happen. They do. The problem is to verify that the cure is beyond all known laws of nature. Did the cancer just disperse, because of a medical law which we do not know yet?

It is impossible to prove that an individual wonderful cure is against all known laws of nature. God's ways in nature are so amazing, and it is so difficult to assemble all the relevant facts of a case, that there will always remain an element of mystery.

Certainty is possible regarding a miracle; but only the certainty which comes from the discernment of faith; that is to say, of a light, an enlightenment, permitting one to be aware of the fact as a sign from God. We find this throughout the Gospels. Many see the miracles of Jesus but give different explanations. Some attribute Jesus' power to demons. Others even try to say that the blind man was not blind at all. Only those with faith saw the reality behind it. They came to believe in the miracles, as they came to believe in Jesus.

The Church, when authenticating a vision, makes a great point of finding out about the spiritual fruits of the particular vision. The miracles at Lourdes, for instance, became taken more and more seriously as people went to the shrine of Our Lady, and grew in holiness and in the life of prayer. It became more and more clear that the same God of love who performed the miracle in the first place, to show his own special power, was continuing that work and causing fruit to be born in good works.

Miracles remind our scientific world that there are things beyond our knowledge. But the importance of miracles is relative. The important factor is communication with God, consisting usually in ordinary signs such as sacraments and holy Scripture. Miracles are extraordinary signs which are helpful for faith, but not central to it.

What is of interest to faith is the manner in which miraculous phenomena reconstruct life; they enable the person concerned to overcome dissociations, conflicts, neuroses (often connected with sin); they develop a feeling for others, union, sharing, reconciliation. Miracles demand humility.

LOURDES – THE FACTS

One of the best-known sites of miracles is Lourdes, in France, where Our Lady appeared to Saint Bernadette in 1858. Since the opening of the famous shrine, 6,000 cures have been certified; only 64 have been officially recognised as miracles since reorganisation in 1946;
- 1,300 cures have seemed sufficiently serious to be the object of a file.
- 57 have been passed on by the Medical Office to the Committees (national or international).
- 19 only have been recognised as miracles by the diocesan bishop.

From 1946 to 1965, there were, each year, one or two cases authenticated. After that there were eleven years without authentication of any miracle.

LIGHT FROM THE COUNCIL

Miracles then, are not a magic way in which we can come suddenly to believe. They are only short steps along the road to faith. Above all, they only help us come to faith in conjunction with a growing personal relationship with Christ. This is made clear by the Second Vatican Council.

Vatican II did not go in for anathemas. Pope John was quite explicit that it should not do so. Its Dogmatic Constitution on the Church says of the miracles of Christ that they 'demonstrate that the Kingdom has already come on earth', but it makes it clear that this is a role which they share with his Word, his Works and his Presence. In fact, it says that the Kingdom is revealed principally in the person of Christ himself, Son of

God and Son of Man who came to serve and to give his life as a ransom for many (*Mark 10:45*) (No 5).

The Dogmatic Constitution on Divine Revelation (No 4) puts the role and importance of miracles in the life of Christ in similar perspective. It says that Christ completed and perfected revelation 'by the total fact of his presence and self manifestation – by words and works, signs and miracles, but above all by his death and glorious resurrection from the dead, and finally by sending the Spirit of truth.' In his 'Evangelization Today' Pope Paul VI lists Christ's miracles – among the 'innumerable

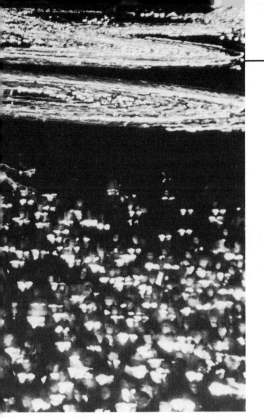

Torchlight procession, nightly at Lourdes.

Many have come to throw away their crutches at Lourdes; even if the panel of experts cannot verify their cure as miraculous, through lack of evidence.

signs which arouse the wonder of the multitudes and at the same time draw them to him in their desire to hear him and to be transformed by his works'.

The Pope points out, however, that for Christ there was 'one sign in particular' which 'stood out among all those to which he attributed a special importance: the weak and the poor were evangelised.

This is also made clear in the Gospel stories of miracles. The writers are leading us away from the wonder as such towards a personal love of our Lord. In the story of the Transfiguration, for instance, Jesus appeared miraculously to his disciples on the holy mountain, together with Moses and Elijah, two Old Testament figures. But finally, the vision went and 'when they looked round, they saw no one with them any more but only Jesus' (*Mark* 9:8).

THE FAGAN CASE

But it remains true that miracles can and do help people's faith even in this sceptical age. One example is the case of the Scotsman, John Fagan.

The story begins in the 17th century, with another Scotsman called John Ogilvie. Brought up a strict follower of the Reformer John Knox, to his parents' annoyance John Ogilvie became a Catholic; and even worse, he joined the hated Jesuit order, who were missionary priests dedicated to face any danger for the Catholic Faith.

After his training as a Jesuit, in 1613, Ogilvie landed back in Scotland. To be caught as a Catholic priest, in those days was a treasonable offence, with a horrible death as a punishment.

For the next year, he travelled in secret celebrating Mass in barns, cellars and woods. One day, a man asked Ogilvie to meet him in Edinburgh to say Mass for a Catholic family.

He said he would meet the priest in the main square. It was a trap. Six of the king's guards leapt on him and he was arrested.

Father John Ogilvie was charged with treason. He was taken to Glasgow, tortured and found guilty. On 19th March, 1615, he was taken to Glasgow Cross and was 'hung, drawn, and quartered'; that is he was hung until nearly dead, then cut down, his entrails removed while he was still alive, and finally cut into four. He was 36 years of age.

What has this horrible death in 1615 to do with a 20th century Scotsman called John Fagan?

In 1929, John Ogilvie was 'beatified'; that is to say, he was declared by the Church to be one of the 'blessed' in heaven, as a faithful martyr. But Ogilvie had yet to receive the Church's highest honour, that of being declared a 'saint'. As a sign that John Ogilvie was truly one of God's specially chosen saints in heaven, the Church required a miracle, given by God as an answer to the prayers of the saint.

The Scottish people began to pray

John Fagan, with a picture of John Ogilvie.

for this miracle. They were not disappointed.

On April 22, 1965, John Fagan, a Glasgow docker, woke in the night with severe stomach pains. His doctor, a non-Catholic, discovered a huge tumour in his abdomen.

John Fagan was a parishioner of a church named after John Ogilvie. His parish priest, Fr Fitzgibbon, gave him a medal of the Jesuit and the whole parish prayed for his recovery.

On March 6, 1967, four days before Ogilvie's feast, John Fagan lay dying. He had not eaten for seven weeks and he weighed five stone.

At 6 am Mary woke from a disturbed sleep. Her husband appeared to be motionless and she took him to be dead. Suddenly, he opened his eyes, propped himself up on his elbows and said: 'Mary, I feel hungry. Could you boil me an egg?' He then amazed doctors by making a total recovery.

John Fagan and John Ogilvie are united over 300 years by a simple faith. Mr Fagan says he doesn't know why he was chosen for the miracle.

This miracle did help some Scottish people pray more fervently. It did make John Fagan and his wife happy, and increased their faith.

On October 17th, 1976, John Ogilvie was proclaimed a saint by the Church.

DAILY MIRACLES

What you must be wondering now is, why miracles do not happen more frequently.

Why did not miracles save the millions who died in Nazi concentration camps? Why are hospitals full of people who will never recover? Why do I not overcome my daily faults, and become a saint? Apart from Jesus the Son of God, why was only Mary given the miracle of a sinless life?

Of course, miracles do happen to all of us.

There is the miracle of birth, the wonder of being. There is the miracle of love, both human and divine. There is the miracle of beauty, the wonderful sound of music. There is above all the miracle of God's grace freely given to us and His very presence in us. And so on, and so on.

What we call miracles, the extraordinary activity of God in the world, only highlight the greater miracles which happen all the time, but are ignored because they are so familiar.

MIRACLES IN ORDINARY THINGS

On the Cross, there were no miracles for Jesus. 'My God, my God, why have you forsaken me?' he asked. There happened then a great miracle. He forgave his enemies, in the midst of all his pain and humiliation. All of us are in one way or another asked to work miracles like that.

The more you can immerse yourself in the mystery of Jesus, God and man, the more you will accept the possibility of miracle-working in his life.

These miracles link up with intercessory prayer. Intercessory prayer means asking God's favour either for ourselves or for others. Some people doubt the value of praying in this way because it seems to them silly to try to change God's plan for individuals or the world.

However, Jesus himself said 'Ask and you shall receive'.

Now, if you look at the miracles of Jesus, you find that on most occasions he is reacting to an intercession. 'They have no wine.' 'Lord, that I may see.' 'Lord, my servant is sick.'

Notice, Jesus couples his willingness to do what is asked with the faith of the asker or receiver.

All prayer of intercession must be made in Faith. In your own life, it is quite right to pray for healing of body, mind and soul – for yourself and others.

But praying in faith, you will find your faith is tested and strengthened, because you have to be still, to wait, perhaps not to get an immediate answer. You must continue trusting, praying in faith. This perseverance can also work on you yourself. Patience in prayer will heal you, give you an inner peace and make you more able to listen to others and help them.

MEDITATION

'Ask and it will be given you; seek, and you will find; knock, and it will be opened to you. For every one who asks receives, and he who seeks finds, and to him who knocks it will be opened.

Or what man of you, if your son asks for bread, will give him a stone? Or if he asks for a fish, will give him a serpent?' (Matt 7:7–10)

QUESTIONS

1. Christ saw sickness as an evil – the 'bondage of Satan' (*Luke 13:16*). Yet those whom he cured had to die. What sign was he giving in healing the sick?
2. Many people expect God to work miracles constantly. They ask 'why did he allow this earthquake, this aircrash, the death of a child?'
   Should a believer expect such interventions? Is it a sign of childlike faith or credulity?

The Mount of Beatitudes, Sea of Galilee.

19-Teaching of Jesus

Jesus taught with authority.
He came to fulfil the Law and the Prophets.
He taught us how to be truly happy.
His teaching leads us to himself, the Way, the Truth and Life.

LIKE THE great Greek philosopher Socrates, Jesus seems to have taught by word of mouth, not by writing. And, also like Socrates, whose teachings are only to be found in the writings of his disciple Plato, the teachings of Jesus of Nazareth are only to be found in the writings of the Christian community which preached his Resurrection from the dead.

How much, then, of the teaching of Jesus recorded in the Gospels is actually his own words, and how much is words put into his mouth by the writers of the Gospels? This is a controversial question, and scholars differ greatly among themselves.

As Christians, we believe that the Bible is the inspired Word of God. But this does not necessarily imply that everything recorded in the Gospel as our Lord's words has to be word for word as he said it. God, in inspiring the Gospel writers, used their human talents, and the normal means of communication.

It is quite acceptable today to report the speech of a person not in actual words, but in the words of the reporter. It was quite acceptable in our Lord's day also. In the Gospels we frequently have what Jesus said, rather than the way in which he said it.

The inspiration of the Holy Spirit enabled the writers of the Gospels to be faithful to what Jesus said, and indeed to what he was saying in the Spirit after the Resurrection to the Christian community of that time, and to us.

The substance of Jesus' teaching is to be found in the first three Gospels, Matthew, Mark and Luke – called the 'Synoptic' Gospels (from the Greek syn-opsis, 'seeing together'). 'Seen together', these Gospels seem to present evidence, that the teaching of Jesus was put into collections before the Gospels as we have them today were compiled. Christians wanted to remember the Lord's words.

The best proof that these Synoptic Gospels are substantially reliable records of the teaching of Jesus is that they 'ring true' when read. A teacher of great genius is behind them, not a community or committee. Matthew tells us that our Lord taught the people 'with authority' (*Matt 7:29*). This authority comes over throughout the Gospels.

THE VARIETY OF THE GOSPELS

The teaching of Jesus is distributed unevenly through the four Gospels.

Matthew and Luke have recorded all the moral precepts of Jesus including his teaching on prayer, chastity, anger, fasting, divorce, money, and discipleship. His parables of the kingdom are also mostly in Matthew and Luke.

Matthew has the bulk of our Lord's teaching, because for Matthew, Jesus is the new Lawgiver. Luke alone has the parables of the Good Samaritan and the Prodigal Son, because for him Jesus is essentially the Saviour, forgiving and merciful to the outcast and sinner.

Mark and John are interested in the teaching of Jesus in a different way.

Mark's Gospel emphasises the miracles. Jesus is the Exorcist, casting out the power of Satan. As far as Mark is concerned, the miracles of Jesus are his best teaching, because thereby the Lord shows that he has come to bring in the kingdom of God by action rather than by words. Mark is clearly not in favour of long sermons.

John, with his long discourses, has more of the teaching of Jesus than anyone but gives few moral commands of Jesus; he expects us to find those in the other Gospels.

John wants us to see Jesus himself. 'The Way'. If we believe that Jesus is the Son of God, then we will not just listen to his words, but we will try to follow them in our own situation.

FULFILLING THE LAW

Sometimes the teaching of Jesus seems incomplete, even 'bitty'. This is because he never set out to provide a complete set of morals for every occasion.

Jesus never considered that he had to give the whole of God's teaching to his disciples. He believed that God's Torah (usually translated 'Law', but better translated 'Teaching') already existed, in what we call the Old Testament. There was plenty of moral teaching already there.

Jesus said clearly, 'Do not imagine that I have come to abolish the Torah or the Prophets. I have come not to abolish but to complete them' (*Matt 5:17*).

The simplest example of such an attitude on the part of Jesus is regarding the precept, part of the Ten Commandments, 'You must not commit adultery' (*Ex 20:14*). Jesus actually made this command much stricter, by covering internal desires as well as external infidelities:

'But I say to you; if a man looks at a woman lustfully, he has already committed adultery with her in his heart' (*Matt 5:27–28*).

TRADITIONS

Jesus' attitude to the Torah seemed revolutionary to his contemporaries, and understandably. By the time of Jesus, a long tradition of interpretation of the Torah had grown up, particularly within the Pharisaic party.

The real difficulty was sorting out what were important commands within the Torah, from the less important. The Five Books of Moses contained legislation for every part of life down to the size of Temple pillars. Out of these hundreds of commands, all given by God, 'Which is the first?' (Mark 12:28), a scribe asks him.

Jesus' answer says nothing new. He quotes two texts from the Torah, the first from Deuteronomy '. . . you must love the Lord your God with all your heart . . .' (6:4–5), and the second from Leviticus 'You must love your neighbour as yourself' (19:18).

Jesus' moral strategy was to lead people back to the Torah; and then to explain its teachings in a new and refreshing way.

His complaint was that some teachers of the Torah had obscured the Scriptures by their traditions. People could even avoid the implications of the command 'Honour your father and your mother' by offering money to the Temple, relieving them of the obligation to help their parents in their old age (Mark 7:8–13).

But Jesus was even more radical in his interpretations of other parts of the Torah.

He taught that some commandments within the Torah of Moses should give way to a more important command. He taught that the law of Sabbath rest, imposed in the Books of Moses on pain of death (Num 15:32–36), could be broken in order to heal a person. 'The Son of Man is master of the Sabbath' (Luke 6:5) he said to his shocked hearers.

Jesus could even cancel some precepts of the Torah, in order to go back to what he saw as a more primitive dispensation. The Books of Moses allowed divorce, provided that the man gave a writ of dismissal to his wife. This was to protect the wife from being reclaimed by her husband, leaving her permanently free to marry another man, and so find some source of livelihood. (Deut 24:1. Note that the wife could not divorce her husband!)

Jesus went right back to Gen 2:24, and nullified the Deuteronomic Code. 'It was because you were so unteachable that he (Moses) wrote this commandment for you. But, from the beginning of creation, God made them male and female . . . So then, what God has united, man must not divide' (Mark 10:8–9). Follow God's law as described from the beginning, says Jesus, and you will not divorce at all.

Jesus' teaching was shocking and surprising. Even his own disciples did not always understand him. But it had an inner credibility. Matthew says 'His teaching made a deep impression on the people because he taught them with authority, and not like their own scribes' (Matt 7:28–29).

His teaching was as effective as his miracles in drawing crowds, and making disciples. A man who could treat the Torah with such apparent arrogance, and yet make such obvious sense of it, must be special.

Jesus' moral package is unbelievably demanding. He wants us to love our enemies. After a lifetime of service of God, we are to say 'We deserve nothing. We are unprofitable servants'. When we fast, we cannot even have the satisfaction of looking miserable. We have to pretend to be happy.

Yet Jesus insisted that his 'yoke was easy and his burden light' (Matt 11:30). There certainly was a feeling of liberation about it, as one began to acquire Jesus' own view of the Torah. But what really must have made the burden light was the fact that Jesus did not see the Torah just as a series of precepts to be learnt off by heart. Rather, Jesus actually lived his own love of God and his neighbour.

THE SERMON ON THE MOUNT

The sayings of Jesus seem very difficult, even impossible to put into practice. He tells us to 'turn the other cheek' (*Matt 5:39*) rather than resist evil. And he told a rich young ruler that, if he wanted to be happy, he would have to sell all he had and give to the poor (*Mark 10:21*).

How can we apply such ideas to our everyday living? Throughout the history of the Church, people distinguished between 'counsels' (advice given by Jesus, e.g. to the rich young ruler) and 'commands' (precepts for all, like the Ten Commandments).

This was particularly so in the Middle Ages, and it created a two-tier Christianity, one for clergy and religious, and another tier (lower) for lay people. Two major parts of the teaching of Jesus are contained in the Sermon on the Mount and in the Beatitudes.

THE SETTING

In the past it was generally believed that the material in the Sermon on the Mount was delivered by Jesus on one occasion. Today it is generally seen to be a collection of key teachings of Jesus spoken on several occasions.

While the 'Sermon' appears to be delivered to the disciples, we learn at the end that 'the crowds were astonished at his teaching' (*Matt 7:28*). The question of whom Jesus directed his message at, or whom Matthew intended to be the audience, is important in interpreting the Sermon. The Sermon addresses anyone who hears it.

HISTORY

The Sermon has elicited a variety of responses. The early Fathers of the Church saw it as applying to all believers.

Luther was driven to distinguish between two kingdoms: the secular, and the sacred. Only the sacred could be ruled by the commandments, and the Sermon. A Christian could kill as a member of secular society but not as a Christian.

Zwingli and Calvin, two leading Protestant Reformers after Luther, went further. They supposed that one could rule a city on the basis of the Sermon, and tried this in Zurich and Geneva.

At the other extreme the Anabaptists, the left wing of the Reformers, insisted on the separation of Church and state, espoused love and passivism, and rejected oaths and violence. A Christian must separate himself from the state, since 'saints' cannot have any truck with 'sinners'.

For the Quakers, too, war and revenge could not be reconciled with Christian practice.

TODAY

It is a mistake to interpret the Sermon on the Mount in one way only, since it is a collection of sayings of Jesus. Each saying must be understood in its own context.

For instance, the Catholic Church has always interpreted the saying on divorce ('The man who divorces his wife and marries another is guilty of adultery against her'; *Mark 10:11*) in the sense that Christ forbids re-marriage after the dissolution of a valid Christian marriage. In this case, we do not merely have an ideal for which we are striving. We have a law left by Christ in order to uphold the sanctity of marriage.

On the other hand, it is clear that some statements of Jesus in the Sermon on the Mount are not legal commands, but exhortations. They serve to instil the spirit of the Gospel in us, but are not to be followed to the letter. For instance, when Jesus said 'if anyone orders you to go one mile, go two miles with him' (*Matt 5:41*), it would be absurd to follow that as a literal command. The person may not wish to go two miles, in which case he would not appreciate the extra distance! In this case, our Lord is giving us an example of how we can turn a situation of frustration – the inconvenience of having to go out of our way – into the possibility of love and friendship.

Finally, it would be foolish to ignore the mediaeval distinction between 'counsels' and 'commands' in interpreting the Sermon on the Mount. We have already seen the way in which the Sermon may give commands. But we must see also the possibility that the Sermon may counsel us, that is, give advice rather than imperatives.

For instance, the saying of Jesus 'Do not worry about your life and what you are to eat . . .' (*Matt 6:25*) has led some Christians to trust God each day for their daily food, without even providing for themselves. The Carmelite nuns led by Teresa of Avila in 16th century Spain did just that. But that may not be God's will for all of us. What it says to all of us is that we must trust God, even if we work for our living, and expect to be paid.

The Sermon on the Mount says different things to different people. But it says something to everyone.

THE BEATITUDES

The core of Christ's teaching is in the Beatitudes. This teaching can only be understood when we try to start living according to Jesus. Otherwise it appears quite illogical, as we can see from the list.

'BLESSED are the poor in spirit, for theirs is the kingdom of heaven.
'Blessed are those who mourn, for they shall be comforted.
'Blessed are the meek, for they shall inherit the earth.
'Blessed are those who hunger and thirst for righteousness, for they shall be satisfied.
'Blessed are the merciful, for they shall obtain mercy.
'Blessed are the pure in heart, for they shall see God.
'Blessed are the peacemakers, for they shall be called sons of God.
'Blessed are those who are persecuted for righteousness' sake, for theirs is the kingdom of heaven.

Blessed are the poor. But not in here . . .

London Stock Exchange. Money is necessary, and today is more and more complex in operation. But how do we achieve a just system of financing, especially worldwide?

'*Blessed are you when men revile you and persecute you and utter all kinds of evil against you falsely on my account.*
'*Rejoice and be glad, for your reward is great in heaven, for so men persecuted the prophets who were before you.*'

The Latin word for 'blessed' is 'beatus'. Beatitudo means 'blessedness' or 'happiness'. And so we have the English word 'beatitude'.

In these Beatitudes, the 'Magna Carta', as they have been called, of Christianity, Our Lord is telling us of joys and rewards beyond the joys and rewards of this world.

Jesus knows our hearts. He made them Himself, for Himself. He designed them in such a fashion that they could never be satisfied but by Himself.

He looked into His own human Heart that was also divine. He knew where His own joy lay. Although He had many friends in this world these were not the source of His joy. This lay in His union with His Father and the Holy Spirit.

The Beatitudes tell us that basic human happiness, not only in the next life but also in this, has its roots in our union with God.

We are all sinners. Only our Blessed Lady observed Christ's teaching perfectly all the time. But if we keep trying to model our lives along the lines of the Beatitudes – if we keep trying to be more detached from this world, if we try to have true sorrow for our sins, if we try to spread peace, to be chaste and keep our hearts intent on God, thirsting for God, if we try always to forgive others and put up with the wrongs done to us – then even in this life we shall know something of the joys of heaven.

The Beatitudes tell us where true joy may be found. By implication, they tell us too where deep misery lies.

If we let ourselves be brainwashed by the media, we can come to think that the worst suffering is to be without food or shelter or liberty.

This is not so. The worst suffering in this life is to be without God. Without God, the whole world cannot make us happy. But if we have God, the whole world cannot take our joy away.

We have in our hearts a void that only God can fill. Creatures and possessions may pretend that they can fill it for us. And God waits.

For years we can struggle against God. We try to bargain with Him, hoping He may reduce His demands, hoping He may let us keep all we have and still have Him. We are afraid of finding ourselves stripped. Yet this is what God requires before He will fill us with Himself, which alone can make us happy. And so, for fear of being unhappy in this world, we run the risk of being unhappy for ever.

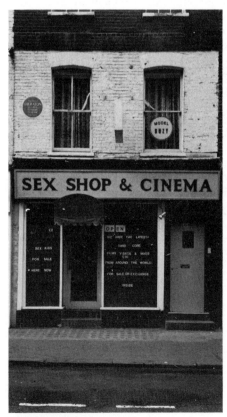

Lust is big business.

LIVING THE BEATITUDES

The greatest danger in Christian life is that you become too good at religion. You keep the rules, you do spiritual exercises. You think you have it all sewn up. The Beatitudes turns all that upside down. 'How happy are the poor in spirit' tells me that the Gospel is for the non-starters; for those who are not very good at religion, or anything else for that matter.

'Blessed' gives the idea that, whatever your situation in life at the moment, happy or sad, you are in a position which makes for ultimate happiness. You are blessed if you are walking the way you should be, the way in which God made you to act.

The Beatitudes may seem foolish. You look at them, and say, 'I can never be a peacemaker. I have to fight for my own corner.' Then, in a sense, you are beginning to live the Beatitudes. You are beginning to realise that you are not worthy of God, and you become poor in spirit! They turn everything upside down. When you think you are not living them, then you begin to realise that perhaps in a strange way you are!

The Church is a church of sinners. One of the earliest heresies was Donatism, people who believed that only faithful Christians should be allowed to remain in the Church. God forgive us if cowards, prostitutes, wealthy stockbrokers, and gamblers feel out of place in the Church.

Note for example that the Beatitudes do not say 'Happy are those who achieve righteousness', but 'those who hunger' for it. Even if we cannot achieve something good – we can yearn for it. Prayer is a most positive way of yearning. We can yearn for our own fulfilment, we can yearn for the hungry to be fed, we can yearn for love in broken marriages. That does not absolve us from doing something about it if we can. But sometimes, we are helpless to do anything.

People who are helpless and weak can be doing more in the eyes of God than those who are strong. But the Beatitudes do not encourage us to wallow in our helplessness, to feel sorry for ourselves! The Beatitudes teach us to yearn for something better and try to achieve it.

They tell our parishes, for example, that we are not following Christ necessarily because we have a marvellous parish council, a well-organised liturgy, excellent parish organisations, and have paid off the parish debt. The greatest danger is always to think, 'I have arrived'. That was the sin of the Pharisee, who recounted all his good deeds before God, while the tax collector simply beat his breast and said, 'God be merciful to me, a sinner' (*Luke 18:13*).

QUESTIONS

1. Choose any one or two of the social or moral concerns of the present day and explain what application of the teaching of Jesus you would make to resolve the issues.
2. Are the Beatitudes a practical guide for the Christian life today? Present a case for and against.

20-Death and Resurrection of Christ

Christ died to save us from our sins.
He made us one with God his Father.
The risen Jesus appeared to his disciples.
We have not seen, but we believe.

WHY DID God do this to me? Perhaps most of us have said this in a time of great stress. A child dies, a family breaks up, a business collapses. As far as we can tell, we have done nothing to deserve it. Then why does God apparently reward with evil the good that we have tried to do?

This question is most of all to be asked about Jesus of Nazareth. Loved by the common people, a healer and one who cast out evil, healed the sick, an inspiring leader, a prophet of God, the Son of God. Yet he was put to death in the most excruciating way invented by man, suspended on a cross.

Why did God allow this to happen to his own Son? The answer must be historical and theological. The death of Jesus happened historically, as a result of a number of religious and political factors.

But Christian faith is that this death of Jesus was part of a plan, the plan of God for the salvation of the world. And, if Jesus' death has a meaning, then no suffering of any person on earth is without meaning any more, because we can all share in the death of Christ, taking up our cross with him.

WHAT HAPPENED?

According to the Synoptic Gospels, it took only one week for Jesus to antagonise the Jerusalem leaders so totally that they determined on his death. In Galilee the opposition had come from the Pharisees and their inability to stomach his attitude to legal observance and re-interpretation of the Law. But now the clash was with the Sadducees, the custodians of the Temple, over the issue of Jesus' authority. After Jesus had solemnly entered the city and taken possession of the Temple on Palm Sunday, the challenge to their authority meant that this unorthodox leader from Galilee had to be removed before he disturbed the delicate equilibrium which left government under the imperial eye of Rome in the hands of the rich high-priestly aristocracy.

So whether it was after questioning by Annas, the godfather figure behind several high priests, or after a formal interrogation presided over by Caiaphas, the high priest, the charge adopted was political, that of being a messiah, at that time the synonym of a rebel leader. Jesus had not fully accepted this role and preferred to preach the realisation of the Kingship of God, his Father.

Pilate, trained in Roman law and used to feuding factions, was obviously uneasy. Three times he tried to throw out the charge. When the Jewish leaders still pressed it, he tried to persuade them to accept this presumably popular figure as the beneficiary of the Passover amnesty. But the Galilaean held no interest for the Jerusalem mob: they wanted one of their own, the rebel Barabbas, released. Still Pilate hesitated till the Jewish leaders played their trump card: if you release this man you are not a 'Friend of Caesar'. If Pilate lost this status by being reported to Rome for releasing a possible rebel leader, he might well lose his job, and even his head.

John represents this scene before Pilate as being the final denial by the Jewish leaders of the kingship of God.

Jesus said, 'I am thirsty' (John 19:28).

The theme of judgement by encounter with Jesus is a thread which runs through the fourth Gospel. The climax comes when Jesus, still robed as King of the Jews, is brought out and rejected. In rejecting him they condemn themselves finally and explicitly as Jesus is seated on the Chair of Judgement (*John 19:13*) and the chief priests proclaim, 'We have no king except Caesar'. If God is not king of Israel, Israel ceases to be as a holy nation. And yet Jesus reigns from the Cross.

THE AT-ONE-MENT

The death of Jesus is central to the New Testament. Without it there is no Gospel, no sacraments and no Church. Yet after two thousand years it remains a mystery. 'Why did Jesus have to die? Why couldn't God let bygones be bygones?' There have been a number of theories and each adds something to our understanding.

RANSOM AND MORAL INFLUENCE

One of the earliest explanations was that Jesus' death was a ransom offered to defeat the powers of evil. The early Church delighted in the idea of God's conquest of the Devil and the triumph of the Kingdom of God over the Kingdom of darkness.

Another theory attractive to the medieval period was Peter Abelard's idea of the death of Jesus as a moral influence. A 12th century scholar, he brilliantly anticipated modern ideas concerning the power of love. As he saw it the death of Jesus did not influence God because how could God need reconciling! After all, it was he who was in Christ. No. Jesus' death constrains and influences us. It draws us to him. As we see that love which drove him to a cruel cross, our hearts and wills melt before the greatness of that example and we are led back to God.

Another set of theories concentrates upon the notion of Christ dying for me. One of them sees Jesus as our representative who as perfect man takes our despair and sin to the cross and dies for us. As the perfect and best he is able to represent us before the Father and open the way to eternal life. This idea is very biblical and accords with the sentiment in Cardinal Newman's hymn: 'A second Adam to the fight and to the rescue came'.

The similar theory of substitution goes a little further and says Jesus is my substitute, dying a death that I deserve. This theory also finds biblical warrant in Paul's language of 'Christ being made sin' (*2 Cor 5:21; Gal 3:13*).

Let us be careful not to separate the death of Jesus from his earthly life. His death is the culmination of his Incarnation. He came to save us all from all that stops us being the people that God longs us to be. He comes to reconcile humankind to God, to heal the brokenhearted and to make all things new. The angel said to Mary 'You shall call his name Jesus because he shall save his people from their sin.' His death was his triumph. According to John's Gospel it is his moment of Glory. 'It is finished!' is the splendid cry from the man on the cross.

SACRIFICE AND VICTORY

He did die for you and me. Even today the language of sacrifice is perfectly understandable. If I am poor and starving and someone offers me food which they desperately need, I can understand how that sacrifice can save me. In a deeper way I can see that if our condition is as serious as the Bible declares, salvation can only come from God. Here then is the basic theology of the Mass. Christ's 'one for all' sacrifice becomes the basis for our celebration.

WHY DID IT HAPPEN?

His death is a triumphant victory. Contemporaries of the early Christians could not understand why the followers of Jesus preached the cross so proudly and firmly. It was as Paul said, 'to the Jews a stumbling block and to the Greeks foolishness' (*1 Cor 1:23*). But it was not a dead saviour they celebrated but a living Lord. The resurrection is the vindication of Christ's ministry in life and death – without the resurrection the death has no power or hope.

There is something compelling and beautiful about the idea of Christ dying for you and me.

CROSS OF GLORY
CROSS OF PAIN

Crucifixion was the most shameful execution, used for slaves. When Paul preached Christ crucified it was a stumbling block and scandal. Even in Christian Liturgy and art it was not until the fourth century that the cross became a widely-used and acceptable symbol and the crucifix with a tortured body became common only in the thirteenth

The Passion Play at Oberammergau.

century. Early representations portrayed the victory of Christ rather than suffering and pain.

An 8th century Anglo-Saxon poem by an unnamed author describes a dream-vision of a glorious cross:

'A gleam with gold it was in every part: the tree of the world: outstretched to its four corners. Where it touched the heavens and the earth gems glowed, and at the heart, there where the two beams met, five precious jewels shone most gloriously. Heaven's multitudes; the hosts of angels worshipped there. They gazed upon it, created for glory before time began. Truly, I tell you, this was no gallows tree, no criminal's gibbet. Rather it is the glory of the heavenly powers, of all the nations of the earth and of the whole creation.

(From *The Dream of the Rood*)

'He is not here: He is risen!'

HE IS RISEN!

The death of Jesus, without the Resurrection, would just have been the end of a beautiful dream. Yet another good man, even perhaps the best man on earth, was put to death by blind, foolish and cruel authorities.

Many sceptics down the centuries have imagined that the resurrection was wishful thinking on the part of the disciples. One critic, Herbert Samuel Reimarus, even suggested that the disciples having been with Jesus for three years, were now disinclined to go back to their fishing, preferring the more intellectual life of a preacher. So they invented the story of the Resurrection, and so got themselves a nice job for life!

Since one of them, James the brother of John, was soon to be killed by King Herod for his beliefs (*Acts 12*), and indeed eventually most of the first apostles were to be martyred, it does not seem that their new life was as easy as all that. Indeed, fishing would have been an easy option in comparison!

But what is strangest of all about the apostles' faith in the Resurrection is that it took everyone, including themselves, completely by surprise; so much so, that the only adequate explanation of this extraordinary faith is that what they said was true. The risen Jesus had appeared to them.

RESURRECTION IN THE OLD TESTAMENT

By the time of Jesus, most Jews had come to believe that, at the end of the world, there would be a general resurrection from the dead. But this faith itself had taken a long time to develop.

What was not expected at all was that the Messiah, when he came, would die and rise again, appearing to his disciples. Some believed that the Messiah, like Elijah, would be assumed into heaven in a fiery chariot. This would be the Ascension of Christ. But not his actual suffering, death, and bodily resurrection. This was totally unexpected.

There were prophecies in the Old Testament about the Servant of God being vindicated by rising from the dead after suffering (*Isa 53*). But this was such a vague idea that it was not until after Jesus had appeared to them that the disciples were able to understand what those scriptures meant (*Luke 24:26*).

HOW IT BEGAN

Jesus of Nazareth died in utter disgrace on a cross, crying out 'My God, my God, why have you forsaken me?'

The Romans frequently imposed this form of execution on slaves, violent criminals and rebels.

Yet shortly after Jesus' death and burial St Peter and others began claiming that he had risen from the dead and should be accepted as the Messiah, Son of God and divine Lord of the universe. The evidence from 1 Cor 15:3–8, the Book of Acts and elsewhere in the New Testament establishes that the preaching of the resurrection went back to the very origins of Christianity.

Both then and now Christian faith stands or falls with the resurrection of Jesus from the dead.

THE APPEARANCES

But why should we today believe that crucified Jesus rose from the dead?

First, we have testimony from some

of the men and women who launched Christianity. Jesus ended his earthly life in slow agony nailed on a cross. But some time afterwards, he appeared gloriously alive to different individuals and groups – several hundred in all. St Paul lists many of these witnesses. He adds his own testimony as a persecutor turned believer: 'In the end he appeared also to me' (*1 Cor 15:5–8*).

Believing in the risen Christ is more than merely accepting the testimony of others to a unique event which took place nearly 2,000 years ago. Easter faith means experiencing the difference the living Jesus can make in our lives now. We experience his powerful presence in the Scriptures and above all in the Eucharist, but also in a thousand other ways. He comes to us in prayer, behind the faces of those who suffer and need our help, in the joys and pains of daily life.

Luke and John also draw attention to the way the risen Lord has been changed and transformed. Closed doors are no obstacle to him (*John 20:19,26*). He appears and disappears at will (*Luke 24:31–36*). People who had known him in his earthly existence fail, at least initially, to identify Him. On the road to Emmaus the two disciples recognise him only in the moment of his disappearance (*Luke 24:31*). Mary Magdalene at first supposes him to be a gardener (*John 20:14f*). Jesus has risen bodily from the dead, but he has become 'gloriously' different.

THE EMPTY TOMB

Closely tied up with the nature of the bodily resurrection is the question of the empty tomb. Some allege that faith in the risen Jesus does not need to affirm his empty tomb. He is risen from the dead but his earthly corpse decayed in the grave. Against this is the evidence

from the Gospels that Mary Magdalene (all four Gospels) with one or more female companion(s) (Matthew, Mark and Luke), visited Jesus' grave and found that it was open and that the corpse had mysteriously disappeared.

There is a reasonable case to be made in support of the claim that Jesus' grave was found empty. Naturally the opponents of the Christian movement explained the missing body as theft (*Matt 28:11–15*). But we have no evidence that anyone, either Christian or non-Christian, alleged that Jesus' tomb contained his remains. Furthermore, it would have been impossible in Jerusalem for the disciples to start proclaiming his resurrection, if his grave had not been empty. Their enemies could at once have produced his corpse.

SIGN

Once we accept the empty tomb, a serious question remains. What does it mean? This empty grave in Jerusalem powerfully symbolises that redemption is much more than a mere escape from suffering and death. Rather it means the transformation of this material world with all its history of sin and suffering.

The first Easter began the work of bringing our universe to its ultimate destiny. The empty tomb is God's radical sign that redemption is not a mere escape to a better world but an extraordinary transformation of this world.

Early Christians knew that if they were wrong about Jesus' rising from the dead, they would be the 'most pitiable' of all people (*1 Cor 15:19*). But they were not wrong. At Mass we continue to cry out with joy: 'Dying you destroyed our death, rising you restored our life. Lord Jesus, come in glory.'

Through the risen presence of Jesus we know that our story will not end in the empty silence of annihilation. The world to which we go is no grey haunt of ghosts, but a richly satisfying existence in which we shall know our dear ones and be known by them. We have the promise: 'If I go and prepare a place for you, I shall come again and take you to myself, so that where I am you also may be' (*John 14:3*). Believing in Jesus' resurrection, we also hope for our own.

He died to save us all. Holy Sepulchre Church, Jerusalem.

LIGHT FROM THE COUNCIL

Not only do Christians believe that Jesus Christ is risen, they believe that he is present in his Church, in her liturgical celebrations. Earlier, the Constitution on the Liturgy spelled this out in great detail (No 7): 'Christ is always present in his Church, especially in her liturgical celebrations. He is present in the Sacrifice of the Mass not only in the person of his minister . . . but especially in the eucharistic species. By his power he is present in the sacraments so that when anybody baptises it is really Christ himself who baptises. He is present in his word, since it is he himself who speaks when the Holy Scriptures are read in Church. Lastly, he is present when the Church prays and sings, for he has promised "where two or three are gathered in my name there am I in the midst of them".'

QUESTIONS

1. **What were Jesus' last words?**
   The four Gospels offer three different versions. Look at Matt 27:46, Mark 15:34, Luke 23:46, John 19:30 and discuss how each of the words recorded by the Gospel writers could serve as a model for personal prayer in a particular situation.

2. **'Christ is in agony until the end of time.'**
   Point to some examples of Christ's agony in today's world. A display (e.g. using newspaper cuttings) could be prepared for your church. This could help a parish celebration of the liturgy of Good Friday to link up with everyday life.

Even the best-intentioned can flag in zeal, and sleep the sleep of the just. A heavy
afternoon session at Vatican II. The Church Human.

21-What is the Church?

We are the Church.
The fullness of visible unity subsists in the Catholic Church.
Other Christians belong to the Church but lack full unity with the
Pope, the Vicar of Peter.

AMONG CHRISTIANS, there are
two views about the church – and
by 'Church' we mean not the
building, nor the Church leaders, but
the people who make up the Church.

One group of Christians (sometimes
identified as 'Protestant' or 'Evangelical') believe that being a Christian is
first and foremost an individual relationship with God through Jesus Christ. The
church is a community of believers who
have come together because they all
believe in Christ.

Put this way, it is not important
whether you are a Methodist, a Baptist,
or an Anglican. What matters is the
personal relationship with Christ. The
various denominations are of human
rather than of divine institution.

The other group of Christians (sometimes identified as 'catholic' or 'orthodox'), believe that being a Christian is
not only an individual matter. From the
beginning, Christ gathered a community round him, called 'disciples'. Among
them he chose twelve 'apostles' whom
he sent out with his authority to preach
and to convert. After his death and Resurrection, these same apostles acted
with the authority of the Spirit of Christ
to found church communities all over
the world.

In this view, 'the Church' is a divine institution, part of the will of Christ; and it is important which church you belong to, because you have to find the church or churches which have this visible link with the original 'apostolic' church founded by Christ. Only there is to be found the true doctrine and the true discipline of the Founder of Christianity, Jesus.

The 'Catholic' or 'Roman Catholic' Church presents a very distinctive claim to being linked with this original apostolic church founded by Jesus Christ. The leader of this Church, called 'the Pope' ('Pope' means 'Father', or 'Papa'), the Bishop of Rome, claims to be the successor of Peter, the leader of the apostles, called 'The Rock' by Jesus himself. In the Catholic faith, to be linked with the Pope in visible 'communion' is an essential part of being fully Christian.

Not all popes have been examples to the flock. Pope Alexander Borgia.

OUTSIDE THE CHURCH NO SALVATION?

We must be clear what the Roman Catholic Church does not claim.

There is a story about a person who went to heaven, and was being shown around by St Peter. When they reached a high wall, the new entrant asked 'What is behind that wall?' St Peter replied 'Oh, all the Roman Catholics. We have to let them think that they are the only ones here'.

Contrary to what many people think, the Catholic Church does not teach that only its members get to heaven. It might have seemed like this, because we used the expression 'outside the Church there is no salvation'. But we are becoming more and more aware that people who are not Catholics are also members of the Church, because they can be united with Christ.

In fact, an American priest was condemned for heresy not too long ago because he insisted that you had to be a member of the visible Church to get to heaven. The Church teaches that any-

one of good will may come to the vision of God in heaven.

The word 'Catholic' (from the Greek Kath holos, 'according to the whole'), means 'universal'. At the time of the 4th and 5th century Councils, where important doctrines about Christ were defined, the word 'Catholic' referred to those Christians who accepted the whole doctrine about Christ. They believed that he was both God and Man, whereas 'heretics' believed only parts of the 'whole' doctrine.

'Roman' also refers to the rite of one section of the Catholic Church. Other sections follow the Armenian, Ukranian, Byzantine or Orthodox rites. All are members of the Catholic Church.

After the Protestant Reformation, when Europe divided into different denominations, 'Catholic' referred to those Christians who accepted the Bishop of Rome as the successor of the apostle Peter. Roman Catholics claim that to accept the 'whole' (Catholic) doctrine of Christ implies visible communion with the Pope. To Catholics that is a vital principle of universality.

The Church does not only contend that anyone of good will may come to the vision of God in heaven. Even more, the Church teaches that any Christian, who is a member of any church, in some sense belongs to the body of Christ, the Church. What we do claim is that only in the Roman Catholic Church is this visible communion complete, because only there is that visible and historical link with the apostolic Church founded by Christ.

THE BODY OF CHRIST

Immediately we have begun to discuss what 'the Church' is, we begin to talk about its leader, the Pope. We have done this because we cannot understand the worldwide (Catholic, 'according to the whole') church without considering the person who is the symbol of our visible unity.

But it is misleading to focus on this without realising that first and foremost the Church is 'the people of God'; and every member of the Church of every race, class, colour and intelligence has a place.

SAINT PAUL

St Paul described the Church as the Body of Christ. He knew of the obvious comparison with the human body in which the well-being or illness of any one member affects the health of the whole body. He was aware of the image, in many societies, whereby a community is seen to be like a living body with all the members having a different function. He was familiar with the biblical relationship between husband and wife becoming one body, one flesh. He had a growing appreciation of the mysterious contact between the body of the Christian and the glorified body of Christ which takes place in the Eucharist (*1 Cor 6,10,11*) and when Christians become one body with Christ (*1 Cor 10:16,17*). He was sure that one day all our bodies will be transformed into the likeness of Christ's glorified body (*Phil 3:21*). This led to his great song of praise of the resurrection when 'this mortal body will put on immortality and this corruptible body will put on incorruption' (*1 Cor 15*).

All these insights led St Paul to see Christians as one body 'in' Christ. He stressed this in the letter to the Romans and his first letter to the Corinthians. In the letters to the Ephesians and Colossians he goes further and describes Christians simply as the body 'of' Christ. In being the one body of Christ, Christians have Christ as their head – from which there is a movement of life into the rest of the members and He directs and co-ordinates their activities. Christ's head-ship is not merely over his Church. It is over the whole of creation. He is the very source and destiny of everything that is created (*Col 1:15–17*).

The unity of both head and members is made possible by the work of the Holy Spirit, because there is but one body and one Spirit (*Eph 4:1–4*). The Spirit of God lives in the Christian as in a temple. He creates and conserves union between Christ and his members.

All this has daily implications for believers. They must live in close dependence on each other and on Jesus Christ. They must respect their bodies which are the dwelling place of the Spirit of Christ. The Christian is not just a body of flesh but a Spirit-filled body. Life in Christ demands a high standard of moral behaviour. The Christian, for example, cannot at the same time share his body with a prostitute and with Christ (*1 Cor 6:15*).

The bread that is broken when Christians share the Eucharist is a sharing, a communion, in the body of the Lord (*1 Cor 10:16,17*). Each Christian has his own role and his own gift, but all gifts must be used for the good of the whole

body. The Christian is called to a full life 'in Christ', and with Christ.

THE MYSTICAL BODY

For centuries, the Church has been called the 'Mystical body of Christ'. This tendency received a new impetus from an encyclical letter of Pope Pius XII in 1943. He stated that there was no more fitting title for the Church. The word 'mystical' was originally applied not so much to the Church as to the body of Christ as received in the Eucharist. Whatever words we use, there is an obvious and intimate link between the body of Christ received in the Eucharist and the community of people we call the Church. Christ has only one body, his glorified body. In it all the mystery, all the secret plan of God reaches its fulfilment. Christ's glorified body is like a magnet drawing not merely all Christians but all of the human family and the whole of the universe into unity with itself.

MODELS OF THE CHURCH

The Constitution on the Church singles out some common scriptural images and symbols of the Church. These include the shepherd's life; the cultivation of land; the art of building; family life and marriage. In every generation, the Church tries to probe deeper into all of these images and uncover something of the riches of God's revelation in Christ (Constitution on Revelation).

Each of us takes a particular starting point, which colours our understanding of the Church.

Some see the Church primarily as institutional; some as a community; some as a herald of good news; some as a servant of God and mankind; some as a people on a journey. All these 'models' should throw light on each other, and they come together when we see the Church simply as a community of disciples of the Lord.

As we explore the mystery of the Church, we are also exploring the mystery of Christ. Who is Jesus Christ? In what sense is he unique?

THE ONE TRUE CHURCH

The uniqueness of Jesus leads to the uniqueness of his Church. Catholics are used to describing the Catholic Church as the 'one true Church'. The bishops at the Council taught that the sole Church of Christ 'subsists in' the Catholic Church which is governed by the successor of Peter and by the bishops in communion with him (para 8).

'Subsists' is a puzzling word. In practice, it means that the Catholic Church sees itself as possessing all the sacramental life and structures willed by Christ. But the bishops declared that many elements of sanctification and of truth are found outside the visible confines of the Catholic Church and are forces impelling towards Christian unity. This statement is one of the great foundation statements for the ecumenical movement. Much of its meaning has yet to be unpacked.

COMMUNION

Being in communion with each other need not mean identical worship, or even belief.

Communion is primarily a gift of God. The Greek word koinonia, as it appears in the First Epistle of St John, means a relationship between persons which comes about because they share mutually in one and the same reality. The reality with which we are concerned is the very life of God made available to us in his mystical body the Church. So the gift of communion is, first and foremost, the gift of salvation, the re-establishment of that relationship between God and men which was once ruptured by sin. But Christ has made it clear that the saving relationship between ourselves and God is re-established precisely in and through our mutual relations, our koinonia, as members of his body, the Church: 'He has willed to make men holy and save them

It is the Mass that matters.

not as individuals without any bond or link between them, but rather to make them into a people who might acknowledge him and serve him in holiness' (Vat II Constitution on the Church, 9).

We must share with, care about, accept responsibility for those others who are members with us of the communion of saints.

We commonly talk about the Euchar-ist as Holy Communion. It is a renewed participation in Christ's life; but clearly communion koinonia should also be the effect, the fruit of Holy Communion. An intensified participation in Christ's life must intensify the shared life which is the bond linking together all the members of the Church. Conversely the sacramental reception of Christ's body and blood can also be seen as the peak of sharing, a process of communion with God and with each other which is going on all the time by virtue of the fact that we are members of the Church.

The word for 'Church' in Greek is 'ekklesia', which means 'called out'. Essentially this means the same as the Hebrew 'qahal'. The idea is that God is calling out his own people to address them, if you like, it is God's own roll call!

God's people become 'Church', therefore, insofar as they respond positively to His call to celebrate His presence, to listen to His Word, and to share in His Life.

CHURCH ON SUNDAY

Every Sunday in this country there are something like four million people, Christians of all denominations, who go to church. We are in a minority. A recent survey showed that while 85% of people in Britain believe in God, less than 10% go to church. Why do we go?

I suppose if we were to take a cross-section of a congregation on Sunday, we would find all kinds of motivations. Those who say I go because I am told I must. Others who go out of conviction that they must somehow express belief in the fact that there is God, and that Jesus Christ is in a special way the Son of God; that he is alive, to the glory of God, and he is at work in the world. Therefore they feel a need to go and worship Him and express their faith in Him, not merely as individuals but as a group.

There is no more fitting day to do it than on Sunday which has become known in Christian language as the Lord's Day because it is the day of the resurrection of Christ.

Even those who go largely through habit gain much from it. The law of the Church, that Catholics attend Mass

each Sunday, is to help form this habit. There are many good things in life which we do by habit. But I think if we really remain in that level of habit and never make the decision our own we are missing out on something important. It is not adequately appreciated by many Catholics that the Church has a wonderful teaching. The Risen Christ is present all the time in the Church, but in a very special way when the Christian gathering comes together to worship Him. It is really the presence of the Risen Lord and our awareness of it that should make a Sunday Mass a living celebration. Ideally people should be so enthusiastic about this that they wouldn't miss it for anything. Jesus Christ is always really present in His Church, through the sacraments and when Christians come together. 'Where two or three are gathered together in my name', says Christ Our Lord, 'there am I in the midst'. Catholics often think of the words 'Real Presence' as applied only to his presence in the consecrated bread and wine which has become the body and blood of Christ. But we cannot appreciate that Real Presence adequately unless we realise that He is present in the people who believe in Him. We are Church. We are the body of Christ.

The next section of 'Faith Alive' will look at what this means.

QUESTIONS

1. What are the essential elements which make a person 'belong' to the Church? Are there different ways and degrees of belonging?
2. Do we think of ourselves first as Catholics or as Christians? Does it make a difference which way we look at it?

22-The Church – Two Thousand Years On

The whole Church is entrusted with God's Word.
The Holy Spirit guides the Church in its history.
The Church is human and divine.
The Church is a Church of sinners becoming saints.

IN THE year 2030, the Church will celebrate two thousand years history, since the first Day of Pentecost, when the Holy Spirit came upon the first apostles and Christian people.

How has the Church survived so long, when empires, political parties and so many philosophies have disappeared. Why, in spite of all the pressures of history, and in particular the pressures of secular and atheistic society in this century, does the Church continue to grow?

One answer is that the faith of Christ and his church takes people as they are, with all their faults and failings, and gives them the opportunity to become truly themselves, children of God their heavenly Father. It is a church for human beings. One of the secrets of its success is that it has so many failures.

It contains many saints and sinners and also saints who are at the same time sinners.

HUMAN AND DIVINE

If you look at the images which come spontaneously into your mind when the word 'Church' is mentioned, the chances are that you will find that you have been thinking about popes, bishops and assorted clerics rather than of yourself and the people on either side of you at Mass last Sunday.

Societies such as the Church tend to be defined by reference to those who hold power within them. This is how the world, especially the media, employs the word 'Church'. The Second Vatican Council, however, strove to correct a centuries-old preoccupation with this image when it used the phrase 'people of

Many Christians died to provide public entertainment here in the Colosseum, Rome, thrown to the lions or crucified.

God', thus making the men and women in the pew the main ingredients in any definition of 'Church'.

THE CHURCH HUMAN

If the Church is to be the leaven in society, it cannot be a purely invisible reality. It has to have a thoroughly human face while carrying out its divine commission. It has to organise itself for action. But the organisation is always secondary to the membership.

Inevitably, if regrettably, it is as an organisation that the world usually sees the Church. Historians are naturally interested in those who have power. Hence we hear of popes and emperors, bishops and kings, abbots and synods, but rarely of the man and woman in the pew. The vast majority of Church members appear in histories largely as statistics.

Lay or clerical, governing or governed, we belong to a society with two thousand years of history. Some of that history is highly creditable, some of it utterly disreputable, but all of it marked by the invisible presence and patience of the Holy Spirit. To look at the Church's course through history is to appreciate that its divine mission has to be carried out in thoroughly human ways.

For centuries the Church provided not only the service of preaching and sacraments but also many of the bulwarks of civilisation such as scholarship, law and civic administration. The problem, then as now, is how to be fully involved in the world while remaining a sign of contradiction; how to use power wisely and responsibly but avoid being corrupted by it.

As the Second Vatican Council put it, the Church, 'although she needs human resources to carry out her mission, is not set up to seek earthly glory, but to proclaim, and this by her own example, humility and self denial' (*Lumen Gentium*, para 8).

Simple honesty compels even the most loyal member of the Church to admit that this ideal has not always been realised. If, however, the Church has often failed in justice, love, and evangelical fervour, it has also promoted repentance and reform.

THE CHURCH OF SINNERS

Most important of all, it has resisted every call to turn itself into a society for the perfect alone. It holds out perfection as a constant ideal, but it does not exclude the great majority who muddle along in spite of failure and low-voltage faith.

When the German philosopher Nietzsche remarked that Christians would have to look more saved if they wanted him to believe in their Saviour, he may have been missing the meaning of salvation. 'I have not come to call the righteous but sinners to repentance' (*Luke 5:32*) was what Jesus had said. It still serves as a claim for his Church.

The story of Jesus has been told and retold in every generation and the Holy Spirit has never ceased from his work of inspiring, forgiving and strengthening.

The Church is a society in which the divine and the human are mysteriously intermingled. History shows that just when the Church seems to have grown old and tired and irrelevant, it has always found the power to rejuvenate itself.

Faith recognises this immediately as the 'power from on high', which Jesus assured his disciples would come upon them shortly (*Luke 24:49*). Since Jesus will be with his Church until the end of time, Christians can confidently look to the coming of that power in every age.

Perhaps we could look a bit more saved.

THE APOSTOLIC AGE

The Holy Spirit came upon the apostles and the Church at Pentecost (*Acts 2*). Peter led the first Christians, all Jews, in Jerusalem. After the conversion of Paul (about AD 33), and Peter's vision in Joppa (*Acts 10*), the mission widened to include Gentiles. The church spread rapidly with Paul's missionary journeys, and by AD 63, when Paul went to Rome, there were Christians in most cities of the Roman Empire.

The first Christians were persecuted both by Jews and the Romans. The synagogue leaders were not prepared to accept Jesus as the Messiah, and resented Christians allowing Gentiles to become members of the new movement without the need for circumcision. There were Jews in most of the cities of the Empire, and friction between Jews and Christians existed from the beginning of the Church.

But persecution by the Romans was much fiercer, and lasted much longer than the early Jewish persecution. In AD 64 Nero accused the Christians of starting a fire in Rome (which he himself might have started), and Christians were tortured to death. What bothered the Roman authorities was the exclusiveness of Christianity, refusing to worship the Roman gods, and particularly the emperor, in addition to their own Christ. For this reason, they were thought to be 'atheists'.

Towards the close of the first century the New Testament was completed and the apostles handed it on to their successors.

THE EARLY FATHERS

Throughout the first three centuries of Christianity, persecution by the Roman Emperors continued to flare up from time to time.

Outstanding teachers appeared whom we call the early fathers. They included Ignatius of Antioch, Justin the Martyr, and Irenaeus. They presented the Gospel in its authentic form to counter both pagan objections, and weird forms of Christianity which began to appear, such as Gnosticism.

Many Christians were tempted to see the world as essentially evil, the only solution being escape from it into a world of 'gnosis' (knowledge). Fathers such as Irenaeus countered this by pre-

senting the true humanity of Christ and the history of salvation, emphasising that God actually entered our world in order to redeem it.

Church discipline at that time was very strict. People had to undergo a long period of instruction (called the 'catechumenate') in order to be baptised. And, should a person fall into serious sin, such as burning incense to the emperor rather than suffer persecution, a long period of public penance was prescribed.

THE AGE OF THE COUNCILS

In 312, the Emperor Constantine was converted to Christianity and from being a persecuted religion, Christianity eventually became the official religion of the Empire. Persecution ended formally with the Edict of Milan in 313.

Christians became powerful, and priests and bishops assumed important social roles. They tended to become a clerical caste. Christianity turned from being a persecuted church to being a persecuting church, synagogues being burnt down with the encouragement of Christian leaders.

The main internal problem was that of the doctrine of the divinity of Christ. A priest called Arius questioned belief that Jesus was truly God, denying that Jesus existed from all eternity with God the Father. A whole series of Councils followed (see section 2, No. 6) which defined the divinity, the humanity, and the one divine personality of Christ. At one time, Arius had the support of a large number of bishops, and the champion of orthodoxy, St Athanasius, seemed to be against the whole world.

Monasticism began to flourish, particularly now that most Christians, their faith no longer being tested by persecution, began to lapse into superficiality in their religious practice. Becoming a monk, often leading a life of great austerity in the desert, was seen as the best way of following the strict demands of the Gospel.

St Anthony of Egypt was one of the best known. He became a hermit but many disciples followed him into the desert and he taught them. He came out of his solitude at the time of the Arian heresy.

THE MIDDLE AGES

With the collapse of the Roman Empire, and Rome invaded by the barbarian hoards (AD 410), the Pope began to assume more political as well as religious authority. Troubles began with the East, since Constantinople, the 'new Rome', felt that their bishop should have primacy now that the seat of the Empire had moved there.

In response, Popes such as Gregory the Great and Gregory VII (Hildebrand) established Europe as a unity under one Catholic Faith, which was seen as the basis of life both religious and secular. Gregory the Great, himself a Benedictine monk, sent Augustine to England in AD 597 in order to convert the country to Christianity. Augustine became the first Archbishop of Canterbury.

In the 11th century, a flood of manuscripts by the Greek philosopher Aristotle came into Europe, and university life began to flourish. At the same time, orders of mendicants such as the Franciscans and the Dominicans rose up to reform the Church. Friars did not live in monasteries, but wandered about begging (hence 'mendicants'), witnessing to the poverty of the Gospel, and preaching the Good News to people who often were neglected by their own pastors. Scholastic theology was the most important academic discipline, because God was seen as the centre of all life, secular and religious.

THE REFORMATION

By the 14th and 15th century, scholastic theology had become decadent, reduced to logic-chopping. People were often ignorant of their faith, the scriptures being read by a tiny literate minority of clerics.

Throughout the late Middle Ages,

King Henry VIII, who declared himself Head of the Church in England, in defiance of the Pope.

groups such as the Hussites, the 'spiritual Franciscans', Lollards, and the Waldensians had protested against the authority of the Church, appealing straight to the Bible and the Holy Spirit in one's own experience. This attack was reinforced by the Humanist movement which encouraged scholars to abandon scholasticism, and to go back to classical Rome and Greek culture to find inspiration for art, culture, and religion.

In the 16th century, perhaps the most turbulent event in the history of the Church happened: the Reformation. Martin Luther, a German Augustinian Friar, defied a papal letter against him, and started an 'Evangelical' church based upon scripture and faith alone. Calvin and Zwingli in Switzerland followed suit. The King of England, Henry VIII declared himself Head of the Church in England, thus defying papal authority.

Rome called a council in 1549, at Trent in northern Italy, near the German and Austrian borders. At first, only a few bishops attended. But it gathered momentum, and became the basis of reform within the Catholic Church, establishing proper catechesis, good training for priests, and adequate apologetics against the views of Protestant Reformers. At this time also the Jesuit order began to flourish, founded by a Spanish aristocrat-become-priest, Ignatius of Loyola. The Jesuits, a mobile and highly dedicated group of priests without either the monastic enclosure or the rules of the friars, became the 'shock troops' of the Catholic counter-Reformation.

THE MODERN CHURCH

In the 16th century, nearly all Europeans would wish to call themselves Christian, whether Catholic or Protestant. But soon, with the growth of scientific knowledge, and the use of the scientific method, belief in God himself came under challenge, and even more belief in direct interventions by God such as miracles and the Incarnation.

In the 18th and 19th centuries, scien-tific and historical method began to be applied in earnest to the scriptures. The reaction of the Church at first was entirely negative, seeing biblical criticism as a threat to the claims of Christ. The same reaction we find in the time of Pius IX against liberal democracy, since the authority of God seemed to be replaced entirely by human freedom; as for instance with the French Revolution.

The response of the Vatican was to clarify the position of the Pope. The first Vatican Council defined the infallibility of the Pope when he makes a solemn declaration on a matter of the faith of the whole Church. This same Council also reaffirmed faith in miracles, and the reasonableness of the act of faith, in the face of modern scientific and biblical criticism.

A new and more positive climate emerged after the First World War,

Pope John XXIII, the Great and the Good, who summoned the Second Vatican Council. Son of a farmer in Northern Italy.

1914–18. Christians became more ecumenical, seeking unity among each other. With the threat of atheistic communism growing throughout the world, Christians became once more a persecuted minority rather than a force-factor in the world. Protestants formed the World Council of Churches; and, in 1960, Pope John XXIII called a General Council at the Vatican to renew the Catholic Church. In spite of all its traumas of the past four hundred years since the Reformation, the Church had grown enormously. Seventy bishops attended the Council of Trent, three thousand were present at Vatican II, now only a minority from Europe.

The growth of the 'institutional' Church has, at times, detracted from the role of lay people. Perhaps the most significant movement in the church recently has been greater recognition of the common priesthood of all God's people, and the part all have to play in the building up of the body of Christ.

SENSUS FIDELIUM

This refers to the Catholic belief that the whole people of God have an infallible understanding of the truth of Christ. Because the whole Church is entrusted with the message of Christ, and is given, by the presence of the Spirit, the competence to keep this message faithfully, and preach the Gospel, the whole body of Christ cannot err in matters of faith.

QUESTIONS
1. 'Perfection is an ideal the Church constantly holds out to us, but it does not exclude the great majority of us who muddle along in spite of failure and low-voltage faith.' People outside the Church often think membership is only for those who can keep the rules. Is that what we believe?
2. How can lay Catholics help to promote and bring about necessary developments in the life of the Church?

23-The Church-What is its Authority?

The church is guided by the Holy Spirit into all truth,
The church is preserved from fundamental error in preaching
the Gospel.
This gift of infallibility is in the whole body of Christ.
But the whole body of Bishops, and the Pope himself, can speak
infallibly under certain circumstances.

THE CHURCH claims that its message, and its life and worship, is not man-made, but comes with the authority of God. Indeed the Church claims that its message itself goes beyond what human beings can work out for themselves; it is about the life of God, and our sharing in that life, here on earth, and for eternity.

This means that the message itself must have the guarantee of God's authority in order to be trustworthy.

God began by giving the message of salvation in the form of a 'covenant'; a deal with Abraham (*Gen 12*) promising him a land and a family, a 'seed' greater than any other nation. God then made a covenant with Moses, giving him the law (the Ten Commandments), guidance for happiness on earth. When the people of God had settled in the Promised Land of Israel, God sent a prophet, Nathan, to tell King David, the Anointed (Messiah), that he had a covenant from God as well. He, David, was to have an eternal dynasty (*2 Sam 7*).

The people were unfaithful to the covenant, and suffered misfortune. But the prophets told of a new covenant, to be made with the 'house' (the dynasty) of David. This covenant would change their hearts, and they would 'know' God Yahweh (*Jer 31:31*).

Then came Jesus, sent from God his Father, a 'son of David' (*Matt 1*). Jesus' miracles, his teaching, and the love he showed to outcasts and sinners, was proof that he was sent by God to found a new kingdom, and to make a new 'covenant' or 'Testament' with the human race. Above all, his resurrection was proof that God was with him, in spite of his dreadful death on the cross, and was a seal of the new covenant.

Jesus sent out his apostles with his authority to preach and to found churches. They 'laid hands on' (ordained) their successors the bishops or 'overseers', to govern the Church in their place. Christ sent his Spirit to be with the whole Church until his final return.

Christ our Lord himself is the sole basis of the Church's authority.

NEWMAN'S DILEMMA

Any organisation – a cricket club, a debating society, a religious order, for example – needs some sort of authority if it is to be and to do what it is supposed to be and to do. It also needs to be able to develop. The more dynamic the organisation the more thrusting will be the seeds of development within it.

The Church is no exception. This is why 'Christ the Lord set up in his Church a variety of offices which aim at the good of the whole Body. The holders of office . . . are dedicated to promoting the interests of their brothers and sisters, so that all who belong to the People of God . . . may . . . attain salvation. (Dogmatic Constitution on the Church, No 18).

In 1845, a young and brilliant Anglican clergyman, who had two years before resigned his ministry as Vicar of St Mary's Oxford, became a Catholic. It was the end of a long agonising over the whole question of authority.

Christianity claims to be based on a revelation. God is not impersonal. He is our Father and has revealed himself in

John Henry Newman. Lead, kindly light . . .

history through the man Jesus Christ. The Bible tells us about him. But how do we know which interpretation of the events and stories in the Bible is the true one? Left to itself the Bible offers a thousand interpretations. Does not the intervention of God in history imply a present informant and guide, and that an infallible one? This was Newman's question. If you take Newman's road, the next question is where is this guide and interpreter to be found and in what form? Not in the Bible. Instead we must look at the Christian churches. Is there one which claims to teach with the same infallible authority as the Apostles and the Fathers? The answer is what it always was – Rome.

But, the Protestant objects. Rome has added to the faith. Newman argued in Development of Christian Doctrine, that Rome had preserved the apostolic faith by developing it. It is the character of true interpretations of the Christian faith that they possess the power to adapt and develop through history.

Thus for example the papacy is a development of Matt 16:18; the Immaculate Conception of Luke 1:28; and liberty of conscience, and the separation of Church and State are developments of Matt 22:21.

Newman's argument is that in matters of religion, the stream is not purest near the source. Instead, religious belief is purer and stronger, when its bed has become deep and broad and full. 'In a higher world it is otherwise. Here below to live is to change, and to be perfect is to have changed often.'

Many people have been faced with that same question as Newman, and have come to a similar answer.

But there is a further problem. In matters of religion, especially that truth given by God which is beyond reason and understanding, our authority cannot make fundamental errors. In other words, it must be infallible.

While on earth, Christ spoke with authority, and those who came to believe in him accepted his authority as infallible, from the Father. But what was to happen after his death? Were his disciples to be left in the cold, without truly trustworthy guidance? This is where the infallibility of the Church comes in.

BISHOPS AND POPE

Paul in his letter to the Ephesians says that the Church, or what he calls 'God's household', is built upon the foundations of the apostles and prophets. Jesus Christ himself being the cornerstone (*Eph 2:20*).

This theme of building of the Church on a secure foundation is more familiar to us from Matthew 16 where Jesus changes Simon's name to Peter (Rock). This change of name assigns him his vocation. Jesus says: 'You are the rock on which I will build my Church' (*16:18*).

Though the emphasis is different, there is no contradiction between these two texts. Peter is himself one of the apostles. Apostles are people sent out as authorised delegates.

The Church is built on them. Building up 'God's household' is always a divine activity in the Old Testament. Even if Peter is the foundational-rock, Jesus himself remains the cornerstone.

Of course Peter has a special place among the Twelve. His name occurs 124 times in the New Testament; John comes next with 38 mentions. Peter is given the specific task of 'strengthening his brethren' (*Luke 22:32*) and feeding Christ's sheep (*John 21:15–17*).

But his leadership role does not cut him off from the rest of the apostles. Neither could exist without the other.

A key passage of Vatican II reflects these New Testament themes: 'Just as the role the Lord gave individually to Peter, the first among the Apostles, is permanent and was meant to be transmitted to his successors, so also the apostles' office of ministry in the Church is permanent, and was meant to be exercised without interruption by the sacred order of bishops' (Church in the Modern World 20).

Note that the special place for Peter is already indicated here: for he is the successor of an individual apostle, Peter bishop of Rome, while the other bishops are successors of the apostles taken as a body.

THE GENERAL COUNCIL

The best expression of the team-nature of the college of bishops is seen in a General Council. At Vatican II, for example, it was impossible to drive a wedge between the successor of St Peter and the successors of the apostles.

Pope John XXIII and then Pope Paul VI 'presided over the whole assembly of charity' and therefore were members of the Council – not above it, still less against it. The whole college signed the Council documents, beginning with Pope Paul.

This is a somewhat ideal picture, and of course a Council cannot be in permanent session. In between Councils, that is, most of the time, there have been famous historical quarrels about just where final authority lay.

There have been two extreme positions, both of which have been rejected by the Church.

COUNCIL VERSUS POPE?

'Councilarism' held that a General Council was superior to the Pope, could on occasions depose him, and was the only way to reform the Church 'in head and members'. In the thirteenth and fourteenth centuries, with popes and anti-popes competing for an office that was often seen as one of domination rather than service, this was an attractive theory.

The opposite position isolates the Pope from the college of bishops, and makes them mere rubber stamps of his authority – branch managers as it were in the multinational corporation that is the Church.

Some interpretations of Vatican I went along these lines, but they were rejected by Pope Pius IX himself in 1875 in his letter to the German bishops.

Vatican II restored the balance between the Petrine ministry and the bishops. Various measures were taken to ensure that they should not drift apart again.

For the first time residential bishops became members of the Roman Curia. A regular Synod of Bishops was set up to express 'continuing collegiality' and make episcopal advice available to the Pope.

These moves were meant to stimulate consultation and communication – the life-blood of the Church. If they have not always succeeded, that can be attributed to human nature: the Church will not reach its final stage of perfection until the end of time.

Bishops of a region are now grouped together in an 'episcopal conference'. This is a revival of something very traditional. They do what patriarchates used to do in the ancient world. The diversity of 'liturgical usage and spiritual traditions', says the Council, shows 'all the more dazzlingly the catholicity of the undivided Church'. (Church in the Modern World 23).

So Catholic unity does not mean being uniform: the Church is the home of 'reconciled diversity'.

The fact that England and Wales form one bishops' conference, while Scotland has its own, illustrates that the Church is ahead of secular society. The reality of a local Church is guaranteed by its episcopal conference.

At the same time diversity exists not for its own sake but for the more effective and adapted preaching of the Gospel. All the European bishops come together in the Council of European Bishops of which the Bishop of Rome, naturally, is a keen member.

Finally, one should add that although bishops are the official 'teachers and witnesses' of the faith of the Church, they do not in any sense 'own the Church'.

Thus the two infallible Marian definitions – the Immaculate Conception in 1854 and the Assumption in 1950 – were not novel doctrines propounded by the Pope after consultation with his bishops: they were valid only as the expression of the already existing faith of the Church, the sensus fidelium or faith-instinct of ordinary believers.

The college of bishops with the pope in its midst exists to serve the whole People of God and give it shape. Authority in the church exists 'so that all may unite freely, and yet in order' (Church in the Modern World 18).

MAGISTERIUM

From the Latin magister, teacher. This usually refers to the official teaching body of the Church, in particular the bishops led by the Pope. But the word essentially refers to teaching authority of the whole Church, of which the bishops and the Pope are the official representatives, in apostolic succession from the apostles and Peter.

INFALLIBLE?

Since it is God's instrument for the achievement of his plan for the salvation of men, the Church, as Church, cannot be teaching fundamental error. Christians gradually realised that an ecumenical council, that is a council representing the whole Church as such and not just some region or section of it, will be protected from error when it commits itself positively to some specific interpretation of revealed truth. Thus after various conflicts in AD 343 a regional council at Sardica recognised the role of the bishop of Rome as final arbiter in a dispute between other bishops. It was gradually perceived that the 'official' solution to such disputes, given in the name of the Church and in the light of the teaching and experience of the Church as a whole, must also be infallible.

But the bishop of Rome, successor of

Peter though he be, is no more protected from greed, pride or ambition than the rest of us. Vatican I defined that Peter was appointed by Christ prince of the apostles and thereby endowed with a primacy of true and proper jurisdiction in which the bishop of Rome is his successor. He thus has power over the universal Church, and possesses that infallibility with which Christ wished his Church to be endowed. These legal phrases have carefully limited the occasions on which the pope can be seen to be enunciating the faith of the whole Church, and thus protected from error.

But infallibility, mere protection from error, does not guarantee the aptness, the clarity or the completeness of a statement. These will often come not from the magisterium of pope and bishops, but from 'the community which must respond to and assess the insights and teachings of ordained ministers'. 'The Magisterium exercises a function of its own which the Spirit has not entrusted to others. But this function demands that the Magisterium draw from the very life of the People of God the reality to be discerned and judged, promulgated or defined, for it must exercise all its activity upon the word as received and lived in the Church' (Jean Tillard, Sensus Fidelium).

SENSUS FIDELIUM
(Understanding of the Faithful)

This refers to the Catholic belief that the whole people of God have an infallible understanding of the truth of Christ. Because the whole Church is entrusted with the message of Christ, and is given, by the presence of the Spirit, the competence to keep this message faithfully, and preach the Gospel, the whole body of Christ cannot err in matters of faith.

The controversial First Vatican Council, 1870, which defined infallibility of the Pope as Catholic Faith.

PRAYER

As Christ's vicars on earth, popes have been responsible for encouraging prayer in general and also in specific form.

Gregory the Great, a Benedictine, reformed the liturgy and gave emphasis to the prayer of the Church, psalms and readings. Innocent III backed the spirituality of St Francis of Assisi and St Dominic, blessing Dominic's preaching of the Rosary. Pope Pius V further stressed the Rosary by instituting the feast of the Holy Rosary, while Pius X made efforts to stimulate the prayer and the worship of the people of God by stressing the importance of frequent Holy Communion. The latest authoritative teaching comes from Vatican II. 'The spiritual life, however, is not limited to participation in the liturgy. The Christian is indeed called to pray with others, but he must also pray to his Father in secret. Furthermore, according to the teaching of the apostle, he must pray without ceasing.'

> **PRAYER**
> *Lord Jesus,*
> *You taught your followers to pray.*
> *The authority of your Church and her teachers always continues to insist that Christians pray, individually and together, at all times. Help me to make prayer a regular, daily part of my life. Amen.*

THE POWER OF THE KEYS

Around the inside wall of the basilica of Saint Peter in Rome, in gilt letters several feet high, runs the inscription, 'Thou art Peter, and upon this rock I will build my Church'. If tradition is correct, as Pope Paul VI asserted, that statement is literally true, since Peter's martyred body lies buried directly beneath the high altar. Which is strange, since the

I will give you the keys of the kingdom.

New Testament makes no clear reference to Peter's presence in Rome, let alone to his having been bishop, pope and martyr there.

The closest allusion we have is a note in the First Letter of Peter (5:13) to the effect that the author sends greetings from the church in 'Babylon' (used in Revelation as a cryptic name for Rome). For the tradition about Peter as it is now widely known and accepted, we have to wait for Eusebius the church historian in the fourth century.

The New Testament does not say much about the position of Peter among the Twelve and in the early Church. Even though the Beloved Disciple John had occupied the place of honour next to his Master at the Last Supper (*John 13:23*) and outran him to the Empty Tomb, he nevertheless deferred to the acknowledged leader of the Twelve and allowed him to enter first (*John 20:4–6*).

When Peter makes his fateful declaration to Jesus, 'You are the Messiah, the Son of the living God' (*Matt 16:16*), Jesus makes it clear that Peter is doing more than act as a spokesman for the Twelve: 'Blessed are you, Simon son of John. For this was not revealed to you by flesh and blood, but by my Father in heaven' (*16:17*). It is in consequence of this declaration by Peter that the Lord addresses to him those words which in recent centuries have become almost *the* Roman Catholic defence of papal primacy: 'You are Petros (the Greek translation of the Aramaic word for rock), and on this Cephas (= rock) I will build my Church' (*16:18*).

When Jesus gave Peter the power of the keys of the kingdom (*16:19*) it would be wrong to imagine that he was thinking of a highly organised institution complete with College of Cardinals and Vatican Curia! Perhaps it would be more realistic to see Peter in a role approximating to that of a chief rabbi of his time, the exercise of whose authority included deciding who could and who could not form part of the worshipping community.

QUESTIONS

1. One of the things which most people know about the Catholic Church is that the Pope is infallible. Not so well known, but equally important, is the teaching which comes from the 'sensus fidelium', by which we mean the widely held beliefs of ordinary people.

   What implications does this have for our responsibility to reflect on our faith and to develop our 'sensus fidelium'?

2. You are asked to introduce a discussion on 'The Role of the Pope and Bishops in the Catholic Church' for an ecumenical study group. How will you do this? Besides your introductory remarks please suggest the discussion questions and/or other material you would provide.

24-Church Rules

The people of God need rules in accord with the Gospel.
The bishops make rules for their own dioceses.
The Pope and Bishops make rules for the whole church.
These are expressed in the Code of Canon Law.

THE CHURCH AND ITS RULES

All religions have basic rules for all their members. Muslims, for instance, have five rules including prayer five times a day, one pilgrimage to Mecca if possible, and keeping the fast of Ramadan. Following these, a person is defined as a 'good Muslim'. On the other hand, a Christian for example, who never went to church, would usually be described as 'nominal' or even as 'lapsed'.

We must be careful before we define whether a person is 'good' or not in terms of whether religious rules are kept. A person may keep all the rules, and be a spiteful or a hateful neighbour. Again, a person may be 'lapsed' from the practice of his or her faith, yet that faith may influence life in profound ways, making that person truly loving and merciful.

Also, to define a religion simply in terms of keeping its minimum obligations would do a great disservice to that religion. Religion, especially Christianity, is the growth of a relationship, a kind of marriage, between ourselves and God our Father through Christ and in the Spirit. And, as with any marriage, just to make it a series of rules is to take the heart out of it.

On the other hand, again as with marriage, no way of life which is permanent can flourish without discipline, without rules; and Christian life is no exception. The Church's rules can help us to be faithful to the covenant between God and ourselves. When life is humdrum, even when we do not 'feel' good about our religion, the rules are there to keep us plodding on.

And again, to treat the Church's rules with contempt can put our spiritual lives in danger. On this earth, life with God is not once and for all, but is a process. Like plants, without nourishment we can die. The rules are there to make sure that such daily nourishment is there for our spiritual lives.

All down the centuries, rules have been given for the daily life of a Christian, in the Catholic Church, with the authority of the local bishop, or, for the wider Church, with the authority of the Pope. These rules vary according to times and circumstances, and changing needs. The latest revision has been published by Rome to enshrine the insights of the Second Vatican Council. The book is called 'The New Code of Canon Law' (it is called 'Canon Law' because each of the 1752 rules is called a 'canon', Greek for 'rule').

Like any code of law, only a small proportion of its rules apply to the life of any individual. Many of the rules in the New Code of Canon Law are not relevant to most of us, referring to the setting up of parishes, taking religious vows, or the organisation of a diocese.

The following canons are relevant to all, or at least to a large number of, Catholic Christians, and arise from our baptism and consequent commitment to live the Christian way in the life of the Church.

Canon Law states that each church member has the duty of witnessing to our faith, together ensuring that 'the Gospel reaches the whole world'.

THE TEN CHURCH RULES

1. All Christ's faithful have the duty to preserve communion with, and promote the growth of, the Church, lead a holy life, and strive that the Gospel reaches the whole world (Canons 209–211, 225).

2. All Catholics are obliged to accept the infallibly declared teaching of the Church (Canon 750), and to follow in obedience the pastors of the Church when they declare this teaching and discipline (Canon 212).

3. They are obliged to receive Holy Communion at least once per year during the Easter season (Canon 920).

4. They must attend Mass on Sundays and Holydays of Obligation, abstaining from such work and business which would inhibit worship on those days (Canon 1247).

5. They are bound to confess all 'grave' or 'mortal' sins, and are recommended to confess 'venial sins' (Canon 988). Grave sins must be confessed at least once per year (Canon 989).

6. Ash Wednesday and Good Friday are days of fasting and abstinence (Canons 1249, 50). Other days of fasting and/or abstinence are reg-

ulated locally. As are all Fridays when the Church insists all Catholics must perform some act of Penance.

7. In order to be married, a Catholic must have been confirmed (Canon 1065), and must be married before a priest and two witnesses (Canon 1108), unless special dispensations have been obtained.

8. All have a duty to provide for the needs of the Church, for its worship and support of its ministers. All must promote social justice, helping the poor from their own resources (Canon 222).

9. All have a duty to grow in the knowledge of Christian teaching appropriate to their capacity (Canon 229); and to educate their children in accordance with the teaching of the Church (Canon 226). Parents are obliged to choose those ways which can best do this (Canon 793), especially by sending their children to schools which provide for Catholic education (Canon 798).

10. Parents are obliged to have their children baptised within the first few weeks of birth (Canon 867), and to ensure that their children who have reached the age of reason are prepared for confession and communion (Canon 914).

LIGHT FROM THE COUNCIL

'Christ the Lord in no way abolished the bountiful heritage of the law and the prophets which grew little by little from the history and experience of the People of God in the Old Testament. Rather he fulfilled it, so that it could, in a new and more sublime way, lead to the heritage of the New Testament. Accordingly, although St Paul in expounding the mystery of salvation, teaches that justification is not obtained through the works of the law, but through faith, nonetheless he does not exclude the binding force of the Decalogue, nor does he deny the importance of discipline in the Church . . .' (Pope John Paul, in the Apostolic Constitution promulgating The New Code of Canon Law).

MEDITATION

I will meditate on your precepts
and fix my eyes on your ways.
I will delight in your statutes;
I will not forget your word.

Deal bountifully with your servant,
that I might live and observe your
*   word.*
Open my eyes, that I may behold
wondrous things out of your law.

QUESTIONS

1. Which laws of the Church have you found most helpful and supportive for your own Christian living? What advice would you offer someone who was finding particular laws irksome?
2. Why does the Church have rules? Are there too many rules? Should we have more rules?

25-The Church-Its Life of Prayer

We should pray each day.
Prayer is relating to God in love.
There is a rich tradition of prayer life in the Church.
Each person has to find his or her way.

THE MOST important feature of any religion is its life of prayer. Religion is the development of a personal relationship towards the mysterious Other whom we do not see, but we know is often more present to us than we are to our own selves.

Why do we pray? Most commonly people pray for things. They pray that God will heal them or make their life prosperous, or even end their life if they

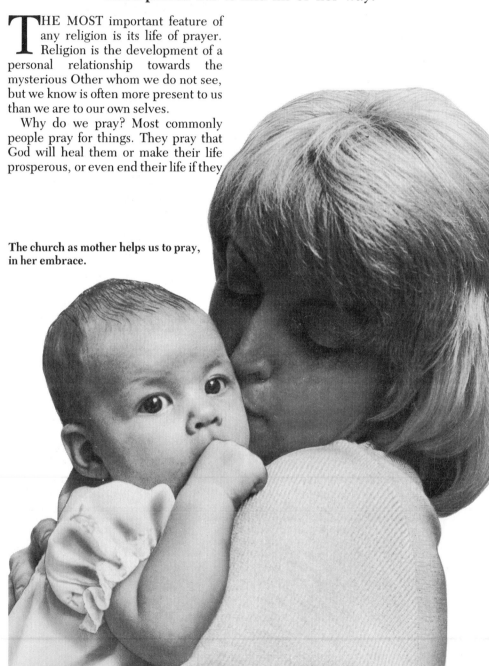

The church as mother helps us to pray, in her embrace.

are suffering terribly. People who never go to church will often pray in times of need.

Some people think it selfish to pray for our own interests. If that is our only prayer, that is a fair criticism. But intercessory prayer is most important, because it shows that we believe that this mysterious One, the creator of the universe, has our interests at heart. And can be 'bothered' by our little interests. Intercessory prayer is at least the beginning of the realisation that God is our heavenly Father who loves us and cares for us.

If this were all that this kind of prayer could do, it would still be worthwhile, because it begins our relationship with God. But intercessory prayer is also based upon the realisation that God actually answers our prayer. How this happens, it is impossible to know. We only see the effects of God's plan in history. But it is important to realise that the ultimate cause is God. His answers are often surprising, sometimes shattering! But answers we do receive, if we are prepared to listen.

However, as we develop our relationship with God, we soon realise that it is selfish just to ask all the time. A baby begins by always crying for mother, for food or comfort. But soon, in a good parent/child relationship, genuine love develops.

So it is with God. The normal development of the life of prayer, in particular if we pray each day of our lives (which is the most recommended practice), leads to genuine love of God, with God's help of course. We soon desire to be with God as much as we desire to be with a loved human being – even though, like human relationships, our love of God has its ups and downs.

The highest form of prayer is what is called the 'mystical experience', the experience of being possessed by the love of God. This mysticism is sometimes accompanied by ecstasy.

These experiences occasionally happen because to grow in the love of God

those who hope in God will regain their
    strength,
   they will sprout wings like eagles,
though they run they will not grow weary,
though they walk they will never tire.
   (Isaiah 40:31).

means that we can eventually fall totally in love with God. And, love can be crazy.

For most of us, and even for those deeply practised in it, prayer is basically a down-to-earth daily affair. Mystical experiences are rare, and they are not the most important thing. What matters is that our prayer life should lead to a union of heart and will with God. And this can happen to everyone.

Prayer is not only a duty. It is our right as human beings to become lovers of the Lord of the Universe.

Many people wonder, 'What shall I say when I pray?' Sometimes, it is best to use your own words, to avoid repetition. But, for those who make prayer a daily practice, we soon find that we run out of words of our own.

THE 'OUR FATHER'

When the disciples asked Jesus 'What shall we pray?', he gave them the most famous prayer of all, the 'Our Father'. We should pray this slowly and reflectively every day of our lives. In the 'Our Father', all the elements of good prayer are present. It is the pattern of prayer. No matter how 'holy' we become, we can never outgrow the 'Our Father'. And no matter how ignorant we might think we are of theology or religion, we can still say the 'Our Father', with meaning, as our Lord's own prayer.

Each petition of the 'Our Father' introduces us to an essential aspect of prayer:

Our Father, Who Art In Heaven

We call God 'Our Father', because He loves us as our creator, and he sent his Son Jesus Christ on earth to be our brother, and to lead us back to the Father. 'Who art in heaven' defines God, not in terms of space 'up there', but as greater than any notion we can have of him. This thought raises up our minds and hearts to the infinite God.

Hallowed Be Thy Name

Literally 'May your name be made holy'. We need in particular to recover the sense of the holiness, the 'otherness' of God. Whenever we utter his 'name' with reverence, we 'make holy his name'. All prayer should begin by quietly placing ourselves in the presence of the all-holy God.

Thy Kingdom Come

Our first prayer is not for ourselves, but for God's kingdom. 'Seek first the kingdom of God, and its justice, and all these things will be added to you', said Jesus, 'and do not worry about tomorrow, tomorrow will take care of itself' (*Matt 6:33,34*). It is daily an act of faith to put God's kingdom first in our lives, and to believe that God will look after our needs.

Thy Will Be Done On Earth As It Is In Heaven

Having addressed the prayer to God the Father in heaven, we now pray that God's will be done here just as it is in God's own presence. We have so much evidence of God's love. Sometimes it is very hard to do God's will. At such times, we remember the words of Jesus just before he was arrested in the Garden of Gethsemane; 'My Father, if it is possible, let this cup pass me by. Nevertheless, let it be as you, not I, would have it' (*Matt 26:39*).

Give Us This Day Our Daily Bread

Having set our minds to seek for God's kingdom, and to do His will, we are prepared to ask for our daily physical and spiritual needs. In asking for daily bread, that does not mean that we are not asking for butter and jam as well! God knows that we need the sweet things in life, in every sense of that word, to make life more enjoyable. But in asking for daily bread, rather than for riches, we are focusing on what we need for this life, rather than for always what we want.

Christ warned continually against avarice, the desire for possessions for their own sake, which causes inequality and injustice and destroys us.

Note also that the prayer says 'Give US our daily bread', not 'Give ME my daily bread'. We pray for others also to have what they need, and this implies that we will try to make that happen.

And Forgive Us Our Trespasses, As We Forgive Those Who Trespass Against Us

Christ gave one condition for forgiveness, that we forgive others their wrongs against us. See the parable he told of the Unforgiving Debtor (*Matt 18:23–35*). Often when we pray, we remember we need forgiveness from our heavenly

Father; and we remember people who have offended us, and who need our forgiveness. It is only in daily prayer that we form the right attitudes, to ask forgiveness from God, and to become forgiving people like Jesus our Lord.

And Lead Us Not Into Temptation, But Deliver Us From Evil

To be tested is a necessary part of everything in life; business, family, school, sport, art, so also in the spiritual life. What we pray in this petition is that God will not allow us to be tempted beyond our strength; but, that He will deliver us 'from the Evil One', that is from Satan the Adversary.

St Paul assures us that 'You can trust that God will not let you be put to the test beyond your strength, but with any trial will also provide a way out enabling you to put up with it' (*1 Cor 10:13*).

God will not desert us in our trial; what this petition secures is that we are aware of possible tests to come, and that we form attitudes of dependence on God, who alone can bring us through.

Amen!

This is a Hebrew word, used continually in our prayers, and often on the lips of Jesus himself and his people the Jews. It means 'trustworthy, reliable, secure'. At the end of our prayer, by saying Amen, we say to God 'I believe that what I have just said and done is right and true. I believe that with your help, I can now put it into practice in life.'

PRAYER TOGETHER

So far, we have been speaking about prayer which we can make on our own, without going to church. Christ said, 'When you pray, go to your private room, shut yourself in, and so pray to your Father who is in that secret place, and your Father who sees all that is done in secret will reward you' (*Matt 6:6*).

But Christ also joined in public worship. Before he died, he established the distinctive form of Christian worship, the Eucharist, Communion, or 'Mass'.

'Worship' comes from 'worthship', an Anglo-Saxon word. Coming together to praise God and to share God's life in communion with each other is our way of giving God his 'worth'. It also fulfils our worth as human beings, to praise God together, acknowledging that as John Donne puts it, 'No man is an island'. We are members of one human race; and we worship God as one people together, responding to His call.

We will deal more specifically with this public worship in a later section, on the subject of the sacraments and the Mass.

'What kind of commitment do I need to begin to pray? And what am I trying to do when I pray?'

We need to pray together as well as alone.

PRAYING LIKE THE FIRST CHRISTIANS?

As well as being the joy and the duty of every Christian, in the history of the Church, prayer has been a specialised vocation, of people who have consecrated their whole lives to God in prayer.

God created us to be holy. It sounds less alarming if we call it 'wholeness', our whole being saying 'Yes' to God in love and joining into union with Him. We cannot slice off a portion of ourselves or of our day and label that 'spiritual'. Our aim is to love God all day.

All the same, we will not recognise what God is asking unless we spend time looking at his Face.

The 'Face' of God is Jesus. He alone has seen the Father, and he reflects Him to us. We look at Jesus in two main ways. First, and most important we see Him and are drawn into His Sacrifice in the Holy Mass. At Mass, Jesus gives Himself, and though we may notice nothing, He slowly changes us into our true selves.

The more faithful we are to the Mass, the more we will understand that we must also pray alone. When we are with other people, we are upheld by their faith and prayer, as well as by our own. Today, most parishes have prayer groups, where we give and receive this support. But it is not enough to pray with other people. If we are to know Jesus intimately then we must come before Him alone.

No one can tell us what to do. An old man once said that he just sat in front of the tabernacle and 'I look at Him, and He looks at me'.

It is the real me who stands before the real God in all spirituality.

OTHER CHRISTIANS

But how does the spirituality of Catholics compare with other Christians? The Orthodox resemble Catholics in attaching great value to the sacraments, especially the Mass; to religious art as inspiration and a focus for prayer, to the use of repetitious prayers (for Catholics the rosary, for Orthodox the Jesus Prayer) as a means of raising the mind and heart to God; and to a warm devotion to Our Lady and the saints.

Protestants base their spirituality on the public and private reading of scripture, on preaching, and on hymn-singing – activities which have recently grown rapidly also in Catholic practice. However, they place a greater emphasis on the conversion experience than Catholics. The development of the ecumenical movement helped Christians of all kinds to appreciate the spirituality of other churches as a valid way of following Christ, and as a source of enrichment for their own spirituality.

CATHOLIC SPIRITUALITY – THE TREASURES OF THE PAST

One of the greatest encouragements to prayer is 'spiritual reading', either of scripture or of one of the great mystics in the history of the Church. When we read one or other of the spiritual giants of the past, we begin to realise that prayer is a rich and varied subject.

Prayer should be the centre of our whole day. We stand before God holding out our lives to his all-seeing but merciful gaze.

All Christians are called to make their lives an extension of their prayer, so that we ourselves become 'a living sacrifice, holy and acceptable to God' (*Rom 12:1*). So the first great commandment is that we should love God with all our heart, soul and mind (*Matt 22:37*).

Some dedicate their whole lives to prayer, for all of us.

TWO WAYS

Early on in the Church two different ways of integrating life and prayer became apparent. The first was for Christians to continue living in the secular world. The baptismal promises to renounce Satan and his works and to devote oneself to Christ express the seriousness with which this lay vocation was taken. This was one reason why many were not baptised as children, but, like St Ambrose, waited until they felt prepared to take on its commitments.

The second way was that of Christians who decided to cut themselves off from ordinary life in order to devote themselves exclusively to following Christ. At first this took the form of a life of solitude, such as that of St Anthony, who seventeen hundred years ago retired into the Egyptian desert. Gradually similar hermits began to form groups which combined solitude with mutual support. A more common type of religious community was the monastery, in which the monks prayed and worked together. St Benedict's Rule in the sixth century provided the classical pattern for this kind of life.

New forms of religious orders developed in response to different needs of the Church. In the tenth century St Bruno returned to the early pattern of the community of hermits when founding his order of Carthusians. In the next century the Cistercians (among whom St Bernard is the best known) sought a stricter interpretation of St Benedict's rule.

A new style of religious order, which aimed at a greater simplicity and mobility than was possible in the fixed life of the monastic orders, emerged in the thirteenth century. The two great examples were the Franciscan and Dominican friars, who provided a model which was subsequently adapted by the many active congregations which have been founded since. Each of the rules was followed by both women and men.

The expansion of religious orders had the unfortunate result that the pursuit of holiness could be seen as a specialist activity of monks and nuns which was beyond the aspirations of the laity. Vatican II firmly rejected this view declaring that 'all Christians in any state or walk of life are called to the fullness of Christian life and the perfection of love' (Decree on the Church 40).

One of the most striking developments since Vatican II has been the flowering of many movements devoted to fostering the holiness of the laity. Possibly more lay-people are devoting themselves today to serious prayer than ever.

QUESTIONS
When and where in our lives do we feel God closest to us? What image of God do we have when we pray? Do we pray to one of the Persons of the Trinity (Father, Jesus, or Holy Spirit)? Is there a particular reason for this?

26-Mary

Mary said 'Yes' to God's messenger.
She is the Virgin Mother of God.
She was conceived without sin.
She is the spiritual mother of us all.

SINCE THE Reformation Mary has been the subject of controversy between the Roman Catholic and other Christian Churches. This is now, largely, a thing of the past, but differences persist. All mainline Christian Churches hold Mary in high esteem and accept that she was the Mother of God, that in Luther's words '. . . the same One whom God begot from eternity she herself brought forth in time'. They differ, however, on what kind of honour should be paid her, on whether to pray to her and on whether she played a part in our salvation.

The position of the Orthodox Churches is close to that of the Catholic Church. In the eyes of the Reformed Churches, however, certain Catholic Marian teachings and devotions lack scriptural basis and involve 'glorification' of Mary. Martin Luther, who wrote warmly of Mary, accused the papacy of his time of 'frightful idolatry'. He would have Christians praise Mary, but not pray to her.

Mary does not figure largely in the theology or in the devotional life of the Reformed Churches, who tend to celebrate only two feasts in her honour, the Purification and the Annunciation. However, individuals and groups in different Churches have been coming closer to the Marian doctrine.

Devotion to Mary has inspired the greatest art, in particular 'icons' (images) in Eastern Christianity. Christians argued that it was not against the Ten Commandments' prohibition to make images of Christ or of the saints, because in Christ God has assumed a truly human shape, which we can represent in art.

MARY AND VATICAN II

The Catholic Church made an important contribution to ecumenical dialogue in the eighth chapter of the Dogmatic Constitution on the Church (Vatican II).

The chapter opens with a reminder that the reason why Christians ought to 'reverence the memory' of Mary is that it was through her that the Son of God 'truly came into our history'. Because (53) she is therefore 'Mother of God and of the Redeemer . . . united to him by a close and indissoluble tie . . . beloved daughter of the Father and temple of the Holy Spirit . . . she far surpasses all creatures, both in heaven and on earth.'

The chapter then recounts what the Scriptures and the Father tell us of the role of Mary in the plan of salvation. In the Old Testament she is 'foreshadowed in the promise of the victory over the serpent', she is 'the virgin who shall conceive and bear a Son' and 'she stands out among the poor and humble of the Lord who confidently hope for and receive salvation from him' (55). For the Fathers she is the Second Eve, through whom life came, as death had come through the first Eve, and she is 'all holy and free from every stain of sin, as though fashioned by the Holy Spirit and formed as a new creature'. Her assent was required to the Incarnation and having said yes 'she devoted herself totally, as a handmaid of the Lord, to the person and work of her Son, under and with him, serving the mystery of redemption, by the grace of Almighty God'.

Mary's role did not finish 'when her earthly life was over', 'Taken up into heaven . . . by her manifold intercession (she) continues to bring us the gifts of eternal salvation. By her maternal charity, she cares for the brothers and sisters of her Son, who still journey on earth surrounded by dangers and difficulties, until they are led into their blessed home . . . This however, is so understood that it neither takes away anything from nor adds anything to the dignity and efficacy of Christ the one Mediator' (62).

On this point the Council is most insistent, for Protestants have contended that Catholic understanding of Mary's role diminished the unique role of Jesus in our salvation. It quotes Saint Paul (60): 'for there is but one God and one mediator of God and men, the man Christ Jesus, who gave himself a redemption for all.' It goes on: 'But Mary's function as mother of men in no way obscures or diminishes this unique mediation of Christ, but rather shows its power.'

In this, Mary is like the Church and the Church is like Mary. 'The Church . . . by receiving the word of God in faith becomes herself a mother. By preaching and baptism she brings forth sons and daughters who are conceived of the Holy Spirit and born to God, to a new and immortal life' (64).

The Council went on to urge 'that the cult, especially the liturgical cult, of the Blessed Virgin, be generously fostered'.

It insisted that all devotion to Mary must lead to Christ: 'let them rightly illustrate the duties and privileges of the Blessed Virgin which always refer to Christ, the source of all truth, sanctity and salvation'. And it warned: 'Let them carefully refrain from whatever might by word or deed lead the separated brethren or any others whatsoever into error about the true doctrine of the Church. Let the faithful remember moreover that true devotion . . . proceeds from true faith, by which we are led to recognise the excellence of the Mother of God and we are moved to a filial love towards our mother and to the imitation of her virtues' (67).

MARY FULL OF GRACE

Mary is different from us. We acknowledge the difference in the Hail Mary: she is 'full of grace' and we are 'sinners'. But we must not think of her exalted state as setting up a barrier between her and us. It is precisely because she is the Mother of God that she is at the centre of the mystery of Christ and the Church and is herself a pre-eminent member of the Church.

The unique privilege of *the Immaculate Conception* prepared Mary for her divine motherhood. It was by virtue of the redeeming power of Christ her Son that she was, from the first moment of her conception preserved free from Original Sin. How are we to understand this?

As G. K. Chesterton remarked there are two ways of 'getting home'. One is to stay there. The other is to wander all over the world till, hopefully, one returns to the place from which one has set out. With the exception of Mary, mankind chose the second course. Through God's grace she always remained 'at home' with Him. She was most perfectly redeemed by not having been allowed

MARY AND TRADITION

The Catholic Church maintains that doctrines about Mary have developed under the guidance of the Holy Spirit, within the tradition of the Church.

Not all the doctrines concerning Mary are contained explicitly in scripture. This raises the whole question of the relationship between Scripture and Tradition in Catholic thought.

God's revelation is handed on, according to Catholic faith, in two interrelated sources, Scripture and Tradition. The Church must teach nothing contrary to Scripture, because Scripture is the Word of God written. Also, the Church's teaching must be related to Scripture, because there is a unity in God's revelation. But, 'the Church does to fall. She was without sin from the first moment of her existence. Our vocation also is to be 'without sin': 'glorious, with no speck or wrinkle . . . holy and fault- less' (*Eph 5:27*). But whereas Mary through God's grace was sinless from the beginning, we with God's grace shall be sinless at the end.

Mary gave herself totally to God and became the Virgin Mother of God through her free consent to His invita- tion. Her bodily virginity symbolises the new creation in Christ and chal- lenges us to live in undividedness of heart and affection of Christ.

Mary is most intimately related to the Church. As the link between the old and new dispensations she receives the Word of God on behalf of Israel and all mankind. In conceiving and giving birth to Christ she realises in her own person the vocation of God's people: to give to the world its Saviour. At Cana Jesus gives his first great 'sign' as the result of her request and changes water into wine. She stands at the foot of the Cross as the Church is born symbolically from Christ's side in the water and blood, symbols of Baptism and the Eucharist which constitute the Church. She is in prayer with the disciples at Pentecost when the Church launches out on its mission which will continue to the end of time.

Finally in her Assumption, Mary anticipates the resurrection of the body. She is the perfect disciple faith- fully following Christ, ready to take risks, and at the same time always learn- ing more about him. In heaven she in- tercedes for us. But we must not think of her as coming between us and Christ in any way. Christ, our redeemer, is im- mediately and personally present to each of us. Nobody comes between us and him. But though he himself is always interceding for us, it is his will that all his saints including Mary should be part of the work of intercession. However, her intercession under Christ is unique because she has given us the very source of all intercession, Christ himself.

Devotion to Mary has its basis in the New Testament: 'all generations shall call me blessed' (*Luke 1:48*).

not draw her certainty about all revealed truths from the holy Scriptures alone' (Vatican II, Constitution on Divine Revelation para 9).

Therefore the Church claims to teach nothing contrary to Scripture about Mary.

MARY MOTHER OF GOD

The Council of Ephesus (AD 431) de- fined that Mary was truly the 'Mother of God' (Greek theotokos). This title 'theotokos' was disputed by the 'Nestor- ians', who held that Mary was not the Mother of God, but simply the 'Mother of Christ' (christokokos), of the man Jesus, to whom the person of the Word of God united himself. This made two 'persons' in Jesus, the man of whom Mary was the mother, and God the Word, which to the Catholic bishops, led by St Cyril of Alexandria, was heretical. Thus from early on, the Catholic doctrine of Mary has defended the true doctrine of Jesus as truly God the Son, the Word made Flesh.

THE PERPETUAL VIRGINITY

'She conceived in true reality without human seed from the Holy Spirit, God the Word Himself, who before the ages was born of God the Father, and gave birth to Him without corruption, her virginity remaining equally inviolate after the birth'.

THE IMMACULATE CONCEPTION

'. . . that the most Blessed Virgin Mary was, from the first moment of her conception, by the singular grace and privilege of almighty God and in view of the merits of Christ Jesus the Saviour of the human race, preserved immune from all stain of Original Sin'.

Pope Pius IX, 1854

THE ASSUMPTION

'. . . immaculate in her conception, a spotless virgin in her divine motherhood, the noble companion of the divine Redeemer who won a complete triumph over sin and its consequences, she finally obtained as the crowning glory of her privileges to be preserved from the corruption of the tomb and, like her Son before her, to conquer death and to be raised body and soul to the glory of heaven, to shine refulgent as Queen at the right hand of her Son, the immortal King of ages'.

Pope Pius XII, 1950

THE 'HAIL MARY'

Second only in popularity to the 'Our Father' as a prayer among Catholics is the 'Hail Mary'. This prayer is often said after the Our Father, to remind us that worship is given only to God, not even to a human being as holy as Mary; and that our devotion to Mary is to our spiritual mother in heaven, part of the 'communion of saints' which we will join one day by the grace of God at the end of our journey on this earth. The 'Hail Mary' is divided into three parts.

The first part, 'HAIL MARY, FULL OF GRACE, THE LORD IS WITH THEE', is a direct quotation of Luke 1:28, when the angel Gabriel appeared to Mary to tell her that she was to bear a son Jesus (we call that the 'Annunciation'). We share Mary's joy at the news that she is to become the Mother of our

Saying the Rosary ('rose-garden') of Mary, meditating on the mysteries of our faith with Mary as it were showing us around. See Appendix for the structure of the Rosary prayer.

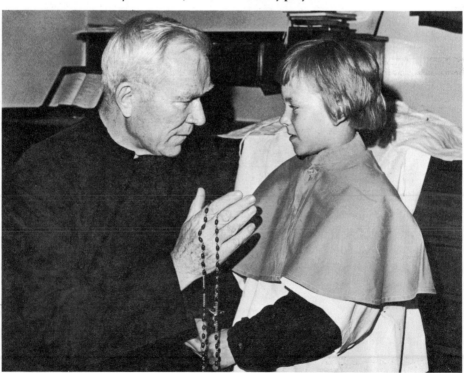

Saviour Jesus Christ, and ask for the same faith that she showed when she replied simply to the angel.

The second part, 'BLESSED ART THOU AMONG WOMEN, AND BLESSED IS THE FRUIT OF THY WOMB, JESUS', is a direct quotation (apart from the last word 'Jesus') of Luke 1:42. This was said to Mary by her cousin Elizabeth, when Mary went to visit Elizabeth. (We call that event the 'Visitation'). Elizabeth was also pregnant, due to give birth to John the Baptist; and so they rejoiced together as proud mothers. But Elizabeth recognises that Mary's son-to-be is to surpass even John the Baptist in God's plan. So she blessed Mary as the 'Mother of my Lord' (*Luke 1:42*); and we join Elizabeth in that blessing, recognising Mary as the Mother of God.

The third part, 'HOLY MARY, MOTHER OF GOD, PRAY FOR US SINNERS, NOW AND AT THE HOUR OF OUR DEATH', has been added by the devotional tradition of the Church. By this, we turn a Scripture meditation on the Annunciation and the Visitation into a prayer, a personal address to our spiritual mother. Just as we ask other Christians on this earth to pray for us, so now we join the 'communion of saints' in heaven by faith, asking the 'Queen of Saints and Angels'

to pray for us. Note that the prayer is going back eventually to God. It does not stop at Mary. She prays for us to God. We ask her the sinless one to pray 'for us sinners' especially 'at the hour of our death'; because we remember that she suffered a mother's agony, as her divine Son was dying on the Cross (*John 19:25–27*). She remembers her sufferings, and shares in ours.

HAIL, MARY, FULL OF GRACE, THE LORD IS WITH THEE. BLESSED ART THOU AMONG WOMEN, AND BLESSED IS THE FRUIT OF THY WOMB, JESUS. HOLY MARY, MOTHER OF GOD, PRAY FOR US SINNERS, NOW AND AT THE HOUR OF OUR DEATH. AMEN.

QUESTIONS
1. How would you organise parish devotions to Our Lady? Explain your aims and what understanding of Mary you would want to develop.
2. Women today are looking for recognition of their value as persons. Is this contrary to the Christian way of life seeing that Mary lived out her life obscurely in a country village?

The Sacraments-
General Introduction

Sacraments are visible signs, instituted by Christ, by which we enter into the mystery of God's saving plan for us.

Christ himself is God's own sacrament. Everything he said and did on earth was a visible sign of God's love. When he went to heaven, he left the Church to be his body, the sign of his rule on earth, his sacrament.

The Council of Trent defined that Christ instituted seven sacraments.

Not all the sacraments are of equal value. Supreme is the Eucharist, the source and the summit of the whole of the Church's life.

Central to every sacrament is the 'sign', for example, water in baptism. Ordinary things of this earth are taken and, joined to a word, for example 'I baptise you . . .' become means of grace.

The sacraments are not magic. Essentially, they are prayers of the Church through Christ to the Father. But, as instituted by Christ, they have the authority of his Word. This effectiveness of the sacrament does not depend upon the worthiness of the minister involved, but achieves its effect 'by the work worked' (ex opere operator): that is, by the power of God.

Each sacrament also must have a minister who represents the action of Christ. Generally, this minister is ordained, either priest, bishop, or deacon. Ordination, itself a sacrament, confers the authority of God upon the ordained person to represent Christ in the sacrament. But two sacraments, marriage and baptism, do not require an ordained minister. The sacrament of marriage is truly the 'lay sacrament', because the ministers of the sacramental union are the man and woman themselves. Husband and wife together 'make' the sacrament.

Baptism, in the normal way, is conferred solemnly in Church by an ordained minister. But, in case of danger of death, any person can baptise, even one who is not a Christian.

For the sacrament to be effective, there must be faith and commitment on the part of the person receiving it. Even a validly conferred sacrament can be fruitless, if the person receiving it is insincere. St Paul reminds the Corinthian Christians 'anyone who eats the bread or drinks the cup of the Lord unworthily will be behaving unworthily towards the body and blood of the Lord' (1 Cor 11:27).

On the other hand, we are all human, and none of us is completely worthy to receive any sacrament. We say before receiving Holy Communion, 'Lord, I am not worthy to receive you, but only say the word and I shall be healed'. The Holy Spirit helps us to receive worthily.

We start by looking at Baptism and Confirmation.

Infants are baptised in the faith of the church, with their parents promising to do all they can to bring the child up to make a personal commitment of faith in due time.

27-Baptism

Baptism is the sacrament of beginning.
Confirmation confers the Gift of the Spirit.
We become members of the Church
and have a share in the eternal life of God.

BAPTISM, CONFIRMATION, AND COMMUNION

Every society has conditions of entry; and some have initiation rituals. Members of Parliament, for instance, go through a ceremony before taking their place for the first time in the House of Commons. Such initiation ceremonies indicate the seriousness of what is being undertaken, give a chance for the new members to demonstrate publicly their commitment, and give them a sense of being welcomed by the community which they have joined.

Since becoming a Christian is not something which we can do by ourselves, but need the help (called the 'grace') of God and of our fellow-Christians, it is most appropriate that God left his Church to perform solemn ceremonies of initiation for new members of Christ's body. In fact, there are three ceremonies, all sacraments, associated with Christian initiation; baptism, confirmation, and Mass or Eucharist.

THE EARLY DAYS

In the early days of the church, most converts to Christianity were adults, making a full, and often dangerous, commitment to Christ, with martyrdom a real possibility. The sacraments of baptism, confirmation, and Eucharist were performed in one ceremony, at the

Easter Vigil, and were great and solemn occasions.

Old 3rd and 4th century churches have 'baptistries', where the candidates were plunged naked into the water, and came up 'reborn to new life'. A white garment was put on them, and then they were 'anointed' with chrism (oil), before receiving the holy bread and wine of communion, the Body and Blood of Christ.

As time went on, and the whole of Europe became at least nominally Christian, more and more infants were baptised, children of Christian parents. By the Middle Ages, infant baptism had become the norm, and adult baptism was becoming more rare.

The result of this was that baptism was no longer the sacrament of the personal commitment of the individual Christian. The children's parents and the church community had to make commitment for them.

Another result was that Confirmation became separated from Baptism, being given later in life, when the bishop visited. While a priest (or indeed a layman in case of urgency) can baptise, the usual rule (now changed somewhat) is that only the bishop is allowed to confirm, the ceremony of the laying-on of hands (signifying the Gift of the Spirit) and anointing with oil. The sacrament of communion also became separated from initiation; although, in the Eastern churches, infants are still given all three sacraments of baptism, confirmation, and Holy Communion. By this century, the Western Catholic practice was fixed this way:

Baptism: infants of up to three months.
Confirmation: from 7 to 14 years.
Eucharist: 7–8 years.

Since the Second Vatican Council, there has been greater emphasis upon adult initiation. While not denying the effectiveness of infant baptism, we may see a much greater number of adult initiation ceremonies, with people receiving as in the ancient practice, all three sacraments together.

BAPTISM – NEW BIRTH, NEW LIFE

Baptism means new birth. It brings us into contact with the power of Christ's redeeming love. That does not mean that others are excluded from it, only that in this sacrament we know for sure that we are made one with Christ. Christ who is the firstborn of creation and the firstborn from the dead brings us into being as a people who now belong to the world of the resurrection where he is Lord and Saviour.

Christ died and rose again. Through baptism we are caught up in that mystery. There is a before and after which marks a real change in our condition. We sometimes use the expression 'before the flood' as an indication that something belongs to a past world now lost to us. The rising waters of the flood destroyed a world bent upon its own destruction. The receding waters revealed and stayed to irrigate a world with hope restored. In baptism we leave behind the world that sin has marred with its alienations. We cannot entirely escape from it. But we join Christ and enter a new world that God is reconciling with his love, where Christ is the instrument of the Father's will.

Grace is the new life through Christ

and the gift of his Spirit. The baptised
have a new relationship with God the
Father.

FAITH

Baptism is for those who have come to
faith. Babies who are baptised must be
brought by those who have faith, or
must be linked in some way to a community of faith so that the gift in them
may grow. Indiscriminate baptism
which takes little consideration of the
presence of faith or offers no prospect of
an environment of faith is misplaced
unless the danger of death makes the act
itself, done in good faith, one which may
stand alone.

It is in the nature of baptism that it
should be celebrated once only for each
Christian, just as it is in the nature of
God that he does not go back on his
word, and it was in the nature of Christ's
sacrifice that it is valid for all time and in
eternity. The bond is as unbreakable.
Failure on our part does not lead God to
revoke it. Rejection only diminishes us,
not his love.

If God accomplishes so much in
baptism, it is easy to see its importance.
The Church has always acted with
urgency, because 'unless a man is born
through water and the Spirit, he cannot
enter the kingdom of God' (*John 3:5*).
But the grace poured out is already at
work. It is seen most clearly in those
who are preparing for baptism and in the
community providing a welcome.

In baptism God is at work, but there
are many human participants. The
minister says 'I baptise' yet it is Christ
who is baptising through him. By his
intention he brings his will in line with
the intention of Christ. The baptised
person is brought into the community
of believers as into a family. Unique
though each new member is, he or she
is now a member of Christ's body,
the Church. The Church is seen in
relationship with Christ as actively
participating in his work of bestowing
new life.

Baptism is a bond between all Chris-

Baptism of adults may be by immersion.

tians, ensuring that all are linked in
some way as members of Christ's
Church. Sadly we do not see one
Church or one communion of Churches
in our world. Catholics believe that the
Catholic Church contains all the means
of holiness and full visible unity, and
that baptism has been their gateway into
that Church. They also recognise the
elements of holiness and unity in other
Churches and pray that their common
baptism may bear fruit in reconciliation.

INFANT BAPTISM

In the new Rite of the Initiation of
Adults, it is becoming clear that the
Catholic Church is placing a new
emphasis upon adult baptism. Baptism
and faith are inextricably united in the
thought of the New Testament. No
faith, no baptism. Thus the norm for
baptism was adult commitment in faith.

But does this deny the validity or the
advisability of the baptism of infants?
Catholic teaching states that it does not.
There is no clear evidence of the

baptism of infants in the New Testament, and little in the early church. That is because the early converts were all adults. But we do see evidence from early on that the children of believing parents were admitted into membership of the church. For instance, we read in Acts that a new convert, the jailer at Philippi, was admitted for baptism, together with 'all his household' (*Acts 16:31*). This may well have included his children, even infants.

The sacrament of Baptism is invalid without the response of faith. But where the infant is concerned, its faith is supplied by the parents, and above all by the church community. This faith, at the beginning given for the child, needs to grow into the full personal commitment of faith through education and formation, above all in the home.

Why are infants baptised? Ultimately, because Catholic faith is that baptism is 'necessary for salvation', 'is the sign and the means of God's prevenient love, which frees us from

In Western countries, Confirmation is usually of young people, and not of infants as with Eastern Christians.

Original Sin and communicates a share in divine life. Considered in itself, the gift of these blessings to infants must not be delayed' (Instruction on Infant Baptism of the S. Congregation for the Doctrine of the Faith, 1980).

What happens to children who die without baptism? This constitutes an enormous problem. One thing is clear; infants who die, clearly without having committed sin, will not go to hell, because no-one goes there except through his or her own fault.

The Christian denomination which puts most emphasis on baptism of adults is the Baptists. They believe that no-one should be baptised who is not able to make a conscious act of commitment to Christ; thus the baptism of infants is excluded. The first Baptist Church in London was formed in 1612 by Thomas Helwys. Today, the Baptists are one of the largest Protestant denominations worldwide.

CONFIRMATION

Because the sacrament of confirmation was originally part of the whole initiation ceremony, theologians have long debated what Confirmation as a sacrament gives that baptism does not. If we say that the Holy Spirit is given at Confirmation, with the laying on of hands and the anointing with oil, making us 'other Christs'; does not baptism give us that gift of the Spirit also?

There is one text in the Acts of the Apostles which tells of Christians, in Samaria, who had been baptised, but who still had to receive the Holy Spirit; for as yet the Spirit 'had not come down on any of them; they had only been baptised in the name of the Lord Jesus' (8:16–17). The apostles went, laid hands on them 'and they received the Holy Spirit'.

From the beginning, therefore, the Church understood that there was a special gift of the Holy Spirit in addition to baptism; we now call this 'Confirmation'. But what is that gift?

Some scholars have seen the special contribution of the sacrament of confirmation as the gift of the Spirit to give us talents to become fruitful members of the Christian community (see 1 Cor 12:4–11, the famous 'charismata'), whereas Baptism is more orientated to the person becoming a member of the Church.

The Church teaches that Confirmation is a strengthening and 'confirmation' of the gifts already received at baptism. Where Confirmation is delayed until teenage life, the sacrament becomes a way in which the young person can make the act of individual commitment to Christ which was made for him or her at infant baptism.

THE GIFTS OF THE SPIRIT

In the early days, and sometimes today, the gift of the Holy Spirit is linked with 'speaking with tongues', that is, an ecstatic state where the person utters strange speech which can only be interpreted by one who has the special 'gift of interpretation'. As with all types of mystical experience, this gift is not to be despised, but is to be treated with the same caution and common sense St Paul shows when dealing with the charis-

matics in Corinth (see 1 Cor 14).

Above all, following Paul's teaching, we are not to seek for these exceptional gifts, but rather for the greatest gift of all, 'love' or 'charity' (see Ch. 13).

In addition, we pray for the 'gifts of the spirit' which the Church's tradition links with the sacrament of Confirmation. These gifts are listed in Isaiah 11:2. Isaiah prophesied in the 8th century BC, foreseeing an anointed

Messiah to come in the line of David, who would have special gifts for ruling his people. With the coming of Christ the Messiah, these gifts are for us all, not just for specially chosen rulers.

THE SPIRIT OF WISDOM AND
    INSIGHT,
THE SPIRIT OF COUNSEL AND
    POWER,
THE SPIRIT OF KNOWLEDGE
    AND FEAR OF YAHWEH.

THE FATHER, THE SON, AND THE HOLY SPIRIT

From the early days, Christians were baptised in the name of the 'Trinity'; a word which is a shortening of 'Tri-Unity'. God has revealed to us that he is three (Father, Son or Word, and Spirit), and one. Hence the Tri- or Threefold Unity.

Christ said to his apostles just before he ascended into heaven: 'All authority in heaven and on earth has been given to me. Go, therefore, make disciples of all nations; baptise them in the name of the Father, and of the Son, and of the Holy Spirit . . .' (Matt 28:19).

By baptism we do not simply become part of a human community. Becoming a Christian is not like joining a club. It is really gaining entrance into a family that has existed from all eternity, a 'family that consists of Father, Son and Holy Spirit'. Baptism is not simply a matter of receiving sanctifying grace. It really gives us a relationship with all three persons of the Trinity, so that we can truly say that we become children of the Father, brothers of the Son, and temples of the Holy Spirit, and this, of course, should affect our prayer. When we say the 'Our Father', we are not speaking to someone who is like a father but to someone who really is our father and who sends the Holy Spirit upon us so that we shall be able to show him the love and reverence which a child should have for its parents.

Does the word 'family' as applied to the Trinity suggest that God is not completely one as we all have to believe? After all, members of a human family are separate human beings however much they may love one another. The whole purpose of loving someone is to come closer to them and yet barriers will always exist that cannot be broken down. We want to be one with them and yet we know that this can never be fully achieved.

What is only a tendency among human beings is a reality on the divine level. There the love is so perfect that there is no place for the separateness that exists between human beings. Love is always self-giving and in the godhead the self-giving is complete. The human parent in his love for his offspring would like to hand on all the qualities he possesses. God the Father does this. He gives to the Son and to the Spirit all the perfections he himself possesses.

Perhaps in conclusion we may dare to say that we cannot fully understand the meaning of love without mediating on the mystery of the Holy Trinity.

GLORY BE . . .

Already, we have given a brief explanation of the 'Our Father' (Ch. 25) and of the 'Hail Mary' (Ch. 26).

Now we come to the third element in what we might call the Catholic 'Trilogy' of prayer, the 'Glory Be':

GLORY BE TO THE FATHER, AND TO THE SON, AND TO THE HOLY SPIRIT. AS IT WAS IN THE BEGINNING, IS NOW AND EVER SHALL BE, WORLD WITHOUT END. AMEN.

Catholics very often say these prayers one after the other.

They go well in sequence, because together they express the whole of the mysterious and wonderful relationship between ourselves and God in the Christian revelation.

First, the 'Our Father' makes us realise that all prayer is to the One God, our Father, who loves us and wants to give us all that is good.

The 'Hail Mary' makes us realise that we never pray alone, even if we are physically alone; because we pray in union with other Christians on earth and in heaven, meditating on the Gospel with the one who first said 'Yes' to the Good News, Mary the Mother of God.

Third, the 'Glory Be' makes us realise that in our prayer, we are caught up in the life of the Trinity, a life which begins on earth, but will continue for ever 'world without end'. Prayer is never just personal reflection. It is giving praise and glory to the Trinity.

It is important to try to understand the words of the 'Our Father', the 'Hail Mary', and the 'Glory Be'. Otherwise, the saying of these prayers could become a routine, a 'vain repetition', against which our Lord warned (*Matt 6:7*).

With care and reflection, the daily recitation of these prayers is a tried way of personal communion with God for anyone who wishes to deepen their relationship with Him.

It is also important to become well acquainted with the 'Our Father', the 'Hail Mary', and the 'Glory Be', before beginning to say the Rosary. The Rosary is built up by using a series of sequences of these three prayers, meditating on the life of Jesus in the Gospel.

With prayer, as with physical growth, it is best to learn to walk before starting to run!

QUESTIONS

1. What do you think about baptising infants?
2. What age do you think people should be confirmed?
3. Investigate the evidence for baptism in the New Testament.

LIGHT FROM THE COUNCIL

The Dogmatic Constitution on the Church (No. 7) says, 'In that Body the life of Christ is communicated to those who believe and who, through the sacraments, are united in a hidden and real way to Christ in his passion and glorification. Through baptism we are formed in the likeness of Christ: 'For in one Spirit we were all baptised into one body' (*1 Cor 12:13*). In this sacred rite, fellowship in Christ's death and resurrection is symbolised and brought about: 'For we were buried with him by means of baptism into death'; and if 'we have been united with him in the likeness of death, we shall be so in the likeness of his resurrection also' (*Rom 6:4–5*).

PRAYER

Come, Holy Spirit, fill the hearts of your faithful, and enkindle them in the fire of your love. Send forth your Spirit and they shall be created. And you shall renew the face of the earth.

28-The Eucharist

We celebrate the Lord's Supper.
The bread and wine become his Body and Blood.
Christ is present in the Eucharist ('Thanksgiving').
We become one with Christ and with one another in Communion.

BAPTISM AND Confirmation can be given to us once only in our lives. Once you are baptised and confirmed, you are always baptised and confirmed.

However, the third sacrament administered at the initiation of a Catholic, Holy Communion, the most important sacrament, an adult is given only for the FIRST time at initiation. The Church intends us to participate in this sacrament as often as we can, daily if possible, but at least weekly, at public assembly in our local ('parish') Catholic Church.

Catholics are obliged by Church law to go to Mass every Sunday. Why is the Mass so important?

THE LORD'S SUPPER

The Mass was first celebrated by Jesus himself, on the night he was arrested in the Garden of Gethsemane (*Luke 22:14–20*). It was the time of 'Passover' (Hebrew Pesach, hence our word 'Pasch' or 'Paschal Mystery'). In this feast, the Jews commemorate the night when the children of Israel, led by Moses, escaped from slavery in Egypt. (The full account of the Passover and the Feast of Unleavened Bread is in Ex 12.)

During the meal, Jesus broke bread, and introduced something quite new when he said 'Take, eat, this is my body'. Then he took a cup of wine and said 'Drink of this. This is my blood, the blood of the new and everlasting covenant, for the forgiveness of sins. Do this in my memorial.'

From the beginning, this service (called in the Acts 'the breaking of bread', *Acts 2:46*) was celebrated on the 'Lord's Day', that is Sunday, to commemorate Christ's Resurrection. In a sense, every Sunday for a Christian is

The Last Supper.

Easter Sunday; because on every Sunday we commemorate that first Sunday morning, when the women, coming to anoint Jesus' body, found that his tomb was empty. This was Jesus' Passover, his passing over from death to life; and the Mass is our 'passing over' from a life of darkness to a life of light and virtue. Such a new life only begins imperfectly on this earth; but there is a promise of final fulfilment in heaven.

'When the people are assembled, the priest enters the church, and goes up to the "sanctuary" – the "stage" of the church, as it were. The priest is a special sign of Christ's presence. He presides over the assembly in Christ's name, and Christ working through him changes the bread and wine into his own Body and Blood.'

THE INTRODUCTORY RITE

We begin Mass making the sign of the cross, 'In the name of the Father, and of the Son, and of the Holy Spirit. Amen'.

As the assembled community we confess our sinfulness and our need of God. The confession reminds us of the eternal mercy of God and of Christ's mission to call sinners back to the Father.

We respond with a hymn of praise 'Glory to God'.

The introductory rite ends with the special prayer of the day. Called the collect – it introduces the theme of the feast or season or the particular celebration, for example a marriage, or a saint's day.

THE LITURGY OF THE WORD

We now listen to the Scriptures inspired by God's Spirit. God himself speaks to his people and Christ proclaims the Gospel. It is important that the readings at Mass are read clearly, with understanding, and that we receive God's word with faith, allowing it to come into our hearts to nourish our lives and make us better followers of Jesus.

The homily (or sermon) is an integral part of the liturgy of the Word and should only be omitted on Sundays and Holy Days for a serious reason.

The homily explains the meaning of the Scriptures, especially the Gospel reading, and tries to show how we can put the Gospel message into practical effect in our daily lives.

Bread for our strength, wine for our joy.

PREPARATION AND OFFERTORY

Representatives of the people then bring the bread and wine for the sacrifice and also the people's gifts in the collection. This symbolises the offering each of us makes of ourselves and all that God has given us.

THE LITURGY OF THE EUCHARIST

This is the central part of the Mass. The priest prays that the Holy Spirit may come down on the gifts of bread and wine to make them holy so that they may become for us the Body and Blood of Christ. Then by the power of Christ's word, the bread and wine are changed into his Body and Blood. At the end of the prayer we join with the priest in offering Christ's Body and Blood to the Father. 'Through him, with him, in him, in the unity of the Holy Spirit, all glory and honour is yours, almighty Father, for ever and ever.' Our 'Amen' is one of the most important of our Acclamations at Mass, since we are giving our assent to all that has gone before. It is our statement of faith in Jesus really present.

CHRIST IS PRESENT
Tradition and Theology

The Church believes that Jesus Christ is really present in many ways. He is really present in the community, for 'where two or three are gathered in my name, there am I in the midst of them' (*Matt 18:20*). He is really present in the Scriptures, and in all the Sacraments. But the phrase 'Real Presence' normally refers to His presence in the consecrated bread and wine at Mass.

The Church has explained this in various ways across the centuries. For the Jews remembering makes the event present again, so Jews who became Christians understood Our Lord to be present through the Church remembering him. Jesus instructed the Church to 'do this in memory of me'. So by this remembering we re-experience his presence and his saving work.

POWER OF GOD

The Real Presence is not magic, but is the result of the effective power of the Word of God. In the beginning, God said 'Let there be light', and it came to be. Everything that God said came to be. That same authority was exercised by Jesus Christ, God incarnate, when he said 'Receive your sight.' 'Be cleansed.' 'Little girl, I say to you arise.' 'Your sins are forgiven.' 'Take up your bed and walk.'

The same authority is exercised in the Mass. When the priest says, 'This is my body . . . this is my blood'.

The most famous explanation of the Real Presence comes from St Thomas Aquinas. Drawing on an earlier tradition, he applied the philosophy of Aristotle (Greece, 4th century BC) to the theological question, to make a distinction between substance and accidents. Substance is what a thing really is, its underlying reality, while its accidents are its shape, weight, colour, taste, smell, etc.

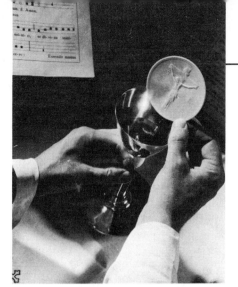

In Catholic theology, the bread of the Eucharist is often called the Host (the Sacrificial Victim), to denote our faith that this bread has become the true body of Christ offered to God the Father for our salvation.

REAL CHANGE

In the action of the Mass, the substance of bread and wine is changed into the Body and Blood of Christ, while the accidents of the bread and wine remain. This is called transubstantiation.

The crisis of corruption in the Church and the Reformation led to controversies about many matters, including the sacraments. For instance, Martin Luther believed in the Real Presence, but he also thought it possible that the bread and wine might be the Body and Blood of Christ, and at the same time continue to be bread and wine.

On 11th October 1551, the Council of Trent issued its famous teaching on the Eucharist, emphatically asserting: 'Bread and wine are changed, converted into the Body and Blood of Christ'. It then adds the phrase, 'which conversion the Catholic Church most fittingly calls transubstantiation'.

The essential Catholic doctrine is that a real but mysterious change, not visible to the senses, is effected by the Holy Spirit at the consecration. The bread and wine become the Body and Blood of Christ.

It is the Mass that matters.

THE SAVING SACRIFICE

The Holy Eucharist – the Lord's Supper, the Mass, the Blessed Sacrament – is a divine jewel, showing many facets to our devotion and belief. It is the Church's great act of liturgical worship. It is our meeting with God, and with one another, for prayer, praise and thanksgiving. It is our way of keeping holy the Lord's Day, and our weekly encounter with the Word of God.

At a deeper level, the Eucharist mystery is the Real Presence of Jesus Christ under the appearances of bread and wine, sanctifying our churches and places of worship, testing our faith and calling us to adoration. It is the sacred fellowship-meal bringing into unity the members of Christ's body, the Church. It is Holy Communion with Christ, not only for the community but for each individual to whom it is a personal gift of grace and divine life. It is the sacrifice of the Mass, by which Christ perpetuates the work of our redemption.

THE ONE SACRIFICE

'Dying You destroyed our death, rising You restored our life . . .' When we say those words at Mass we proclaim the centrepoint of our Christian faith. Jesus of Nazareth, the incarnate Son of God, became one of us in order to live with us, die for us, and raise us up to live with God. Through his death upon the Cross he cleansed our human nature from the deadly contagion of sin, and conquered the evil which separates us from God; through his victorious resurrection he revivifies those he has redeemed by imparting to them the power of his own divine life.

All other sacrifices are mere shadows of the reality (*Heb 7–10*). They cannot contain the meaning of the divine mystery of Christ's death and victory, which is the one true saving sacrifice that reconciles men to God.

Central in Christ's saving sacrifice was his self-giving love, his merit and obedience to his Father's will, his example and moral influence for mankind. But central also is the divine power that works through the dying and rising of God made man. This power changes mankind and the created world; it inwardly transforms with a share of his divine life those whom he justifies by faith and love – even the infant at the baptismal font – and energises them with the Spirit.

Through the mystery of Christ's death and resurrection the work of our redemption was accomplished once and for all. He entrusted to his priestly Church the power of making it available and operative in all times. 'Our Saviour instituted the Eucharistic sacrifice of his body and blood, so that he might perpetuate the sacrifice of the Cross through the centuries until his coming' (Vatican II, Sacrosanctum Concilium 47). That is the meaning of the Mass.

'As often as the sacrifice of the Cross, in which "Christ our paschal victim was immolated" (1 Cor 5:7), is celebrated at the altar, the work of our redemption is made operative' (Lumen Gentium 3). Those words of the Council repeat the constant belief and teaching of the Church through the ages.

LIGHT FROM THE COUNCIL

There is a modern ring to what the Dogmatic Constitution on the Church, No 8, has to say about the redemption, and yet it is a very ancient truth. 'Christ', it says, 'carried out the work of redemption in poverty and oppression', adding that the Church 'is called to follow the same path if she is to communicate the fruits of salvation to men and women'. It goes on to say that, in the words of St Paul, Jesus, through God, 'emptied himself, taking the nature of a slave' and, 'being rich, became poor'.

The Constitution on the Liturgy speaks of 'the work of Christ in redeeming humankind and giving perfect glory to God' and says of it: 'He achieved his task principally by the paschal mystery of his blessed passion, resurrection from the dead, and glorious ascension, whereby "dying he destroyed our death, and rising, restored our life"' (No 5).

The General Catchetical Directory, No 54, has this to say about the mystery, under the heading 'Jesus Christ Saviour and Redeemer of the World': 'The mystery of Christ appears in human and world history, subject as it is to sin, as the mystery not merely by the incarnation but of salvation and redemption.

'God so loved sinful humanity as to give his Son to reconcile the world with himself. Jesus, therefore, the firstborn of many brothers, holy, innocent, immaculate, freely obedient to his Father out of filial love, accepted death for the sake of his brothers and sisters as their Mediator, death being for them the wages of sin. He redeemed the human race from slavery to sin by his holy death and he poured out the spirit of adoption on it, establishing a new humanity in himself.'

PRIESTHOOD

The Council teaches: 'The common priesthood of the faithful and the ministerial or hierarchical priesthood, though they differ not merely in degree but in their essential nature, are however directed to one another . . .' (Lumen Gentium 10). All the baptised share in Christ's priesthood, and so have their part in offering the Eucharistic sacrifice.

But the power to consecrate the Eucharist and to actuate the sacrifice is divinely committed to bishops and priests.

WHY WAS JESUS CONDEMNED?

According to the Synoptic Gospels, it took only one week for Jesus to antagonise the Jerusalem leaders so totally that they determined on his death. In

Galilee the opposition had come from the Pharisees and their inability to stomach his attitude to legal observance and re-interpretation of the Law. But now the clash was with the Sadducees, the custodians of the Temple, over the issue of Jesus' authority. After he had solemnly entered the city and taken possession of the Temple on Palm Sunday, the challenge to their authority meant that this unorthodox leader from Galilee had to be removed before he disturbed the delicate equilibrium which left government under the imperial eye of Rome in the hands of the rich high-priestly aristocracy.

So whether it was after questioning by Annas, the godfather figure behind several high priests, or after a formal interrogation presided over by Caiaphas, the charge adopted was political, that of being a messiah, at that time the synonym of a rebel leader. Jesus had not fully accepted this role and had preferred to preach the realisation of the Kingship of God, his Father.

Pilate, the local Roman governor, was trained in Roman law and used to feuding factions, but he was obviously uneasy when Jesus was brought before him by the Jewish leaders for the death sentence. They had no power to impose this themselves. Three times he tried to throw out the charge. When they still pressed it, he tried to persuade them to accept this presumably popular figure as the beneficiary of the Passover amnesty. But the Galilaean held no interest for the Jerusalem mob: they wanted one of their own, the rebel Barabbas, released. Still Pilate hesitated till the Jewish leaders played their trump card: if you release this man you are not a 'Friend of Caesar'. If Pilate lost this status by being reported to Rome for releasing a possible rebel leader, he might well lose his job, and even his head.

John represents this scene before Pilate as being the final denial by the Jewish leaders of the kingship of God. The theme of judgement by encounter with Jesus is a thread which runs through the fourth Gospel. The climax comes when Jesus, still robed as King of the Jews, is brought out and rejected. In rejecting him they condemn themselves finally and explicitly as Jesus is seated on the Chair of Judgement (*John 19:13*) and the chief priests proclaim, 'We have no king except Caesar.' If God is not king of Israel, Israel has no reason to exist, and ceases to be as a holy nation. And yet Jesus reigns from the Cross.

THE COMMUNION RITE

After saying or singing the Lord's Prayer together, and prayer by the priest, we offer each other the sign of peace, that peace of God, wholeness of heart and mind, which Christ came to give. The sign of peace is a final preparation for us to receive in Holy Communion the Body and Blood of Christ. Catholics are taught to receive Holy Communion with great devotion, because the bread and wine has become the very Body and Blood of Christ.

There are certain conditions we are supposed to fulfil before we can receive the sacrament of Holy Communion worthily. We must, for example, be in a state of grace, that is free from grave sin.

There is an old story of an atheist, who, on hearing about Catholic belief in the Eucharist, said, 'If I believed what you believe about Holy Communion, I would be coming into church on my knees, on all fours, not walking in upright!'

The following is a translation of a beautiful old Latin chant, set to anthem by Mozart. It would make a very good meditation after receiving Holy Communion.

O. Sacrum Convivium

O Sacred Banquet,
In which Christ himself is received!
The memory of his Passion is recalled.

The mind is filled with grace,
And the promise of future glory
Is given to us. Alleluia!

THE MASS IS CALLED

THE LORD'S SUPPER: referring to the night when Jesus celebrated the first Mass with his disciples.

HOLY COMMUNION: the act of receiving the Body and Blood of Christ.

THE EUCHARIST: the central part of the rite, the Prayer of Thanksgiving or Blessing, when the Words of Institution are recalled.

THE MASS: a word meaning 'dismissal', most likely coming from the Latin ending to the liturgy. 'Ite, Missa est', which means literally, 'Go, you are dismissed'. Some scholars think that people started calling the whole service 'the Mass' because in the early days, people who were not fully in communion with the Church were 'dismissed' after the homily.

QUESTIONS

1. Work out a way of explaining to young people who complain that Mass is boring why the Eucharist is so important within a Christian community. Why not find some young people and ask them what they think of your idea?

2. Are there any ways in which the Sunday Eucharist in your parish could become more truly a celebration for the community? What kind of things prevent it from being so? Could you offer any helpful suggestions to your priest or liturgy committee?

Consecrated bread is reserved in a safe called the 'Tabernacle', a word which reminds us of the sacred tent in the desert, which contained the presence of Yahweh (see Exodus 33:7–11).

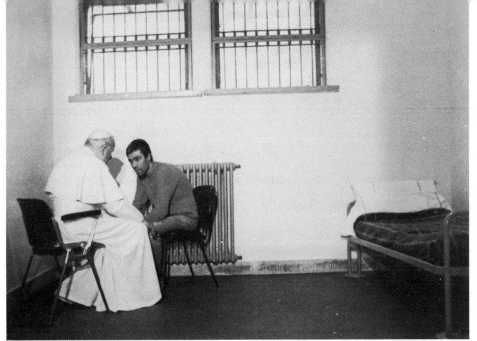

Love your enemies. The Pope talking to Ali Agar, who tried to assassinate him.

29-Penance and Reconciliation

**Christ came to forgive us our sins.
He left us the sacrament of reconciliation.
This is for times when we fall
to bring us back to God and to our neighbour.**

EVERY SOCIETY that we join, every skill that we learn, has to have built-in ways of putting things right when they go wrong.

A person who starts knitting has to learn what to do when a stitch is dropped. A golfer soon has to learn how to get himself out of a sand-bunker.

A Christian, likewise, may have great euphoria and intention never to do wrong when he or she is initiated into the Church in adult life but he or she is only too aware of how easy it is to sin. And the Church has the proviso ready for this; the sacrament of penance, confession, or reconciliation.

If we call it 'confession', this will underline the aspect of our willingness to bring this matter to the Church's representative, the priest. If we call it 'the sacrament of penance', this will emphasise our willing attitude to be prepared to be 'converted', and change from self to God's way. And if we prefer

(as many do today) to call it the 'sacrament of reconciliation', this will emphasise that the effect of this confession and change of heart is to be one with God and with our neighbour again.

The earliest records we have of what later became called the 'sacrament of penance', in the New Testament, show clearly that in the early days it was a form of excommunication for some serious and public sin.

St Paul, for instance, tells the Corinthian Christians (c. AD 57) quite categorically to 'turn out of the community' (*1 Cor 5:2*) a man who has committed incest. 'You must banish this evil-doer from among you' (*1 Cor 5:13*), thunders Paul, quoting the Law of Moses (*Deut 13:6*).

Attitudes today appear to be much softer. Perhaps we have gradually realised that we are all black sheep in some way. But the same basic elements remain; a consciousness that sin, especially serious sin, alienates us not only from God but from his people; the even stronger realisation that by repentance, change of heart, the worst sinner can come back.

The apostles and their successors have power to 'bind and loose' in the name of the Christian community. They can act on behalf of Christ and of his Church, in imposing the conditions of return to the fold, and of guidance for the reinstatement of the repentant sinner.

But how has the sacrament of penance with the modern confessional come to look so different from the time of Paul?

PENANCE YESTERDAY

The Apostles did not use the word confession. They simply called on people to repent and be baptised (*Acts 2:38*). It was not long before some kind of special service, or process of reconciliation, featured in the Church. A second-century writer said, 'You shall confess your sins in the Church, and neither shall you go to your prayer in a bad conscience' (*Didache IV.14*). But how the Christian confessed at that time, we do not know. We do know, however, that, as well as some form of confession of sins, there was a period of penance, followed by an act of reconciliation. Like baptism, this could happen only once in a person's lifetime.

By the fourth century, the Church was developing Reconciliation. Confession of sin in some form was made to the bishop; the sinner was consigned to the ranks of the official penitents, which meant exclusion from Eucharist and community (a kind of portrayal of the real effect of sin) for a period of penance; reconciliation took place by the imposition of hands on the head of the penitent by bishops and priests in the presence of the community. Eventually this took place during Lent with the service of Reconciliation on Holy Thursday.

In Ireland and Britain there was a different system. More detailed confession of sins was made to any priest; absolution was immediate and only then followed by a penance. This could be repeated as often as the sinner needed Christ's forgiveness. Irish missionaries carried this practice to mainland Europe, where the practice of public Reconciliation had declined. The 'new' form of Reconciliation, despite condemnations from local Councils, caught on and, in time, developed into the present practice of 'Private Confession'.

PENANCE TODAY

The Sacrament of Reconciliation today can be celebrated in many ways. The familiar 'private confession' is still private, but sometimes has a reading from the Bible to show how repentance is a response to God's call and how we should examine our hearts in the light of God's Word, not our own weakened will. The priest grants absolution – an act of reconciliation with God and the Church. The barriers of sin are broken down. The sinner comes away, happy in the forgiveness of Christ.

A second form of the Sacrament is the penitential service which is celebrated with the assembled community. The only thing that is private is the confession of sin and absolution. This form of celebration is a powerful sign that reconciliation comes through the Church, the community, which we have damaged by our sins. Together we listen to God's Word, examine our hearts, pray for our forgiveness and that of our brothers and sisters and are reconciled with them and with God.

The third form of the Sacrament has no individual, detailed confession of sin and has a general absolution. It is intended primarily for situations in which there are not enough priests to hear individual confessions. Because the Church teaches that the individual confession of all serious sins is required by divine law, a penitent conscious of such sins should confess those sins privately to a priest, even after having general absolution.

SIGN AND REALITY

Reconciliation is a Sacrament, and therefore a sign; a sign that Jesus came into this world to reconcile us to God and our neighbour. Any celebration of Reconciliation, either when the penitent is alone with a priest, or when the community assembles together, is a celebration of the mercy and love of God which we see and experience in our lives. What is more, it is a sign that brings about what it signifies, and thus the repentant sinner is actually forgiven, reconciled. And it does not end there. Celebrating Reconciliation, especially by a community together, builds up the whole Church into a living, effective sign to the world of the presence in its midst of the redeeming Christ.

Confessing sins makes us aware of our weaknesses and sharpens our sense of responsibility for our actions before God and the Church. But perhaps at times we have placed too much emphasis on the confessing and obscured the forgiving. Sacraments are, above all, celebrations of the actions of Christ. Joy, not fear, should be the hallmark of Reconciliation. Jesus ate and drank with sinners. His three parables recounted in Luke 15 all end with a party. If we were to rediscover that sense of joy in the Sacrament of Reconciliation, we might be better signs of God's loving forgiveness and bring to the world that healing it needs.

WHY GO TO CONFESSION?

If a Christian has not committed a serious sin, there is no obligation to seek absolution in the Sacrament of Reconciliation. It is sufficient to confess sins privately to God or publicly at the beginning of the Mass for the forgiveness of venial sins or of imperfections.

But the Church offers the gift of the sacrament of reconciliation for our personal growth in Christ even when we are not in a state of mortal sin. To come to the sacrament once a month, or at major seasons, is a unique way of realising the joy of Christ's forgiveness.

BENEFITS

- The act of going to confession makes me look more carefully at my life and prepare an examination of conscience.
- I am able to discuss problems with the priest. Often, problems become worse when they are not discussed early.
- The priest undergoes a long training in theology, psychology, and counselling.
- I have the benefit of complete confidentiality. The priest will never reveal anything that I have done or said, even to the police. He is bound by the strictest law of secrecy.
- After I have confessed my sins, the priest gives me personal encouragement which helps me to grow in the Christian life. He then gives me a

'penance' to show my willingness to live a new life.
- When the priest gives me absolution, I experience the forgiveness of Christ. The word of forgiveness is spoken to me personally, by the Church's representative.

Often, people stop going to confession because they no longer feel that it is of benefit. Sometimes, this might be the fault of the priest, who might be unsympathetic. If so, go to a better confessor.

The fault might also be that of insufficient preparation on the part of the penitent. Some basic guidelines for the fruitful use of the sacrament are:
- Make a careful examination of conscience, using perhaps a good booklet such as 'A Penitent's Prayer

book' by Bishop David Konstant (CTS). Do not make this just a 'shopping list' of sins, but ask the Holy Spirit to reveal ways you have failed to live up to the fullness of life in Christ.

● Never be frightened to be frank about your sins, if something is on your conscience. You will probably be surprised to learn that the priest has heard it all before, and it is not nearly as bad as you thought.

● The New Rite recommends reading a passage of Scripture before going into the confessional.

● Do not expect to 'enjoy' going to confession, any more than you enjoy going to the dentist, or to the doctor. But you may well feel liberated after you have received the forgiveness of Christ. Like all healing, the process may be painful, but the result is joyful.

● Never be frightened of routine. We all have some faults which cling like leeches. The story goes of a man going into the confessional and saying to the priest, 'Same old sins, Father'; to which the priest replied, 'OK, then. Same old penance.'

LOVE AND CONFESSION

Perhaps we may have been told as children, 'If you are naughty God won't love you.' That was wrong. God always loves us. Our sins harm our love, not God's.

We want to love God. So we are sorry. There cannot be sorrow without love. It is always important to remember that we come to the sacrament for love. We feel guilty. It is right because we have done wrong. But it is knowing that God's love is still there that really matters, not our guilt.

WHAT SHALL I TELL?

We know we should tell all the serious sins in confession, but what about the things which are not so important? We twist the truth a little to keep ourselves out of trouble. We slip home from work early. We forget our prayers. Do we need to confess these things?

The answer is 'No'. Our friends do not expect an apology for every little thing that goes wrong.

But some of these smaller things do trouble us. They tell us that we are not loving enough. We should tell these. It also helps to say why we think they are happening. Not to make excuses, but to give simple reasons. For example, I told a lie to get my own way.

We are human and we need to know that we are forgiven. When Jesus was

on earth he met that human need in people. He said, 'Your sins are forgiven' or 'Your faith has made you whole' or simply 'Go in peace'.

He left the Church His power to forgive. 'Whose sins you shall forgive they are forgiven.' That is why we confess to God and to the Church through the person of a priest.

As the minister of Jesus the priest says 'through the ministry of the Church, may God give you his pardon and peace' and then 'I absolve you from your sins, in the name of the Father and of the Son and of the Holy Spirit'.

'Why should they change the Rite of Penance? I'm certainly not going to change my sins!'

WHAT PENANCE?

But there is something else that is needed. When we apologise to a friend we often take a present. We want to 'make up' for what went wrong. How can we make up to God? The best penance is a good life. In the sacrament we promise that we will do better.

But we still want to do something ourselves. So we accept 'a penance'. Usually some prayers.

The Eastern Church looks at penance differently. For them it is more like a medicine than a making up. It is something which will help to make the person a better Christian. Perhaps we ought to expect to be given something to do rather than just prayers.

We go to confession because we need to apologise and be forgiven. We often share in each other's sins. So the Church recommends services of reconciliation and penance, especially during Lent and Advent. We think together of our sins, and our need to be forgiven.

Together we give thanks for being forgiven, and for being reconciled with God and each other.

A PRIEST'S EXPERIENCE

Jesus came to preach repentance – to take away the sins of the world. One cannot but be filled with joy in being his instrument in this. All Our Lord's parables on repentance end with a celebration – 'Rejoice with me because what was lost I have found'.

Each person is unique but there is a sameness in the human condition and most of us have a prevailing fault or sin, or at least sinful inclinations against which we may have to struggle. But penitents who repeat the same sins or faults need counselling from the priest on grace-filled means to grow in the opposite virtue. Both sin and virtue are habits and can be changed by grace-filled determination.

All confessors are unshockable. They have heard everything.

So often hearing confessions is a witness and revelation more of people's holiness than sinfulness. This is bound to help the confessor in his growth. Also, while strictly keeping the seal of confession, his experience in listening and guiding one such penitent must help him in dealing with others.

Confessions can also be heard out of doors.

LIGHT FROM THE COUNCIL

'The mercy of God laid down that, in order to receive the remedy of the sacrament of Penance, the Christian should confess to a priest each and every grave sin which he or she can recall after an examination of conscience.

'Further, frequent and reverent recourse to this sacrament, even when only venial sins are in question, is of great value. Frequent confession is not mere ritual repetition, nor is it merely a psychological exercise. Rather it is a constant effort to bring to perfection the grace of our baptism, so that, as we carry about in our bodies the death that Jesus Christ died, the life that Jesus Christ lives may be more and more manifested in us. In such confessions, penitents, while indeed confessing venial sins, should be mainly concerned with becoming more deeply conformed to Christ and more submissive to the voice of the Spirit.'

PRAYER

An ancient practice in Christian prayer is to give some time each evening to an examination of the day gone by. This falls into a pattern of good and bad happenings, actions, words, thoughts and so on.

It is a review of the day in the presence of God. You open yourself so that the searchlight of his goodness and love lights up your personal human response to the day.

The object of the exercise is to reconcile your way of life during twenty-four hours with the will of God, his love and his service. This is not an exercise in guilt, but a genuine and positive assessment of your success or failure – or even indifference – as a follower of Jesus Christ.

PRAYER

Lord Jesus Christ, Son of God,
have mercy on me a sinner.
You were sent to heal the contrite,
Lord have mercy.
You came to call sinners,
Christ have mercy.
You plead for us at the right hand of
the Father,
Lord have mercy.

Never forget this great day.

30-Marriage

**Marriage is a covenant between man and woman.
It is a sacrament of love instituted by Christ.
The sexual act is a sign of permanent union of life and love.
For this reason, it is limited to marriage.**

THE BIBLE

The basic attitude of the Bible to marriage is fully stated on the first page. The Lord said that it was not good for the Man to be alone; he could not flourish and develop without a companion. And this companion was the Woman with whom he becomes one 'flesh'. 'One flesh' means more than a physical union; it embraces the whole being, so that man and wife are depicted as one physical and psychological unit, one living, thinking, planning whole. This teaching is re-affirmed by Jesus when he annuls the regulations of the Deuteronomic Law permitting divorce.

The second account of the Creation, then, treats only the unity between man and wife; the first account, concerned with the stability and perpetuation of every species, leads on directly from the sexuality of human beings to the command to be fruitful and multiply. The two dimensions are there in the two accounts.

Apart from this basic teaching on marriage, perhaps the way which most clearly indicates how it is to be treasured, and how warm and vital it must be, is its use as a figure of God's love for his people. The prophet Hosea first, but after him almost all the prophets, sees that the most burning and faithful human married love is only a shadow of God's love for Israel. Although the prophets' intention is to illustrate the divine reality by the human relationship, the dignity of the human bond grows by the illustration itself. God's unbreakable fidelity, his boundless devotion, his refusal to let go of Israel, has its strongest image in Hosea's pursuit of his faithless wife (*Hos 2*) or the parable of the love-affair with the abandoned foundling (*Eze 16*).

In the New Testament similarly, devotion of husband to wife, and his lavish care for her, is used as the image of Christ's devotion and generous self-giving to the Church for which he sacrificed himself (*Eph 5:25–31*).

Such is the ideal of devotion and generosity of spouse to spouse, voiced of course, in that socially male-dominated world, in terms of devotion of husband for wife. Custom might dictate that the dominant part was played by the husband and that infidelity was more severely punished in wife than in husband. But, alone of the peoples of the Mediterranean or Near-Eastern world, Israel knew that the basic equality of partnership could not be revoked, after the creation narrative provided woman as a companion, one flesh with her husband.

MARRIAGE FOR LIFE

The Church teaches that marriage is for life; 'those whom God has joined, let no man put asunder', said Christ. This is no easy task; but it has been achieved, through God's help, by millions of couples. Here is the testimony of two couples, one recently married and the other married for many years.

'When we first met and fell in love, we thought loving would be easy. But as we got to know each other better, we came up against flaws which we hadn't realised were there. In the close contact of marriage it is not possible to be always beautiful, kind and good – the cracks appear.

We snap when we're tired after a sleepless night with the baby; we look drab without make-up or a shave.

It is inevitable that anger erupts every now and again. We have had to learn not to worry about our own self-esteem, to say sorry and to forgive, or to compromise, or agree to differ and respect each other's opinion.

"Un"-married love is full of romance – country walks, long heartfelt talks by the fire late into the night, quiet meals for two.

Married love, however, has to make room for money worries, crying babies, housework, and hard days at the office. Often we have had to deliberately set aside time for romance, talking and relaxation.

Time also has to be made for separate activities – and we have to learn to accept the other person's needs for their own space. Marriage sounds like hard work. But if you put a lot into it, you get even more out of it.

Tolerating each other's drawbacks is the beginning of a stronger and more meaningful love than simply being 'in love'. It is love with no strings attached.

The result is a relationship which is honest and open, strong and secure. We can talk easily, share everything, face anything. No other relationship has the freedom, and at the same time the security, of marriage. It is basking in the sunshine of warmth and acceptance.

As you grow older, and change, you can grow together through continual communication and no secrets. There is a unity of thought that does not always need words, an understanding in a look or turn of the head.

Marriage makes you feel like the most important and special person in somebody else's life – and that feeling must surely be worth any amount of hard work.'

MEANING OF LOVE

'We have been married for a blessed 34 years – and now with our four children themselves married, one grandchild and another on the way we thank God for the many gifts He has showered upon us and for the way that He is still teaching us daily to live our lives as "two in one flesh".

At the time of our wedding we were Anglicans, but we had no clear idea of what was entailed in living the Christian life. Like many of our contemporaries we probably considered it to be a moral and decent attitude towards each other and our neighbours with an occasional nod towards a probably existent God. So we opted for a marriage in church which was beautiful, truly a sacrament. This we understood more deeply after our reception into the Roman Catholic Church three years later.

By saying that we received a sacrament and that those years were blessed we are not trying to say that we were spared the angers, misunderstandings, frustrations, resentments and all the other pains inherent in our fallen and sinful state – rather we say that the Lord has taught us to profit and learn from them by trying faithfully to respond to the grace that He showers upon us. To truly and sincerely repent of our sinfulness to Him and to each other and joyfully to accept forgiveness and enlightenment.

The unity we have found physically, mentally and spiritually grows each day. Our relationship to each other as brother and sister in Christ is integral to our feeling for each other as man and wife. We thank God for His gift for the joy we have found walking together in faith and trust because of Jesus Christ, who has taught us the meaning of love.'

Although external pressures have certainly contributed to the increase in divorce it must also be recognised that many people are totally unprepared for the intimacy and reality of marriage. They may marry too young. They may marry for the wrong reasons. Perhaps they are lonely, on the rebound, anxious to leave home, pregnant, or it may be simply because all their friends are getting married. They may be inflexible,

The strength of the body and blood of Christ in communion for the newly-weds.

incapable of coping with change, unused to expressing how they feel and unpractised in the ability to communicate with each other. Their self-esteem may be damagingly low; 'How can I tell him his friends make me feel small? I feel so stupid all the time. He'd only laugh. He never listens to what I say.'

Moreover partners bring to their relationship their own unique experience of life which will be different. They will have different experiences of family, different values, expectations, and styles of behaviour. Many will have learnt from inadequate models inappropriate, ineffective and sometimes destructive ways of both relating and communicating.

It is not always easy to share prayer in married life. Having common belief obviously should make it simpler. This is one reason why the Church prefers and encourages marriages between Catholics rather than mixed marriages. But sharing belief does not guarantee sharing practice. People can lapse and give up praying while still believing. Some people can be deeply in love and have a very wide understanding and union, but nevertheless find prayer together embarrassing and even counter-productive.

The habit of prayer together and going to Mass together should begin before marriage and continue within marriage. This helps the couple to grow together.

Sharing a Gospel passage is one common basis for prayer and meditation. Sharing ups and downs, talking and praying them over, is another way. In past days, many families said the rosary together. It is possible to share music in a prayerful way or even simply be together closely and silently, after a brief turning to God – say by sharing an 'Our Father'.

Prayer with children in a family is a sensitive area, particularly if there are different ages. It is important for parents to pray with children. But this must be simple and loving. They must be allowed their own expression in words and ideas, even if they are a bit off-beat. Children should not have long tedious prayers, but should learn to pray in love and trust.

If one partner will not or cannot share prayer with the other, the praying partner must not give up his/her prayer.

WHAT IS MARRIAGE FOR?

A married couple learn to sustain each other in every aspect of life. In order for any human being to do this there is usually a long and sometimes painful process of learning, which first tests, and then deepens the love each has for the other.

Second there is healing. After the 'honeymoon period', faults can soon begin to be revealed. A priceless grace of married life is for each to accept the other as he or she is. This acceptance is itself a primary form of healing. Mutual confidence develops, and one can help the other to overcome fears and anxieties.

Third, there is growth. As the years pass, crises arise, and the couple can guide each other through them.

SEXUAL LOVE

In Christian teaching, the sex act has often been viewed negatively merely as a remedy for lust. But the current secular fashion of talking about 'having sex' rather than sharing love sees it as mainly for pleasure, often with a very tenuous relationship with lifelong love.

The Second Vatican Council prefers to refer to sex more personally as 'conjugal love', which it sees as noble, and as a fundamental part of the mutual self-giving of the spouses. That is why the Council, in line with constant Christian tradition, limits sexual love totally to married life, excluding all sex outside marriage. Seen in this way, chastity is not just a negative rule, but rather an expression of human integrity.

It is the control of our bodies in order to truly love God and other people.

'By their very nature, the institution of matrimony itself and conjugal love are ordained for the procreation and education of children, and find in them their ultimate crown' (Church in the Modern World, para 48). Nevertheless, the Council, as does previous teaching, accepts that the couple themselves have to decide the size of their family after consideration of all their circumstances, so that birth regulation is part of Catholic married life.

What the Church does not allow is the prevention of conception by artificial means, a ban reiterated in the encyclical Humanae Vitae published by Pope Paul VI in 1968. Natural rhythm methods, which are becoming more effective, are allowed within the context of family planning. However this remains one of the most difficult aspects of the teaching of the Church.

Recent Vatican rulings also exclude surrogate motherhood and in vitro fertilisation because the child born is not the fruit of the married love of the parents.

What of married couples who are unable to have children or those who are beyond the age of fertility? A couple who make love, while knowing that conception is impossible, are not ruling out the possibility of conception by their own action. Their act is still open to life morally speaking.

In this case, what they are offering each other is thanksgiving for each other's presence and the hope that they will continue to sustain each other. Sometimes they use the act to be reconciled after conflicts; they affirm each other's sexual identity as man and woman and they confirm at regular intervals that they are the most important force in maintaining the stability, permanency and exclusive faithfulness to each other.

The Church teaches consistently that sex is morally justified only within marriage. But this is not because sex is seen as something dirty, to be avoided unless a child is thought of. Rather, it is because the sex act is a share of the creative love of God, that it is only permissible within the context of persons committed to each other in marriage, and open to God's gift of new life. In that context, it is a joyful act of union between two people, for which thanks to God are due.

But why cannot sex be just a means of people enjoying themselves? Pope John Paul II, when he was Bishop of Cracow in Poland, dealt with this problem in a book now published in English as 'Love and Responsibility' (Collins, London, 1982).

The Pope begins with the idea of love between persons. A human person, made in God's image, says Wojtyla, can never be used as a means to an end. Our bodies are themselves an integral part of our being persons – thus we must not use our bodies, or other persons' bodies, merely for pleasure. As St Paul says, 'Your body, you know, is the temple of the Holy Spirit . . . That is why you should use your body for the glory of God' (*1 Cor 6:19–20*).

When the married couple follow the laws of nature, which, as Wojtyla explains, is not only biological but is a law of 'existence and procreation', genuine love between them is the result. They

are not merely using each other for pleasure. There is a union of love between them, a sharing of God's own creative love.

That is why, in Catholic morality, the sexual act must be open to procreation.

'When a man and a woman consciously and of their own free will choose to marry and have sexual relations they choose at the same time the possibility of procreation, choose to participate in creation (for this is the proper meaning of the word procreation). And it is only when they do so that they put their sexual relationship within the framework of marriage on a truly personal level.'

This is the reason why, in Catholic teaching, all other forms of sexual activity both within and outside of marriage (contraceptive intercourse, masturbation, adultery, homosexuality) are seen as wrong; because they do not measure up to this 'personalistic norm' of an act open to procreation within marriage.

Not all these acts are equally wrong. Adultery, for instance, is worse than sex between unmarried people, because the marriage bond is being broken; but there is a disorder in any sexual act which is not within marriage.

SEX AND HUMAN GROWTH

While the Church is strict and totally unyielding on the question of the objective right-and-wrong of sexual morality, two thousand years' pastoral experience of dealing with imperfect Christians makes the Church understanding.

The sexual urge is very strong, and manifests itself in each of us in different tendencies, whether heterosexual, homosexual, or towards solitary sexual activity. Indeed, in many people, a complex mixture of tendencies manifest themselves at various times. The instinct itself is God-given, even though sometimes turbulent.

Even if we give in to temptation, we must not immediately assume that we

Happy Landings,
we hope and pray.

have committed a mortal sin. Particularly where bad habits are concerned, or acts done almost spontaneously, the 'full deliberate and consent' (necessary for a mortal sin) is often lacking. Our Lord did say, 'the spirit is willing, but the flesh is weak' (*Matt 26:41*). This is why the confessional, or counselling of one kind or another, is vital. Left to ourselves, we can become riddled by quite unnecessary guilt. Often, we need another person to make us realise that we are not as bad as we thought.

These tendencies can all be used creatively, whether we are married, single or celibate. For example, we must never despise a person because he or she has homosexual tendencies. The tendency is in itself not wrong. Homosexuals can be friends without sexual activity. Friendship in itself is a gift of God. Only homosexual acts are wrong.

Undoubtedly, one reason for the increasing numbers of marriages breaking down today is the belief that 'anything goes' where sex is concerned. Marital infidelity is very often accepted as a way of life.

ANNULMENT

The Church teaches clearly that a couple who are divorced cannot remarry. Yet some Catholics and some non-Catholics are allowed to marry in Church after they have received a Church annulment or dissolution of their first marriage. What is the real difference between a civil divorce and a Church annulment?

Marriage is a special and solemn agreement between a man and a woman to enter a lifelong partnership which of its very nature is faithful and permanent, open to the possibility of children, and is for the mutual benefit and support of each other. When a couple give a proper and considered consent to marriage they are promising to remain faithful to each other 'for richer or poorer, in sickness and in health, till death us do part'. Once having given that consent, it is essential that they stick to it, for their own good, for the good of the children and society. That applies to any marriage properly entered into whether the couple are Christians or not.

But for Christians, this agreement is also strengthened by the grace of the sacrament. Once a marriage is solemnly and properly entered into, and has been consummated, it cannot be dissolved under any circumstances because it is a solemn covenant made before God and the Church. That is why the Church does not accept that a couple can re-marry after a civil divorce, because by granting a divorce, the State is claiming to break the bond of an existing and valid marriage.

This is substantially different to a Church declaration of annulment. When the Church declares a marriage to be null and void, it is a formal declaration by the Tribunal Judges that what appeared to be a marriage on the face of it, was in fact no marriage at all – it never existed in reality despite appearances. Therefore, the couple concerned are not bound in marriage, and are in fact free to marry. The essential difference then is that by a civil decree of divorce, the State claims to break the bond of an existing marriage, whereas by a declaration of annulment, the Church judges that there was no marriage from the beginning.

The process of annulment looks at the consent a couple gave to their marriage. A marriage comes into being when the couple mutually exchange their con-sent. But if there is some radical defect in that consent then the marriage is in reality non-existent, despite the outward appearances. There are many reasons why such consent can be defective, even though the couple enter into the marriage in good faith and with the intention of making it last. It is the job of the Church Marriage Tribunals to determine if the consent was invalid.

The breakdown of a marriage involves a great deal of suffering on the part of the couple, their children, and their families and friends. The Church, with a mother's love for her children, has for centuries used the annulment process to heal and strengthen the broken without abandoning the values of the Gospel in regard to Christian marriage. It is true that the number of such declarations has risen sharply throughout the Church in the last twenty years, but this is simply the Church responding to an increasingly acute pastoral problem, namely, the rise of breakdown in marriage. But whilst the Church is deeply concerned for those involved, she also has the serious duty to protect and strengthen the institution of marriage and so witness to the world its inherent value.

QUESTIONS

1. What are the main influences against marriage and family life in the modern world? What does Christianity offer to help people face and overcome them?
2. The pastoral care of married couples is the responsibility of the whole parish. What do we do in our parish to help foster and strengthen our married couples? What else could be done?

Life at the seminary is not only praying. There is a lot of work to do.

31-The Ministerial Priesthood

The priest is the consecrated minister of God's people.
The priestly ministry was instituted by Christ.
The priest's task is to celebrate God's love and forgiveness.
The priestly ministry should be rooted in prayer.

IF ANYONE becomes a priest because he thinks that they only work one day per week, Sunday, he will soon be disillusioned. The priest's work is varied, demanding, lonely and often very hard, with its own particular tensions. In fact, many priests at one stage or other during their ministry will be tempted to give up.

What keeps them going, and still more, happy and fulfilled in their vocation? Basically, the priesthood is being in love with and loving the Church, God's people. Paul wrote to the Ephesians that 'Christ loved the Church and sacrificed himself for her . . .' (*Eph* 5:25). Just as Christ's love led him to die

on the cross, so the priest gives his life to help people draw closer to God, and into communion with each other.

The priest's ordination consecrates him in a special way to the Church, as the leader, and the representative of Christ in the Christian community.

It is in the Mass, the Eucharist, that the priest's role is most fully expressed. He represents the whole community in offering the one sacrifice of Christ to the Father. All Christians are 'other Christs'. But at the Eucharist the priest fulfills the role played by Jesus at the Last Supper, giving himself to his disciples.

And furthermore, the priest's role at

the Mass symbolises his role throughout his life. At Mass, he represents Christ offering the perfect worship to his Father. The priest then helps God's people in their daily lives to form a community of love, sharing, and witness, lives which themselves are offerings pleasing to God.

The priest's life, like all professions, is often humdrum, and concerned with mundane affairs like raising money for the upkeep of the church. He is something of a GP, expected to be counsellor, friend, small business manager, spiritual director, preacher, parish politician, school governor, school teacher, youth club leader, registrar, employment referee. No task, however secular or unusual, which builds up the Christian community, is foreign to the priestly ministry; provided that his prayer life, the heart of his vocation, is not neglected. As in marriage, a priest who loses his love of God and his people has lost everything.

THE PRIESTHOOD IN HISTORY

It has been said that, 'The priesthood is the second oldest profession'.

This may not be very complimentary to priests, to put them second historically to the ladies of the night. But it makes a valid point, that nearly all ancient civilisations had a man, or woman, whose role it was in that community to offer worship to their god in their name.

Because sacrifice is central to most religions, the priest's job was to offer the sacrifices prescribed by that religion. His duties also included teaching and handing on traditions. The priest also exercised a role of leadership. When Christianity flourished, it developed its own priestly system.

In the 16th century, Europe suffered its greatest religious cleavage, the Protestant Reformation (see Ch. 22). One of the most important issues dividing Protestants and Catholics was that of the nature of the Christian priesthood. Should the Christian Church have priests, just like most other religions?

The Protestant Reformers answered with a definite 'no'. They believed that Jesus Christ was the only priest.

The Catholic reply, given in the 23rd Session of the Council of Trent (1563) was totally opposite. 'Since, in the New Testament, the Catholic Church has received from Christ the holy, visible sacrifice of the Eucharist, it must also be acknowledged that there exists in the Church a new, visible and external priesthood into which the old one was changed.'

For over four hundred years, this controversy has raged between Christians. The Catholic Church maintains that Christ did initiate in his Church (either while on earth, or after his Resurrection, through the Spirit) a permanent order in the Church, which we now call the order of bishops, priests, and deacons. This permanent order took time to develop; but its main lines were established by the end of the first century, with Ignatius of Antioch.

Only those in Holy Orders, in fact bishops and priests, can offer the sacrifice of the Eucharist for and with the

The priest has a special ministry to the sick and suffering.

people of God, and represent Christ in the sacraments.

But, in an ecumenical age, we are beginning to realise that we have much to learn together with other Christians, without compromising our faith. The Second Vatican Council saw the need to realise much more profoundly the insight that all Christians, both priest and lay, have a vital role in the whole 'priestly people of God'. A priest is ordained 'to preach the Gospel, to shepherd the faithful and to celebrate the divine worship' (Lumen Gentium, para 28, CF. p. 509). A priest's role is complex and varied.

THE COMMON PRIESTHOOD

St Peter wrote to the early Christians: 'You are a "chosen race, a royal priesthood, a consecrated nation, a people set apart" to sing the praises of God who called you out of the darkness into his wonderful light' (*1 Pet 2:9*). He borrowed the description of Israel, the People of God, from the book of Exodus (*19:5f*), which sets them apart from the rest of the nations and gives them the role of priest among the earthly kingdoms. Because of her special relationship to God, Israel is allowed to 'draw near' to Him to do 'service' for all the world (see *Isa 61:5f*). Peter applies this description to the new People of God who are incorporated into Christ by their baptism, and in whose unique priesthood they have a share.

The New Testament idea of priesthood moves the emphasis away from the duty of priesthood in the individual sense to a sharing in the being and mission of Christ, the sole priest of the New Covenant. Each and every Christian, therefore, participates in the prophetic, priestly and pastoral identity and activity of Jesus Christ.

The ministerial priesthood was instituted by Christ, and is exercised in various 'orders' (bishops, priests, deacons). They share Christ's office of mediator, shepherd and head. 'These

members in the society of the faithful would be able by the sacred power of their order to offer sacrifice and to remit sins.' The ordained are living images of Christ's headship over the common priesthood. They are required to teach and to build up the Church at local, diocesan and international levels.

THE PRIESTHOOD OF THE LAITY

All Christians share in the mission to preach the gospel. 'The laity, too, share in the priestly, prophetic and royal office of Christ and therefore have their role to play in the mission of the whole people of God in the Church and in the world' (Decree on the Apostolate of the Laity, 2). The Church has an involvement in the renewal of the temporal

At the Maundy Thursday Liturgy in his Cathedral, each priest renews his vows to be a good and faithful servant of God and his people.

order of the world and in this the laity has a special role. 'By their very vocation the laity seek the kingdom of God by engaging in temporal affairs and by ordering them according to the plan of God' (Laity, 31).

The difference in nature and function between the common priesthood and the ministerial priesthood exists only to ensure a more complete collaboration in one mission. Their common goal is the evangelisation, sanctification and transformation of the world.

CELIBACY

One of the most controversial aspects of Catholic life is that priests cannot marry. Why is this so?

Celibacy is not 'required by the nature of the priesthood itself' (Decree on the Priestly Ministry and Life of the Second Vatican Council, para 16). In the New Testament, and in the early Church, many bishops and priests were married; and today in the Eastern discipline of the Catholic Church, not to mention in the Eastern Orthodox Churches, many priests, even the majority, are married.

The law, then, could change for Catholic priests in the West. The law could even have changed at the Second Vatican Council should the bishops have decided it; as they decided to change the law that Mass should be celebrated in Latin. But they decided against change in the law of priestly celibacy.

Even in the Eastern Churches, priests cannot marry after ordination, only before it. This tradition, that men in orders should not marry, but are 'married to the Church', goes back to about the eleventh century. And, where the Catholic Church in the West has occasionally allowed relaxation in the law of celibacy (as for instance when ministers of other Churches have become Catholics and want to become ordained priests), it has only ever allowed married men to be ordained. It allowed men, whether bishop, priest or deacon, to marry after ordination. To do this they must receive a dispensation from the Pope himself and renounce active ministry.

This tradition, as the Vatican Council states, 'is in many ways particularly suited to the priesthood' (para 16, op. cit). It is following the example of Christ, who 'prized highly that perfect and perpetual continence which is undertaken for the sake of the kingdom of heaven'. It is easier for priests to keep close to Christ with undivided love. They are more free, in him and through him, to devote themselves to the service of God and people.

Is a celibate life more difficult than a married life? All states of life, married, single, or consecrated celibacy or virginity, have joys and difficulties. Each of us has our gift; and we should pray for each other to be faithful to it.

Priests are conscious that celibacy could lead to a self-centred life, without the demands of a close family relationship; or even to running away from close friendship. This underlines the need for the priest's training to provide means of personal as well as academic growth.

LIGHT FROM THE COUNCIL

A priest must know the people to whom he ministers! He must live among them, and yet must also be a man apart. Vatican II speaks of this tension in the life of a priest in its Decree on the Ministry and Life of Priests 3:

'Priests come from the people and are appointed for them in the things that pertain to God, that they may offer gifts and sacrifices for sins. Yet, they live with men and women as with brothers and sisters. So also the Lord Jesus the Son of God, a man sent by the Father to men and women, dwelt among us and willed to be made like to his brothers and sisters in all things save sin. The apostles in their turn imitated him, and St Paul the teacher of the Gentiles, the man "set apart for the Gospel of God" (Rom 1:1), declares that he became all things to all that he might save all.'

The priests of the New Testament are set apart in some way in the midst of the People of God, but this does not mean that they should be separated from people, but that they should be completely consecrated to the task for which God chooses them. They could not be the servants of Christ unless they were witnesses and dispensers of a life other than that of this earth. On the other hand they would be powerless to save men and women if they remained aloof from their lives. Their very ministry makes a special claim on them not to conform themselves to this world; still it requires at the same time that as good shepherds they should know their sheep and should also seek to lead in to it those who have left or do not belong to this fold.

Priests will be helped by cultivating those virtues which are rightly held in high esteem in human relations. Such qualities are goodness of heart, sincerity, strength and constancy of mind, careful attention to justice, courtesy and others, which the apostle Paul recommends when he says: 'Whatever is true, whatever is honourable, whatever is just, whatever is pure, whatever is lovely, whatever is gracious, if there is any excellence, if there is anything worthy of praise, think about these things' (Phil 4:8).

PRAYER

Priests should be men of prayer. Their relationship in prayer with God is at the heart of their ministry. The Church tries to ensure this by outlining a prayer pattern for the priest's day. He must say the Daily Office (the breviary composed of psalms and readings and divided into the Office of Readings, Morning Prayer, Prayer during the Day, Evening and Night Prayer).

The Office is sometimes said or sung in common – as in a religious community – or said privately by the individual priest.

Daily meditation is also encouraged.

A main part of priestly ministry is preaching the Good News of Jesus Christ. In order to preach Jesus authoritatively and winningly, the preacher must know Jesus through revelation, service and prayer. The old tag is that no one gives what he has not got. Hence this intimate knowledge of Jesus Christ is essential for the priest in his role as leader, teacher and spiritual guide.

Jesus was asked by his followers to teach them to pray. He did. The priest also has the responsibility to 'teach' others to pray. To do so, he should be knowledgable about how others pray and have prayed – which means reading spiritual writers, the mystics, etc.

But reading is not sufficient. The priest must be experienced in and regularly living a life of prayer. Falling away in prayer means falling away in ministry.

Finally, prayer will affect the way a priest celebrates Mass, administers the sacraments, counsels and teaches people.

PRAYER

Lord give us holy priests, men of prayer, understanding, care and loving wisdom. Amen.

VOICE OF THE PEOPLE

'There is a great happiness in being a priest. It is a wonderful life – to offer the sacrifice of the Mass, administer the sacraments from birth to death, be the instrument of reconciling people with God, and the one who helps with God's grace to heal the suffering and the unhappiness of families. It is a very active life, one which I would never want to give up.'

THE ORDINATION OF WOMEN.

The Catholic Church, in common with Eastern Orthodox Christians, allows only men to be ordained, resisting the more recent tendency within some other Christian denominations to begin to ordain women also.

The tradition of only ordaining men to the ministerial priesthood goes right back to the time of Jesus himself, who chose only men to be his apostles. The priest, especially in the Eucharist, represents Christ, who is God become MAN, not God become WOMAN. This does not mean that women are not important in the church. On the contrary, apart from Christ himself, we believe that the most important role of all in God's plan was given to a woman, Mary, who bore the Son of God in her womb; a role, indeed, which no man could have fulfilled.

(See the Vatican 'Declaration on the Admission of Women to the Ministerial Priesthood' 15.10.1976.)

QUESTIONS

1. Two convert Anglican clergymen, both married, have been given permission to be ordained Catholic priests. What advantages would married priests bring to the ministry and what disadvantages? Would you like to see the practice of married priests being more widespread in the Church?
2. Refer back to the list of things which the priest does. Which of these could not be done by women priests? What would be the benefit to the Church if women could be ordained?

Most people who go to Lourdes are not cured of physical sickness, but receive
spiritual health and strength to face their problems.

32-Healing

ANOINTING

The Church has a ministry of healing.
The sacrament of anointing is for all sickness of body,
mind, and spirit.
The Church encourages scientific medicine.
But sees healing as going beyond human understanding.

THE SACRAMENT of the Sick –
formerly called Extreme Unction
– is healing in a special sense.

All the sacraments heal. Marriage
heals selfishness; Confirmation heals
fear of witnessing; the Sacrament of
Reconciliation heals sinfulness.

Healing is promised by Jesus: 'I came
that they may have life, and have it to
the full' (*John 10:10*). There are many
ways in which we can lack fullness of
life. Bitterness, sickness, sin, guilt,
weakness of many forms, can crush our
spirits. We can become crippled in our
relationship to God, to ourselves, to
others.

Jesus did not promise to remove the
cross from our lives. On the contrary.
But the cross can heal, allowing life to
the full.

The sacraments are a means of bringing us into wholeness, even in incurable illness. We receive healing also from others through acceptance, care, friendship. Prayer and scripture too are healing.

Healing is not the same as curing. Few may be cured at Lourdes, but many are healed there. Some evils are incurable, like loss in bereavement. But the pain of death can be lessened. New peace and courage are found. From the distress of bereavement people can look outwards again. They are healed by God, by time, by others.

The Bible is about healing. Fallen human nature is wounded, and many encounters of life keep that wound open: the pain of childbearing, the brambles and thistles of life, the sweat of toil. And yet even with this curse comes the promise of a remedy, when the offspring of the woman will bruise the serpent's head.

Later on, this healing is associated with the messianic era. A sign of the coming of the glory of the Lord will be that the eyes of the blind will be opened and the ears of the deaf unsealed (*Isa 35:5*) – signs which Jesus explicitly notes that he has fulfilled when he alludes to this passage for the messengers of John the Baptist (*Matt 11:5*). As the consciousness of sin grows deeper, especially in the writings of and after the exile, such as Baruch 1–2, 4–5, the longed-for healing is expressed more and more in terms of healing from sin.

He is responding to the needs which are thrust before him. For contemporary Jews sickness was the punishment for sin, and for Jesus healing from sin and from infirmity are inextricably intertwined: 'Which is easier to say to the paralytic, "Your sins are forgiven" or to say "Get up and walk"?'

The apostles continue this healing mission, and again the healings by Peter and Paul are signs of their deeper mission. They are repeating and continuing the healings of their Master,
as is seen from the details of their miracles: it is Jesus Christ who cures in the Acts, and Peter's 'Tabitha, stand up' echoes Jesus' own 'Talitha, stand up'. In the list of gifts of the Spirit healing takes its place with teaching, guidance and tongues as one of the key activities in the work of the organic body of Christ.

THE SERVICE OF HEALING

The anointing of the sick is a sacrament which looks to one basic New Testament text – James 5:14–15. James asks 'Is any one sick among you? Let him call for the elders of the Church, and let them pray over him, anointing him with oil in the name of the Lord; and the prayer of faith will save the sick man, and the Lord will raise him up; and if he has committed sins, he will be forgiven.' There is, behind this text, the whole concern of Jesus for the afflicted and the weak, and his ministry of healing and reconciliation among them.

Some points should be noted in James's text as guidelines for our celebration of anointing. First. Who are called? Not the members of the community, interestingly enough, who had the gift of healing, but rather the elders (the words we now translate as 'priests'), in other words the people who represented the unity of the community and ensured its fidelity to Jesus. Their coming to be with the sick member is a sign of solidarity of the community with one unable to come to its gatherings.

Second. What does this community delegation do? The primary thing it does is, it prays. The salvation of the sick person is attributed by James to 'the prayer of faith'. This prayerful visit is a focus of the prayer of faith by the community for the sick brother or sister, and this prayer is very powerful (indeed this thought leads James to digress on the power of prayer in the last few verses of his letter).

Third. The anointing with oil is carried out in the context of this prayerful concern. It is not a magic action with

secret power all on its own. The anointing communicates by the sense of touch. Its soothing and refreshing quality expresses the reaching out of the community of faith to the individual.

Finally, the anointing is done 'in the name of the Lord'. This refers to the Lord Jesus, who under this title is the one who humbled himself even to accepting death, and was raised up by the Father (*Phil 2:5–11*). The Church claims the power ('name' involves the whole power of the person) of Jesus who suffered and was raised up, and applies it to the sick Christian; its promise is that the sharing of life and destiny which he or she has entered into in baptism will be present and evident also in sickness and failing health, and ultimately result in the Christian being 'raised up' with Jesus, as James promises.

To think that the sacrament has 'worked' if the sick person gets better and that it has somehow 'failed' if this does not happen is a misunderstanding of the sacrament. The victory of Christ is not conditional but absolute. It is proclaimed to the sick person as a truth of faith, and the response of faith is elicited by the action and prayer of the Church. It is faith in the power of the Risen Christ, who will conform our mortal bodies to the image of his glorious body (*Phil 3:21*). Despite sickness and suffering, despite death itself – which none of us can cheat – we rest safe in the confidence that our ultimate destiny is assured in Christ.

One of the prayers after the anointing expresses the solidarity of the community of faith:

'Father in heaven, through this holy anointing grant N. comfort in his/her suffering. When he/she is afraid, give him/her courage, when afflicted, give him/her patience, when dejected, afford him/her hope, and when alone, assure him/her of the support of your holy people, through Christ our Lord. Amen.'

USE OF THE SACRAMENT

The Christian community and its priests have two important duties concerned with this sacrament. One, they should encourage the sick to receive it. Two, they must protect the sacrament from being trivialised.

The rite of anointing gives the key by using the word 'danger'. Danger does not mean a threat to life, but rather is a threat to the person. Illness can weigh down the whole person: people can be at risk in relationship to God; their life is disrupted; they cannot look outwards; they no longer find a meaning for their lives.

Obviously people who are gravely ill, physically or psychologically, and those very weak in old age should be anointed. Less serious illness can be a danger to wholeness, so that people lack fullness of life. Examples might help. Physical illness: chronic arthritis, certain forms of diabetes, angina, debilitating migraine. Illness with psychological factors; severe depression, alcoholism, acute anxiety or fears that interfere with normal living. There are also difficulties that appear spiritual, but have psychological roots: scrupulosity, and severe sexual problems.

For short illnesses the sacrament should normally be given once. Through the anointing of the sick and by other gifts to his Church, Jesus offers fullness of life no matter what our situation may be.

The sacrament of the sick is healing in a special sense.

THE DOCTOR

Modern life threatens wholeness; it fragments and divides. We are valued for what we have, not what we are. Advertising proclaims that happiness consists in having more money and more possessions. Evil catches the headlines for all to copy; good is usually left out. We are treated as if we had no mental or spiritual life, as mere mechanical things.

All this causes stress. Some diseases such as migraine or asthma result partly from a physical cause and partly from stress. Other troubles such as sleeplessness and loss of appetite, reflect the patient's lifestyle and background, his aims in life and his beliefs. Though the doctor must be clear and firm in his own beliefs in order to help the patient reconstruct his life, he will not seek to impose his own faith on his patients.

Wholeness for the Catholic doctor himself means that he is not just a doctor during the week and a Catholic only on Sundays; he is at all times a Catholic

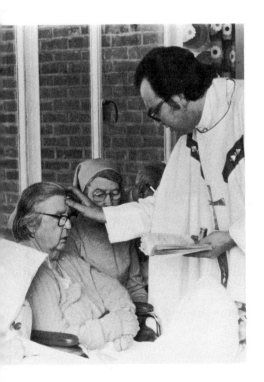

doctor. He will have a Christian relationship with his patients and will value them as individuals – from conception till death. Practices such as abortion and euthanasia will therefore be repugnant to him. However, if a patient has, through ignorance, fear or panic, chosen a wrong way out of a dilemma, he will not abandon them.

In every case his aim will be to restore the patient to that harmony of the physical, mental and spiritual (though the spiritual is strictly beyond the doctor's concern) which is wholeness – which foreshadows the ultimate supernatural wholeness promised by the Resurrection.

Medicines and illness from the Book of Ecclesiasticus Ch 38

Treat the doctor with the honour that is his due,
in consideration of his services;
for he too has been created by the Lord.
Healing itself comes from the Most High,
like a gift received from a king.
The doctor's learning keeps his head high,
and the great regard him with awe.
The Lord has brought forth medicinal herbs from the ground,
and no one sensible will despise them.
Did not a piece of wood once sweeten the water,
thus giving proof of its power? (*Ex* 15:23–25)
He has also given some people the knowledge,
so that they may draw credit from his mighty works.
He uses these for healing and relieving pain;
the druggist makes up a mixture from them.
Thus, there is no end to his activities;
thanks to him, well-being exists throughout the world.
My child, when you are ill, do not rebel,

but pray to the Lord and he will heal
you.
Renounce your faults, keep your
hands unsoiled,
and cleanse your heart from all sin.
Offer incense and a memorial of fine
flour,
make as rich an offering as you can
afford.
Then let the doctor take over – the
Lord created him too –
do not let him leave you, for you
need him.
There are times when good health
depends on doctors.
For they, in their turn, will pray the
Lord
to grant them the grace to relieve
and to heal, and so prolong your life.
Whoever sins in the eyes of his
Maker,
let such a one come under the care of
the doctor!
*Written in the second century BC.
Translation from the New Jerusalem
Bible.*

MIND AND BODY

What do we mean by healing? The
World Health Organisation has defined
health not as the absence of disease but
rather as 'A state of complete physical,
mental and social wellbeing'. Viewed
this way, healing can be defined as the
process whereby people are helped to
realise their full potential as human
beings in a world where ill-health cannot be totally eradicated.

Traditionally, doctors and nurses
were regarded as the healers, and
medicine and nursing the 'caring
professions'. Present-day medical tech-
nological development has converted
them into 'the curing professions' to the
detriment of the sick.

There is a subtle difference between
'cure' with its mandate to eradicate the
disease or defect and 'care' which by its
holistic approach to the patient, heals
although it may not necessarily always
cure. The Chinese, with their ancient
civilisation, believe that the best doctors

use no medicines and instead, heal by
the care they take to give advice on
healthy living.

In contrast to this understanding of
healing, medical services worldwide
today limit the definition of healing to
the prevention and elimination of
disease, mainly of a physical nature.

That this approach to healing is un-
satisfactory is now becoming evident
by the proliferation of other 'healers'
(alternative medicine and prayer
groups) who aim to offer a holistic healing to disillusioned patients.

The whole person is made up of a
body, the physical tangible part, a soul
(psyche), the area of the conscious and
even vaster subconscious mind and
finally a spirit which is what makes one
human and in the image of the Creator.
It is difficult to imagine a satisfactory and
efficient healing process which divides
these five components; yet this is what
modern medicine tends to do.

VOICE OF THE PEOPLE

When a young doctor, I went to work in a
hospital in Africa. One day a new
witchdoctor set up his 'practice' near to
my clinic and was doing a very good
'trade', with many of my own patients.
One morning one of these 'shared
patients' came back to the clinic for a
consultation. From the array of charms
and amulets worn, it was evident that she
had paid him a visit; so to put her at ease
and to get some idea of the treatment
received, I asked whether she considered
him competent. Her reply, 'he says he is
better than you since he treats body and
spirit while you only treat the body', made
me analyse my medical practice and
converted me to holistic healing which I
have since practised with immense
gratitude and satisfaction.

It was somewhat ironical that I, coming
from a Christian background, steeped in
the healing power of God in the Old and
New Testament, had to learn what healing
meant from my pagan neighbours!

In our health system doctors are
trained to treat disease; to cure but not
necessarily to heal. They make decisions

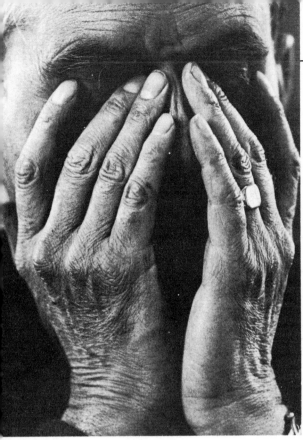

How long, O Lord?

about health and disease and thanks to modern technology effectively cure pain, influenza and life-threatening conditions. Some diseases, however, they cannot treat. For instance, the various forms of mental illness, congenital defects physical and/or mental, stress-linked situations which may include moral, social and political components and the ill health associated with the normal process of ageing and dying.

Since these cannot be 'cured' the doctor feels a failure; the best he can do is to eliminate the patient from society either permanently by euthanasia or temporarily by confinement to an institution. The true malaise of modern medicine is a failure to understand its relationship with healing. This is not only frustrating for the patients – it is also demoralising for medical personnel.

Patients yearn to be treated as human beings and not another number. They sense, although many have lost their Christian tradition, that healing has to touch body, psyche and spirit since all of these are inter-related. They know that modern medicine does not do this, hence their frustration and continued sickness. So they turn to alternative medicine, and prayer to achieve the 'inner healing' which eludes them in present day hospitals and clinics.

Sometimes it is forgotten that medicine owes its greatest debt not to Hippocrates, but to Jesus. It was the humble Galilean who more than any other figure in history bequeathed to the healing arts their essential meaning and spirit. Physicians would do well to remind themselves that without His spirit, medicine degenerates into a depersonalised methodology, and its ethical code becomes a mere legal system. Jesus brings to methods and codes the corrective of love without which true healing is rarely actually possible. The spiritual 'Father of Medicine' was not Hippocrates of the Island of Cos but Jesus of the town of Nazareth.

Jesus worked many miracles of healing. Some prayed to him – that is asked him – for a cure. Before healing them he recognised the faith of those asking for his help. He prayed and laid hands on them. He spoke on one occasion of the need for prayer and fasting.

Miracles of healing are well attested from the early Church till today.

The sacrament of the anointing of the sick (which for years was kept in practice for the moments of dying) is in reality a healing sacrament. Here and at any time, prayer for healing should be an accepted part of our plea to God – our intercessory or petitionary prayer.

In recent years much more has been happening in the healing ministry through the charismatic movement, prayer groups and healing services. Remarkable things are claimed. There is no doubt that God can and does heal. There is also no doubt that the Spirit blows where he wills. Prayer for healing is a prayer of faith in which we should hope and trust in God and the power of the Spirit. But always we must pray with Christ, 'Your will, not mine, be done'. God can surprise us either in healing or not healing. But pray in faith.

The healing we should pray for is not only physical but also mental, psychological and spiritual. For instance, in praying for someone terminally ill with cancer, a cure is possible, so pray for one. But also the sick person, friends and relatives need to face death and may need prayerful help in adjustment. The bereaved need another sort of healing in which prayer should play a part.

Prayers
Lord, he whom you love is sick.
Lord, that I may see.

QUESTIONS
1. Choose one example of healing from each of the four Gospels which you think gives a clear idea of Jesus' attitude to healing. Explain your choice and what each one adds to a complete picture of Jesus the Healer.
2. Vatican II reminded us that the sacrament of the Anointing of the Sick is not for those only who are at the point of death. What suggestions can you offer about how this can be taught and practised in a parish?

'It is part of God's plan that we should combat all illness and should prudently seek the blessings of good health. We will thus be able to play our part in secular society and in the Church. However, we should always be willing to complete what is lacking in the sufferings of Christ for the salvation of the world, as we look towards the liberation of all creation in the glory of the sons and daughters of God.

'Further, sick people have this role in the Church; to put others in mind of the essential, the higher things, reminding them that through the mystery of Christ's death and resurrection our mortal life is given back to us.'
From the Introduction to the Rite of Anointing and Pastoral Care of the Sick.

33-Spiritual Warfare

DISCERNMENT AND THE STRUGGLE WITHIN
There is a 'war' going on in each of us.
The Spirit of God versus the Spirit of Evil.
God gives us discernment.
So we are able to win the war.

THE CHURCH is quite un-ambiguous in its affirmation that a conflict exists at the highest level, that is, at the spiritual level, between God on the one side, and the devil and his angels on the other.

Of course, it is not a struggle between equals. Christian faith rejects this utterly. The devil is only a rebellious spirit created by God. There is no question of him winning the final conflict. The gates of the underworld can never hold out against the Kingdom of God (*Matt 16:18*).

TEMPTATION
Temptation is when we are 'tested' to choose evil rather than good. Why do we choose evil? Because it looks good at the time. Original Sin weakens our resistance to temptation, but does not destroy our free will. Sin is still my decision; we cannot pass the responsibility for our evil choices over to anyone or anything else, even to the devil.

What is the devil's role in temptation? Scripture calls the devil The Tempter. He aggravates the situation by en-couraging us to choose evil. Jesus calls him the father of lies (*John 8:44*). He distorts our ideas of what is good, true or right.

To see more clearly the devil's role in temptation, read the story of the Temptation of Jesus (*Matt 4:1–11*). Jesus was, as the Epistle to the Hebrews tells us, 'tempted in every way that we are, though he is without sin' (*Heb 4:15*). And 'because he has himself been through temptation he is able to help others who are tempted' (*Heb 2:18*).

Jesus' temptations are described in Matthew's Gospel as three, usually in-terpreted as the temptations of The World, The Flesh, and the Devil.

THE WORLD
The devil tempted Jesus to take over the world by evil means. He claimed that he owned 'all the kingdoms of the world and their splendour. I will give you all of these', he said, 'if you fall at my feet and worship me' (*Matt 4:9*). Jesus shut the devil up with 'You must worship the Lord your God, and serve him alone' (*Deut 6:13*).

The Devil of course was telling a lie. The world belongs to God, not to him. However, he was speaking a half-truth. As a consequence of Original Sin, and human decision against God, the devil is able to influence human society. We pray that as Christians we will reject the false values of the world.

THE FLESH
Christ is tempted to turn stones into bread, to satisfy his hunger. He replied, 'Man does not live on bread alone, but on every word that comes from the mouth of God' (*Deut 8:3*).

Within us, given by God, are power-ful desires, good in themselves; desires to eat and drink in order to preserve our life, and desires for sexual intercourse in order to increase and multiply the hu-man family. The instincts are in them-selves good. What is wrong is to respond to them in such a way as to abuse our bodies, or destroy others.

The 'sins of the flesh', gluttony and sexual impurity, are not to be lightly treated as so often they are today in the media. The 'little bit on the side', and 'the night out with the boys' can so often lead to families split by divorce, and lives ruined by alcoholism.

The Church has great experience in dealing with sins and sinners particularly in the sacrament of reconciliation, and realises that the 'sins of the flesh' are very often the result of weakness and bad habit, rather than of deliberate malice. 'The spirit is willing, but the flesh is weak' (*Matt 26:41*). We pray for Christ to help us in our particular weakness never to be discouraged in our attempts, by prayer and self-denial to 'use your body for the glory of God' (*1 Cor 6:20*).

THE DEVIL

The devil took Jesus to the highest point of the Temple. 'Throw yourself down. Does not Scripture say "He will put his angels in charge of you to guard you".'

Not only would it have 'tested' God and proved Jesus' powers, but it would have made a spectacular beginning to his public ministry.

Jesus replied 'You must not put God to the test'. As the obedient Son he would live in faith, trusting the Father's will even to death on the cross.

The devil in fact was asking Jesus to commit suicide to disobey the commandment 'You shall not kill' (in this case himself), demanding God his Father to save him 'on the way down'.

Christian morality is based upon reason. We are responsible for our actions. We have no right to do what is in itself evil, as Jesus was tempted to do, expecting God to extract us from our folly.

The first criterion of action is 'Is it right? Or is it clearly wrong?' God has given us the Ten Commandments; 'you shall not kill', 'you shall not steal', 'you shall not bear false witness', 'you shall not commit adultery'.

Very often, people are tempted even in the name of God to act contrary to

Christian art has always been fascinated by devils and witches.

these commandments. Many wars have been justified on a religious basis. As Scripture says, even Satan can appear disguised as an angel of light (*2 Cor 11:14*). If we follow Jesus in his temptations, we will always 'see off' the devil by quoting the Law of God, and then following it.

DEMON POSSESSION

The existence of 'the Devil and his
angels' to use the Lord's phrase (*Matt
25:41*), is established by Scripture and
the constant teaching of the Church.
And it is possible for them today, as in
New Testament times, to occupy or possess the body (not the soul) of a human
being. But this is very rare and not
something that Christians should become obsessive about. The Christian,
born of God's love, redeemed by the
Blood of Christ, consecrated by the
waters of Baptism and nourished with
the Lord's body, should be worried by
theories of Demonic possession.

The external manifestations of demonic possession and psychological illness can be very similar. Sound medical
guidance and skill in the discernment of
spirits is necessary to help distinguish
between the two. All natural explanations should be examined before con-
cluding the Devil is the cause of some
distressing state. Pope John Paul recently reminded us that 'It is not always
easy to discern the preternatural factor
operating in these cases and the Church
does not lightly support the tendency to
attribute many things directly to the
Devil'.

Solemn exorcism, that is, directly
commanding the Devil in the name of
the Church, is reserved for priests
specially appointed by the local Bishop
and marked by piety, knowledge, prudence and integrity of life (Canon 1172).
On the other hand, all of us can pray for
deliverance from evil spirits; 'Deliver us
from evil' is the Lord's own prayer.

There is an area in between in which the answer is not so clear. We have to tread cautiously in the dark world of demonic activity. Where evil influence is suspected, expert guidance should be sought.

VICES AND CORRESPONDING VIRTUES

Pride	Humility
Covertousness	Liberality
Lust	Chastity
Anger	Meekness
Gluttony	Temperance
Envy	Brotherly Love
Sloth	Diligence

THE SPIRITUAL WAR

St Paul's advice for spiritual warfare is given in Ephesians 6:10–20. 'Put on God's armour so as to be able to resist the devil's tactics.'

'Stand your ground, with truth buckled round your waist, and integrity for a breastplate. Wearing for shoes on your feet the eagerness to spread the gospel of peace and always carrying the shield of faith so that you can use it to put out the burning arrows of the evil one. And then you must accept salvation from God to be your helmet and receive the word of God from the Spirit to use as a sword.'

THE GOOD ANGELS

'We believe in one God, Son and Holy Spirit, creator of things visible – such as this world in which our brief life runs its course – and of things invisible – such as the pure spirits which are also called angels –' (Profession of Faith of Pope Paul VI, 1968).

The Pope is repeating the constant tradition of the Church; that God created both the visible world, of which we are part, and also a world of invisible spirits, whom we call angels (messengers). The Church also believes, with the testimony of Scripture, that these invisible spirits can help us personally in our lives.

'There is a "war" going on in each of us'.

Scripture is mysterious about angels. In the early books of the Old Testament, God himself seems to take a human shape. In the book of Genesis, 'Yahweh appeared to Abraham', in the form of three men standing before him (*Gen 18:1–2*). The 'angels' in this case are simply the human shape of God.

It was not until the later Old Testament period (after the Exile, 597 BC) that the angels, as messengers of God, began to work overtime. Post-exile Jews thought of God as more distant, and angels functioned as intermediaries, dispensing God's message. It is here that we encounter the famous names of angels, such as 'Raphael' (healing of God), 'Gabriel' (God's might), and 'Michael' (who is like God?).

Scripture is less interested in describing who the angel is, and more interested in describing the function of angels, as 'spirits whose work is service' (*Heb 1:14*). They still perform that function for us. The idea of guardian angels, taught to Catholic children down the ages, goes back even before Christian times.

There is the beautiful story of Tobit, a loyal Jew who falls into misfortune, and who is helped by the angel Raphael, who comes disguised as a man looking for work (*Tob 5:7*). Eventually, the angel tells him who he really is. 'I am Raphael, one of the seven angels who stand ever ready to enter the presence of the glory of the Lord' (*Tob 12:15*).

A little boy was once asked, 'Who are guardian angels?' He thought for a moment, and then replied, 'Guardian angels are people who help you'. This is not a complete theological description; but Tobias would say that there is at least a measure of truth in what the boy said.

Angels often appear in very heavy disguises!

Opposition Tactics

In the Screwtape Letters, written in the 1940s, C. S. Lewis used fiction to teach basic truths of spiritual warfare. A senior devil, Screwtape, writes to Wormwood, his nephew, a novice in the business of temptation. The 'Enemy' he refers to is God. Here he explains a general rule:

'In all activities of mind which favour our cause, encourage the patient to be un-selfconscious and to concentrate on the object, but in all activities favourable to the Enemy bend his mind back on itself. Let an insult or a woman's body so fix his attention outward that he does not reflect "I am now entering into the state called Anger – or the state called Lust". Contrariwise let the reflection "My feelings are now growing more devout, or more charitable" so fix his attention inward that he no longer looks beyond himself to see our Enemy or his own neighbours.

Do what you will, there is going to be some benevolence, as well as some malice, in your patient's soul. The great thing is to direct the malice to his immediate neighbours whom he meets every day and to thrust his benevolence out to the remote circumference, to people he does not know. The malice thus becomes wholly real and the benevolence largely imaginary. There is no good at all in inflaming his hatred of Germany if, at the same time, a pernicious habit of charity is growing up between him and his mother, his employer, and that man he meets in the train. Think of your man as a series of concentric circles, his will being the innermost, his intellect coming next, and finally his fantasy. You can hardly hope, at once, to exclude from all the circles everything that smells of the Enemy; but you must keep on shoving all the virtues outward till they are finally located in the circle of fantasy, and all the desirable qualities inward into the Will. It is only in so far as they reach the will and are there embodied in habits that the virtues are really fatal to us. (I don't of course, mean what the patient mistakes for his will, the conscious fume and fret of resolutions and clenched teeth, but the real centre, what the Enemy calls the Heart.) . . .'

Your affectionate uncle,
Screwtape.

HOW DO I GET WISE?

'Discern' comes from a Latin word 'to separate, to keep apart, to sift'.

The dictionary says: Discern: distinguish, see the difference between; perceive clearly with the mind or senses, make out by thought, or by gazing, listening.

In Baptism we have chosen to follow Christ. He is the Way, the Truth, and the Life (*John 14:6*). But because of the complexity and sinfulness of human nature, at times we lose sight of Christ and His way. To be a discerning person in the Christian sense means to keep our gaze fixed on Jesus, to go to Him and learn from Him (*Matt 11:28–30*).

But how is it done? How and where do I find God's will? Ben Sirach (*Eccles 37:12–20*), a wise Jewish writer of the 2nd century BC, gives us the answer. Listen to others, listen to our own heart, listen to God, listen to reason:

OTHERS

But have constant recourse to some devout person, whom you know to be a keeper of the commandments, whose soul matches your own, and who, if you go wrong, will be sympathetic.

REASON

Reason should be the basis for every activity, reflection must come before any undertaking.

In everyday life this means that we need some small oasis of calm to be able to listen, in other words, moments of quiet prayer. And of course there is also common sense.

We need a true understanding of what is sinful and what is not. St Paul advised the Galatians, 'Let me put it like this: if you are guided by the Spirit you will be in no danger of yielding to self-indulgence, since self-indulgence is the opposite of the Spirit, the Spirit is totally against such a thing' (*Gal 5:16–17*).

All sin is self-indulgence. The way of recognising the activity of the evil spirit is in the effects of self-indulgence. Hatred, wrangling, jealousy, bad temper, sexual irresponsibility, drunkenness, anger. Paul gives a comprehensive list (*Gal 5:19–20*).

This is the opposite of the action of the Holy Spirit, which leads us to grow in love with all its facets: joy, peace, patience, kindness, goodness, trustfulness, gentleness and self-control (*Gal 5:22–23*).

These are all one fruit. The person who is trying to follow the way of Christ reflects His light in this many-faceted loving way.

YOUR OWN HEART

Finally, stick to the advice that your own heart gives you, no one can be truer to you than that; since a person's soul often gives a clearer warning than seven watchmen perched on a watchtower.

GOD

And besides all this beg the Most High to guide your steps into the truth.

CONCLUSIONS

● To discern means 'to see the difference between good and evil: between what is of Christ and what is not, what is loving and what is self-indulgent'.

It means to have our eyes fixed on Christ. To listen to His Word, to our own hearts, and to our neighbours and their needs. It is the gradual unfolding of the Father's loving will for me through which I find my true happiness.

A PRAYER FOR DISCERNMENT

Cardinal Newman, in his hymn, 'Lead, kindly Light', prays: 'Keep thou my feet; I do not ask to see the distant scene; one step enough for me'. And he continues: 'I loved to choose and see my path; but now lead thou me on'.

If prayerful discernment is my daily way of life before the Lord, then when big decisions have to be made, I will not be frightened or panic. I simply continue to be open to the action of the Holy Spirit in my life. My basic question is still the same: what will lead me to grow in love towards God and my neighbour?

Holy Michael, Archangel, defend us in the day of battle; be our safeguard against the wickedness and snares of the devil. May God rebuke him, we humbly pray: and do thou, prince of the heavenly host, by the power of God thrust down to hell Satan, and all his wicked spirits who wander through the world for the ruin of souls. Amen.

From the Romal Missal

PLACE FOR PRAYER

St Peter, writing to the exiles in parts of the Mediterranean says: 'Be sober and watchful. Your adversary the devil prowls around like a roaring lion, seeking someone to devour. Resist him, firm in faith' (*1 Pet 5:8–9*).

In prayer there are many different 'moods' – exaltation, depression, warmth, coldness, love, and perhaps sometimes rightly, we blame ourselves – I'm tired, I've lost faith, I can't pray.

This chapter is saying to you very simply – No! It is not necessarily your fault – there are influences warring against you to prevent your growth in God.

This area is a minefield! You may ask – is it my imagination? Am I just slack and indulgent? – and so on. Here you really can gain a great deal from having a spiritual person to whom you can go – to put your problem, to hear what helpful suggestions he/she may have.

- The fact of the matter is that though all can pray, you are not by any means the best judge of how things are going.

Sometimes you will find great temptation to give up an exercise which seems a complete waste of time. There may be occasions when the pressure of life seems to put prayer very low in the priority of life. There may be an attack on your faith, killing all motivation to turn to God.

If you submit yourself as part of your life to a wise and holy person, whether things are going well or badly, you will find that he or she can often discern something in you yet hidden from you.

Lord, when I am at war with myself, you and the world, send me a someone by the power of your Spirit to lead me and guide me. Amen.

QUESTIONS

1. What evidence do you find of the seven deadly sins in society? What remedies can the Christian community offer?

2. Compare the accounts of the temptations of Jesus in the Gospels of Ss Matthew, Mark and Luke. Why do you think St John does not include this episode in his Gospel?

At this point in the journey of a 'catechumen' (that is, one being instructed) towards initiation into the Church, there is an important and moving ceremony, performed by the bishop, called 'Election'. The candidate is 'chosen' now to become a member of the Church; and a period called 'Purification and Enlightenment' is entered into, where the candidate examines his or her conscience in preparation for receiving baptism. This is one of the prayers said over the candidate at this time, to help in his or her spiritual warfare:

God of power,
you sent your Son to be our Saviour.
Grant that these catechumens,
who, like the woman of Samaria,
  thirst for living water,
may turn to the Lord as they hear his word
and acknowledge the sins and
  weaknesses that weigh them down.

Protect them from vain reliance on self
and defend them from the power of Satan.

Free them from the spirit of deceit,
so that, admitting the wrong they have done,
they may attain purity of heart
and advance on the way to salvation.

We ask this through Christ our Lord. Amen.

Why, Lord, did you let it happen?

34-Suffering

Suffering comes to all of us.
God allows it.
But not without promising an even greater good
To come out of it.

SOME PEOPLE argue that the existence of so much suffering is a reason to believe that God does not exist.

'If an infinitely good God exists', the argument runs, 'why does he allow such horrible things to happen such as the Nazi holocaust?'

The question is not new. St Thomas Aquinas, in the thirteenth century, said 'If God existed, surely no evil would be found?'; and came up with this answer: 'It relates to the infinite goodness of God, that he permits evil to exist, and from it brings forth good' (Summa Theologiae, Q.2., A.3, ad 1).

For Aquinas, God in creating the world with finite creatures had to allow for the possibility of evil. Only God himself is infinitely good, with no possibility of evil. That possibility of evil becomes even greater with created beings such as us humans, with free will.

The goodness of God, therefore, consists of God's being able to organise a world in which, whatever evil choices are made by human beings, and whatever natural disasters occur (disasters, that is, for some people. Disasters for some may be lucky for others), all will in the end come to good. That is why our faith in the Resurrection of Jesus is so vital in order to understand suffering in the world; because that is the final part of 'the plan'.

One problem, however, with St Thomas Aquinas' explanation is that it cannot explain why a particular form of suffering afflicts one person, and not another. Why do some become rich and famous, while others starve to death? Why do some have good health all their lives, while others have long and crippling illnesses? Why do some people die immediately without suffering, while others hang on for years in pain and loneliness?

With our limited knowledge, we cannot explain this. What we can say is that God loves each of us personally, and gives us the cross which is right for us. There is a story of a man having a dream going to Joseph the carpenter to change his cross, which he thought was too heavy to bear. Joseph took his cross, and asked the man to choose another. After a long time, the man finally took one. 'That is just right for me', he said. Joseph replied with a smile, 'That is the one you brought in.'

As Paul who suffered greatly in many ways, physically, psychologically and spiritually, said, 'We are well aware that God works with those who love him, those who have been called according to his purpose, and turns everything to their good' (Rom 8:28).

Contrary to legend, Job did not have much patience. But he did have a lot of courage; and faith.

Terrorism is another blight on modern life.

THE PATIENCE OF JOB

The story of Job, included among the 'Wisdom' books of the Old Testament (see Ch. 7), probably written about the fifth century BC, proves that very point.

Why should my baby be born with a handicap? Why should my child be killed or maimed in a motor accident? Why should my wife die of cancer? Why should my parents become senile and need constant care when so many others live unscathed and happy?

The misery of such tragedies makes a test of faith. Can a loving God really permit such agony? Is not the world in fact ruled by unreasoning chance and marauding forces of evil?

Job, lost in the darkness of misery, made worse by its suddenness, is at grips with just such a doubt, and yet he clings firmly to trust in God.

TRUST
Naked I come from my mother's
  womb,
Naked I shall return.
Yahweh gave, Yahweh has taken
  back.
Blessed be the name of Yahweh.
              (Job 1:21)

Starvation is hideous suffering endured by at least half of the world's population today.

The problem is set in the ancient times before there was any revelation of the love of God leading to the promise of a redeemer.

Success and happiness were measured largely – as often nowadays – in terms of material possessions, a strong and prosperous family. Job's comforters (who in fact torment him) try to persuade him that he must somehow be to blame, either he or his family, for the tragedies that have befallen him. Just so we nowadays try to persuade ourselves that tragedy must somehow be deserved, and search our own consciences, too late, for guilt. If we can find some guilt – the drink before driving, the smoking during pregnancy – at any rate the affliction becomes intelligible and so to some extent mastered.

Job can help us in two ways. Firstly, he sturdily and stubbornly rejects the spurious solutions, and yet blindly clings to his conviction that God, the very God who has afflicted him, will somehow stand at his side to vindicate and re-establish him. At some moments he begs to be free of God's relentless gaze, free to shrivel up in his own misery. At others – and so basically this is his attitude – he shouts defiance:

'I know that I have a living Defender, and from my flesh I shall look on God' (*19:25–26*).

It is an unreasoning stubborn faith in God's love and fidelity, not bolstered by any promise of rewards or punishments beyond the grave. No doctrine of the future life had as yet been revealed to Israel, and Job must make sense of his situation without it.

But secondly, and perhaps this is the greatest of all the contributions of the Book of Job and allied to its wonderful literary quality, the final experience of God (*38–41*) makes all reasoning superfluous. God knows and God controls. Man is ignorant and powerless. In these chapters Job, and all those who come to realise with him the awesome power of God, gain a new dimension to their understanding of God and the world: there is no question of God justifying himself in human terms, and somehow no need for him to do so. His sovereign control of the universe is allied to his sovereign care for every element of it.

There is one dimension of the mystery of suffering which remains closed to Job, and which comes to us through the mystery of the Cross, though it glimmers already in the later chapters of Isaiah. This is that suffering willingly accepted in love and obedience can somehow bring life to others. This first comes to expression in the poem of the Suffering Servant of the Lord in Isaiah 53. Then it inspires the whole of Jesus' concept of love as service, illustrated most perfectly by his washing the disciples' feet at the Last Supper. Finally it is systematised by Paul's teaching that we all form one Body of Christ, in which the different limbs and members contribute to each other and fill up the measures of the sufferings of Christ. United in the bond of Christ, suffering accepted by one member can bring health and vigour to others who share in Christ's life.

Job's Confession

I know that you are all-powerful:
what you conceive, you can perform.
I am the man who obscured your
   designs
with my empty-headed words.
I have been holding forth on matters I
   cannot understand,
on marvels beyond me and my
   knowledge.

                (42:2–3)

Structure of the Book of Job

1–2 Folk-tale: Job the wise is tested.
Centred on a folk-hero of antiquity. Can hardship and deprivation topple the faithful servant from his fidelity to Yahweh?

3–37 Dialogue: advice in difficulties.
Job's three friends, Eliphaz, Zophar and Bildad advise him to admit his guilt: he must have sinned to deserve such suffering, even if he is not aware of it. Job protests his clear conscience and his certainty that somehow God will vindicate him.

28 A poem on Wisdom (*added later to the book*):
'Where does Wisdom come from? Where is intelligence to be found?'

29–31 The discourses of Elihu (*added later to the book*):
A new character arrives and gives his view of the matter.

38–41 Yahweh's answer:
God answers Job by showing the depths of his unfathomable wisdom and control of the universe. A high point of the Old Testament on the majesty and awesomeness of God.

42 Conclusion of the folk-tale:
Job the wise is rewarded by the redoubling of his wealth and prosperity.

For Jesus his death was an integral part of his ministry. To evade the Cross and leave a holy man who worked marvellous cures, preached incisive parables and offered sound moral advice is to do violence to the whole purpose of his mission.

It is one thing to endure the stress of, let us say, an Army officer training when there is a goal in view which will bring a sense of achievement and open up new horizons and a new career. Similar endurance with no known goal is quite a different experience.

What was the cause of Jesus' agony in the Garden? Some theologians have speculated that he foresaw all the terrible crimes which would be committed and the resulting number of souls in Hell.

But maybe Jesus suffered from an agony of indecision. As a man he was terrified at the thought of crucifixion. It was as a man also that he chose the will of the Father.

How we react to the appearance of the Cross in our own lives is a very individual affair.

LIGHT FROM THE COUNCIL
Through Christ and in Christ, the riddles of sorrow and death grow meaningful. Apart from His gospel, they overwhelm us (Pastoral Constitution on the Church in the Modern World, para 22).

Prompted by the Holy Spirit, the Church must walk the same road which Christ walked; a road of poverty and obedience, of service and self-sacrifice to the death, from which death He came forth a victor by His resurrection (Decree on the Church's Missionary Activity, para 5).

QUESTIONS
1. Do you find Job a 'model of patience'?
2. Do you find an answer to the 'problem of suffering' in that book?

35-Counselling

**Wisdom is a gift from God.
All of us share in it.
No one has a monopoly of the gift.
Sometimes, we need the wisdom of others.**

IN BUSINESS, there are said to be only two kinds of people; the quick and the dead.

The world admires the 'smart' and 'clever'. The Scriptures speak of one who is 'wise'. What is the difference?

'Wisdom' and 'understanding' in the Bible are gifts of God, which come from prayer and from reflection. They do not necessarily guarantee riches or a good career. But they help us through the most difficult periods of our lives. God guides us by giving us his own Spirit.

God's wisdom comes to us through other people, as well as through our own reflection. We would be foolish to reject the advice of our friends, and of professional counsellors, spiritual directors, or doctors. 'No man is an island' wrote John Donne (1572–1631).

But modern counsellors do not think of themselves as giving advice. They prefer to see themselves as enabling a person to find the resources within himself or herself to come through a difficult situation.

When we receive the word from someone else, we find that it is really already in our mouths and in our hearts, deep in our own selves (*Rom 10:8*).

'Growth begins when we start to accept our own weakness.'

We are never meant to 'go it alone'.

The informal help and advice we get from our relatives and friends is an invaluable support to healthy living. However, many people go through a phase in their lives when they feel the need of formal counselling.

We must understand the uniqueness of each individual and respect their journey. Counsellors seldom tell people what they ought to do or how to live, but encourage them to decide themselves on the 'right' course of action.

A counsellor is someone who is trained to sensitively accompany another person on their journey for a time. They will meet regularly to help them to clarify an area of darkness or indecision in their life. It is a unique relationship of privilege and trust, specially set up so that the 'client' has the undivided attention of the 'guide' for a stated time.

For counselling to be effective, it has to be freely chosen because of a felt need, even if that need cannot be clearly stated.

Counselling is available for anybody who is facing problems which threaten to overwhelm them. Many marriages have been saved and enriched when couples were willing to seek the help of a Marriage Guidance Counsellor. Death, especially sudden and tragic death,

Counselling begins with recognition of need.

often has traumatic effects on a family or individual. A sympathetic counsellor can help a person to come to terms with grief and loss in a healthy way. Crisis counselling is available in many places at no cost through voluntary organisations and religious bodies as well as through the National Health Service. There are also many counsellors in private practice.

What is often not understood by people in general is that a crisis usually indicates or heralds a time of growth. Even very painful experiences such as an accident or the death of a loved one can, with time, be seen as a growing point.

There is a natural tendency within us towards growth and we can either suppress it or cooperate with it. What seems to be a problem can take me to the threshold of a new level of living.

Some people have no specific problem, yet they feel depressed or only half alive. Others feel restless and dissatisfied but cannot say why. Yet others have vague longings for something more in their lives, which they cannot articulate. Such people can benefit greatly from counselling.

Often, the people concerned know that their full potential as human beings is being blocked somewhere. They need skilled help to unblock it. The result of counselling in such cases is often dramatic.

HEALING

Far from becoming more dependent, people who are counselled generally become more free, more in charge of their lives.

Christian counselling can be healing and life-giving. It can help captives to liberate themselves and the downtrodden to stand up and enjoy their status as children of God.

John had been given eighteen months to live. He was terribly depressed. His counsellor thought it would be of help for him to come to terms with death. In fact, he learnt to live more fully in those final months of his life. Things which had caused him anxiety during his very active life became a source of joy. For the first time in his life, he began to see and appreciate the roses he pruned. He became aware of his feelings and his relationships deepened. Talents that he had not explored began to develop. He began to paint and carve with great satisfaction. Finally, spiritual matters preoccupied him and he showed extraordinary patience in his last weeks of suffering. In spite of his suffering he described his final years as having a heightened quality of life.

Mary came for help because she could not understand her own behaviour. She was married and valued her husband and marriage yet she was having an affair. At the final session, after a year's counselling she was able to say 'I feel so much more confident in myself and my ability. My life is more enjoyable because I'm not frightened of others and I can state my opinion in any company. I've learned to love and my marriage is really very precious to me.' Needless to say the affair petered out.

When the disciples walked towards Emmaus after Christ's death, sharing their disappointments and loss, the risen Christ came up and walked with them. Christian counsellors believe that as they sensitively walk step by step with a person, Christ becomes present to bring strength and healing and hope.

As Christ broke the bread at Emmaus and his friends recognised Him, so the counsellor helps a person to break open the meaning of their own feelings and words so they can come to recognise the path God is calling them to follow.

WHO NEEDS COUNSELLING?

Not everybody in the Church needs or wants a weekly session with a spiritual director or requires regular counselling.

Where most Catholics can expect to encounter spiritual direction and counselling is in the sacrament of reconciliation. Since the rite has been renewed and 'confession boxes' have begun to be replaced by 'reconciliation rooms' a good deal more counselling and spiritual direction is being given in the context of the sacrament.

The instruction on the administration of the sacrament, the introduction to the New Order of Penance, says, briefly, that the priest should offer the penitent 'suitable advice to help him/her begin a new life and if necessary instruct him/her on the duties of the Christian life' (No 18).

More importantly, it describes the

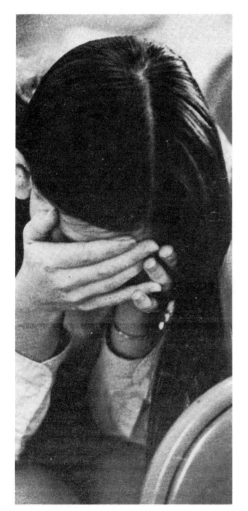

Counselling is self-discovery through sharing.

ideal spiritual context in which the counselling or spiritual direction should take place. It recommends prayer to the Holy Spirit 'for light' (No 15) and it recommends the reading of scripture, which 'enlightens the penitent for the discovery of his sins' (No 17).

All counsellors require the qualities prescribed for a confessor, of whom it is said (No 10,a) that 'if he is to diagnose sicknesses of souls, and if he is to be a wise judge, he must acquire the requisite knowledge and prudence by assiduous study under the guidance of the Church's magisterium and especially in prayer to God. For the discernment of spirits demands an intimate knowledge of the working of God in the hearts of men and women, it is the gift of the Holy Spirit and the fruits of charity'.

'But have constant recourses to some devout person, whom you know to be a keeper of the commandments, whose soul matches your own, and who, if you go wrong, will be sympathetic.'

The idea of one person helping another with problems is not new. The above quotation from the Wisdom of Ben Sirach (*37:15*), or 'Ecclesiasticus' as it is sometimes called, encourages the reader to seek a wise friend; written in the second century BC. Throughout the history of the Church, Christians have been encouraged to find 'spiritual directors', often, but not always, a priest. What is new is the application of modern counselling techniques in a 'one to one' situation, provided as a service in the Church, for example, for a married couple.

PRAYER
Lord, help me find someone who can help me to grow in knowledge and love of you – who will encourage me to pray – who will suggest to me how I follow you – the Way the Truth and the Life. Amen.

Counselling

This is a profession or vocation, not necessarily within the Church at all, whereby one person trained for the job helps another person to find a way forward in life at a time of personal difficulty.

Spiritual Direction

This is a ministry, usually within the Church, whereby a person with spiritual gifts helps another person to relate their life to God in love and prayer. A 'spiritual director' may be a priest, but could be any Christian with such spiritual experience.

Confessor

This is a priest or bishop, administering the sacrament of reconciliation (or 'confession' as it is usually known). The priest's conversation with the penitent may involve (and often does) both counselling and spiritual direction; but the essential elements are the repentance of the penitent, and the absolution from the priest.

QUESTIONS

1. To whom do you turn when you are in trouble?

2. How have your experiences of suffering and personal difficulty helped you to become more aware of the needs of others?

36-New Creation

Baptism is being born again with Christ.
This is a new Exodus.
We celebrate the birth of the new member.
We pray for the Spirit to come upon all of us.

AN ADULT Catholic today is encouraged, after a period of formation which we have described in this book, to make his or her commitment to the Catholic Church at the Easter Vigil, the most important liturgical celebration in the Church's calendar.

In military terms, this would be called a 'passing out parade', when the soldier has finished basic training, and passed the exams. The celebration must be the best possible, to indicate how important is this step into the full ranks of the army.

St Paul describes the commitment of the Christian using military terms. He says that we wrestle, not against flesh and blood, but against spiritual wickedness (*Eph 6:12*). For this reason, we must put on the 'whole armour of God', the virtues, and stand fast in the day of battle (*Eph 6:13*). He tells Timothy, his pastoral assistant, to fight like a good soldier of Jesus Christ (*1 Tim 1:18*) 'with faith and a good conscience for your weapons'.

Finally, seeing the end of his own life perhaps drawing near, Paul says 'I have fought the good fight to the end; I have run the race to the finish; I have kept the faith; all there is to come for me now is the crown of uprightness which the Lord, the upright judge, will give to me on that Day; and not only to me but to all those who have longed for his appearing' (*2 Tim 4:7,8*).

There will be many battles ahead. But, this night, the whole of the Christian community assembled for the Easter Liturgy, are celebrating 'the Exodus' of a new Christian from the slavery of sin to new life.

Christ our Light. The Paschal Candle.

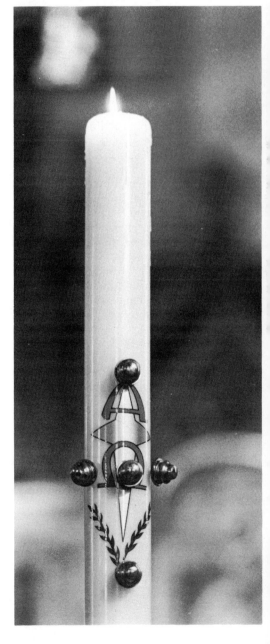

THE NEW EXODUS

On the first Easter Sunday evening, our risen Lord met two of his disciples on their way to Emmaus. The Gospel tells us that, 'beginning with Moses and all the prophets, he interpreted to them in all the scriptures the things concerning himself'. As they reported afterwards, 'he opened to us the scriptures' (*Luke 24:27,32*). During the night of Holy Saturday we read the same scriptures – the Old Testament – by the light of the Paschal Candle, the light of the risen Christ, so that they may be opened to us. Read in the light of the resurrection, they tell us what we are celebrating.

It is a baptismal service, because, as St Paul says, 'you were buried with him in baptism, in which you were also raised with him' (*Col 2:12*). The readings were all chosen to shed light on different aspects of baptism. Read in the light of the risen Christ, the Old Testament readings are meditations on the sacrament in which we become one with Christ in the mystery of his death and resurrection.

The most important is the one about the Exodus from Egypt, the story of Moses and the Israelites crossing of the Red Sea. St Peter, St Paul, and after them the whole of tradition see the miracle of the Red Sea as an image of baptism. The font is the Red Sea through which those to be baptised later in the service will pass, as, by the power of God, they escaped from Pharaoh and his armies, the devil, sin and death, to join in the great procession of those coming 'forth from Egypt', from the world of 'darkness and the shadow of death'.

The story tells us many things about baptism, but here we can only touch on one. Through the waters, the Hebrews escaped from slavery into freedom, into a new life of liberty. And so do we in baptism. It is the start of our journey out of death into life. St Basil the Great says, 'the Hebrews came out of the sea whole and safe; we also come out of the water as living men from among the dead'. It is

liberation from the tyranny of death. With St Paul the baptised can cry out, 'death is swallowed up in victory. O death, where is thy victory? O death, where is thy sting?' (*1 Cor 15:54,55*).

We are freed from the domination of death because baptism gives us a share in the divinity and life of our risen Lord, who, 'dying, destroyed our death, and rising, restored our life'. To be freed from the power of death and share in his life is the liberation and freedom given in baptism. Death has become for us the way to life, as it was for Christ.

But just as the Hebrews entered fully into freedom only when, after wandering in the desert, they crossed the Jordan into the Promised Land, so do we enter more deeply into our freedom when we cross into eternity. That is the second stage of the Exodus which begins at baptism. The traditional Psalm for a funeral procession is the Psalm of the Exodus, 'When Israel went forth from Egypt' (*Ps 113*), which links together the crossings of the Red Sea and the Jordan, Baptism and Christian death, two stages of the journey into freedom.

The final stage of our liberation, the 'glorious liberty of the children of God . . . the redemption of our bodies' (*Rom 8:21–23*) comes at the resurrection, when Christ will come again 'to raise our mortal bodies and make them like his own in glory'. The Exodus that began at the font will have reached its goal. Our freedom will be perfect.

THE FIRST EXODUS

The Exodus ('departure') of the children of Israel from slavery in Egypt is the most important event in their history. No scholar doubts that the story of the escape has a factual basis. The only adequate explanation for the story acquiring such a fundamental importance in tradition is that it actually happened. The escape from Egypt led by Moses, and the wilderness wanderings, formed the nation.

But when and how did the Exodus happen? What route did the escaping

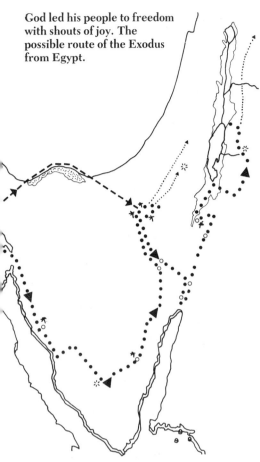

God led his people to freedom with shouts of joy. The possible route of the Exodus from Egypt.

From Egypt, the Israelites escaped into the Sinai Desert, where they wandered until Joshua led them into the Promised Land of Canaan. They remembered the Exodus and Wilderness Wanderings as the time when God was specially with them, and as an assurance that he would not abandon them now.

Every year the Jewish community remembers the Exodus at the Passover celebrations.

TERRIFYING ORDEAL

'The awesome and holy rite of initiation'. This is the way fifteen hundred years ago the great preacher St John Chrysostom described the rites of baptism. 'Awesome' is too weak a word to express the effect the preacher had in mind. Speaking in Greek, he used a word which expresses awe which is so intense that we come out in goosepimples: 'spine-chilling' would not be too strong a translation.

BEGINNINGS

Can we expect baptism to make such an impression on the catechumen today? Perhaps not. Many things have changed since the end of the fourth century. At that time it seems to have been usual to wait until people had grown up before baptising them, but nowadays most people are baptised at an age when the rite is much more likely to induce crying than awe. Again, the rites were wrapped in such secrecy that no one was allowed to be present at baptism or the central part of Mass until they were themselves baptised; on Sundays the catechumens would hear the readings and the sermons, but as soon as they had been prayed for in the bidding prayers they would have to leave. In some places, such as Jerusalem and Milan, this secrecy was maintained so strictly that no explanation of the rites was given until the days following the baptism. The ceremonies and the words of the rite themselves were considered so powerful that they would make a deep and lasting impression on the

Israelites follow? All these questions will probably never be answered with certainty. The evidence in Scripture is difficult to interpret, and the Israelites, living in tents, left few remains for archaeologists to pick up thousands of years later.

The Book of Exodus says that the Israelites escaped miraculously across the 'Sea of Reeds' (*Ex 13:18*). This is not the same as the Red Sea on the modern map. Rather, it is most likely one of the Egyptian lakes, perhaps Lake Timsah, which are full of reeds, and could suddenly become dry land due to change of wind. Another possibility is the salt marsh of Bardawil, separated from the sea by a narrow sand-spit, which is generally a dry salt crust capable of bearing men and light animals but occasionally flooded.

neophytes, even before their meaning was explained.

The Rite of Christian Initiation of Adults has attempted to reintroduce many of the features of the fourth-century rite. Although conditions in the twentieth century make it impossible for the rites to strike the candidates with the same sense of glad surprise as they did fifteen hundred years ago, if the ceremonies are imaginatively performed they can still inspire some of the holy awe of which St John Chrysostom spoke.

The long process of catechumenate reaches its climax on Holy Saturday. For several months the candidate has been gradually introduced into the Catholic understanding of Christian revelation and the life of the parish. Since the beginning of Lent, there has been intense preparation. On three consecutive Sundays the Scrutinies and Exorcisms have clarified, purified and strengthened the candidate. They have solemnly been entrusted with the Creed and the Lord's Prayer.

During preliminary rites the candidate professes faith in the Church's Creed. Recalling the action with which Jesus restored speech and hearing to the deaf mute, the priest has touched their ears and lips and sang, 'Ephphetha: that is, be opened, that you may profess the faith you have heard, to the praise and glory of God'.

VIGIL

The marks of the glorified wounds are pressed into the Paschal Candle, which stands for the risen Lord. The candle is lit from the Easter fire, and the deacon proclaims three times, 'Christ our light'. The candidate lights a little candle from the great candle which stands for Christ, and holds it while the deacon sings the song of praise, the Exulet. This praises the night which is the hinge of history, commemorating the release of the Israelites from their captivity in Egypt, as well as the rising of the Saviour from the dead.

A series of readings often recapitulate God's saving action in history. Water often plays a part in these accounts: the primal water of creation, the Red Sea in which the Israelites' enemies were drowned, the clean water with which God promises to purify his people. After hearing St Paul telling the Romans that in their baptism they have died with Christ and risen with him, the candidate listens to one of the Gospel accounts of the Resurrection.

BAPTISM

The priest blesses the water, dipping the paschal candle into it to recall how Christ's immersion in the Jordan is the source of blessing for all baptismal water. The candidate promises to reject Satan and is anointed as a sign of the strength that is promised in the fight against evil. In the early Church the candidates faced the west to make these renunciations, because the west signifies the darkness which is the characteristic of the devil; they then turned to the east, the source of light, and pledged loyalty to Christ.

The candidate is given a white baptismal robe, the sign that in baptism all sins have been washed away. (In the early Church the candidate would have continued to wear the robe throughout Easter week.) One godparent passes a candle lit from the paschal candle, while the priest encourages the candidate to keep the light of Christ always burning in their heart.

Next the candidate is confirmed. Remembering the descent of the Holy Spirit on the apostles at Pentecost, and recalling that the Holy Spirit came down on Jesus after he was baptised in the Jordan, the priest prays that they may receive the same Spirit to strengthen them to be a fearless and effective witness of Christ.

There remains the great joy, when for the first time the candidate receives the Body and Blood of the risen Lord.

The Baptistry at Pisa.

Profession of Faith at the Easter Vigil

Said by all present: The new candidate has already renounced sin and asserted faith in Christ. Now, all those present renew their baptismal promises.

Priest: Do you reject sin, so as to live in the freedom of God's children?

All: I do.

Priest: Do you reject the glamour of evil, and refuse to be mastered by sin?

All: I do.

Priest: Do you reject Satan, father of sin and prince of darkness?

All: I do.

Priest: Do you believe in God, the Father Almighty, creator of heaven and earth?

All: I do.

Priest: Do you believe in Jesus Christ, his only Son, our Lord, who was born of the Virgin Mary, was crucified, died, and was buried, rose from the dead, and is now seated at the right hand of the Father?

All: I do.

Priest: Do you believe in the Holy Spirit, the holy catholic Church, the communion of saints, the forgiveness of sins, the resurrection of the body, and life everlasting?

All: I do.

Priest: God, the all-powerful Father of our Lord Jesus Christ, has given us a new birth by water and the Holy Spirit, and forgiven all our sins. May he also keep us faithful to our Lord Jesus Christ for ever and ever. Amen.

QUESTIONS

1. How relevant do you find the image of the Exodus for understanding the meaning of Easter?

2. Why do you think people want to become Catholics, or indeed to profess any faith?

37-Ecumenism

Christ calls all Christians to be one.
There are many painful divisions among Christians.
The ecumenical movement seeks to overcome these divisions.
Its goal is visible unity in the one Catholic Church.

THE MOVEMENT for Christian unity is one of the most important happenings in the twentieth century.

It is generally called 'the ecumenical movement'.

'Ecumenism' comes from the Greek word 'oikumene', meaning 'worldwide'. It is close in meaning to 'catholic' ('according to the whole', 'universal'). Thus an 'Ecumenical Council' means 'A Worldwide Council' as distinct from a local synod.

The 'ecumenical movement', therefore, exists to make the Church more 'worldwide', more 'whole'. To become one means to go out to each other in universal worldwide love.

When did the ecumenical movement start? When did Catholics and Protestants stop sniping at each other and start talking and praying that Christ's prayer, that 'they all may be one', be fulfilled?

Perhaps the beginning was at the 'grass roots', or rather the muddy and smelly trenches of World War One.

It was there that Catholics and Protestants began to discover that the man next to you might go to a different Church, but still got cold, wet feet, and shook with fear before going over the top to certain death. Never before had so many men shared so closely a common misfortune. Religious differences paled into insignificance.

The closest daily contact Christians have with each other is not in official dialogues between Church leaders. It is in inter-church marriages. It is during coffee break at work. It is when a Catholic nurse in hospital rings a Methodist minister to ask him to visit one of his parishioners who is seriously ill. It is when a group of Christians of various denominations agree to pray together in a situation of need.

This is where the real problems are courageously yet charitably faced. The hurt of not being able to receive communion together; the painful decision about where the children are to be christened and educated; the joy when realisation dawns that, despite differences, there is a deep and basic unity in Christ, even if that unity is not yet perfect, or perfectly realised.

CHURCH UNITY – A BISHOP'S STORY

The spiritual writers tell us that we would not be seeking God if in some sense or other we had not already found him. So it is with Church unity. We would not be seeking unity with each other if, as we shall explain, that unity were not already in some sense a reality.

'Remember the rock out of which you are hewn', says the psalmist. I was brought up to love the Catholic faith as a gift from God. As a boy and young man I had little opportunity for meeting Christians of other denominations, nor was I encouraged to do so. But under the guidance of the teaching of Vatican II, and as a priest, I gradually came to meet and appreciate Anglican and Free-Church Christians. Instead of looking at doctrines and attitudes that divided us, I began to learn how to appreciate the many Christian truths that united us.

Our common baptism and reverence for the Word of God in Scripture already unites us in a profound love of Jesus Christ. But above all, it was friendship and prayer that changed my attitude to Ecumenism. When I saw the manifest Christian goodness of so many fellow

**How good, how delightful it is for brothers to live in unity.
The Pope visiting the Archbishop of Canterbury.**

Christians I realised that it must be the will of Christ that we should be more fully reconciled and that I should play my part in bringing about the unity for which Christ prayed.

Gradually I have found my earlier suspicions removed, my reluctance to collaborate with others overcome, and now I have a heartfelt and sincere desire to work and pray in any way I can for Christian unity. It is the will of Christ and the will of the Church that this should be.

Catholic Principles of Ecumenism

The Catholic Church asserts that the unity Christ willed for His Church exists in the Catholic Church. It is essentially a communion of faith, hope and love, whose principal cause is the Holy Spirit. The Church is also intended by Christ to be visibly united in the profession of the same faith, the celebration of the same Sacraments, in the unity of the one people of God.

...AND THIS IS WHERE WE HOLD OUR CHURCH UNITY MEETINGS

In order to bring about and maintain such unity, Christ endowed His Church with a threefold ministry of Word, Sacrament and leadership, first entrusted to the apostles with Christ at their head and then continued in the college of bishops under the Pope. When Catholics pray for the restoration of full communion with other Christians, they are praying for that unity which the Church believes Christ willed and which is found in all its essential characteristics in the Catholic Church. 'It is through the Catholic Church alone that the whole fullness of the means of salvation can be obtained' (Decree of Ecumenism No 3).

However the Church of Christ also exists in a certain way outside the visible boundaries of the Catholic Church. Other Christian communities also have means of sanctification and Christian truth. Through their belief in Christ, and their baptism, Christians separated from us are already our brothers and sisters in imperfect communion with the Catholic Church. In varying degrees there exist either in doctrine, discipline or structure of the Church, obstacles, some of which are serious ones, to full communion with the Catholic Church. The ecumenical movement is striving to overcome these. There are three principal ways in which this is brought about: theological dialogue, mutual and loving collaboration and prayer.

Theological Dialogue

Dialogue is taking place between various Churches. One example is the work of the Anglican–Roman Catholic International Commissions (ARCIC-I and II), set up by successive Popes and Archbishops of Canterbury.

The first ARCIC examined the Eucharist, Ministry and Authority, and by their common study, theologians of both Churches have discovered convergence and agreement in doctrine on these issues. The second ARCIC continues this work and has already issued a statement on Salvation and the Church which puts into a new context a theological disagreement which was at the heart of the Reformation.

The Anglican and Roman Catholic Church have already so much that points to a common faith. For example, there is agreement on the authority of Scripture; and a common faith in what is proclaimed in the Apostles and Nicene Creeds. There is acknowledgment of salvation as a gift given in Christ, and a common understanding of the vocation of the Christian community brought about by baptism and faith. There is also agreement on the centrality of the Eucharist and a belief in apostolic preaching guarded by the bishops in continuity with the Apostles.

But substantial difficulties remain concerning the focus and exercise of authority; certain moral issues; dogmatic definitions concerning Mary, Mother of Christ, and the reconciliation of ministries, of which a particular obstacle would be the ordination of women in parts of the Anglican Communion. But in spite of difficulties and obstacles, the theological dialogue will and must continue because it is a work of the Holy Spirit.

Prayer and Mutual Collaboration

The heart of the ecumenical movement is spiritual ecumenism and particularly common prayer. The most profound statement of the Vatican Council's Decree on Ecumenism is that 'there can be no ecumenism worthy of the name without interior conversion. For it is from newness of attitudes of mind, from self-denial and unstinted love that desires for unity take their rise and develop in a mature way. We should therefore pray to the Holy Spirit for the grace of genuine self-denial, humble and gentle in the service of others' (para 8).

Everyone has a part to play in the ecumenical movement and all Catholics should be encouraged to collaborate in any way with our fellow Christians. The enemies of ecumenism are suspicion, inertia and impatience. We must want Christian unity and overcome the suspicions of the past. We must work and pray for unity and trust in God who draws us in Christ to be fully reconciled with each other.

VOICE OF THE PEOPLE
In 1976 Archbishop DEREK WORLOCK was appointed to the Roman Catholic archdiocese of Liverpool. The Anglican Bishop, DAVID SHEPPARD had arrived in the city a year earlier. Since then the two have developed a distinctive and practical ecumenism. They explain what inspires and encourages them.

'When we both came to Liverpool in the mid-1970s, people seemed to assume that our way of life and style of work were so separate that it was frequently necessary to introduce us one to the other. In fact we had known each other slightly in the East End of London. The needs of Liverpool were clear to both of us, so it was natural enough that we should respond to those needs together. The fact that we enjoyed each other's friendship and trust was a help but was not the cause of our partnership. That was due to our baptism into Christ's life and mission. Our working together might prove effective in itself. It was even more important to try to speak together in the name of Christ, if we were to throw the light of the Gospel on the problems of the people whom we were called to serve.'

SOCIAL, SPIRITUAL AND DOCTRINAL

Christians often learn to give common witness through trying to tackle together the needs of others. Working together in different circumstances leads Christians to experience the need to pray together: to worship and grow together in the spiritual life. Sadly, although there is so much that can be done together, so much in our spirituality and devotion which we can share, before long certain barriers become apparent. Some appear insuperable and although we can pray about it, it is evident that the difficulty is rooted in a doctrinal difference which must be studied, prayed about and resolved. So it is not a question of acting together and ignoring theological problems. All three kinds of ecumenism – social, spiritual and doctrinal – are necessary.

PRAYER AND SERVICES

Some of the difficulties which can arise, such as that which is the focus of attention at the moment, the ordination of women, may seem insoluble. It is a grave problem and one in which we must be sensitive to one another as well as to the teaching authority of the Church. But that does not mean that all work for Christian unity is at a standstill. Christ prayed for it and, no matter what the difficulties, we must continue to try to find the way forward, always with due regard to the conscience as well as the traditions of others. Pray harder, study more intently and work more closely together is the only possible answer. Then offer all your efforts to God.

Christ prayed that we might be one so that the world might believe. Many people today have lost all knowledge of their faith. Good people do not presume to recognise Christ in the ordinary circumstances of their daily lives. They tend to think of God as someone only for church-goers. In the name of Christ we must reach out to them, in service, in understanding, in humility, and wherever possible together.

WHY NO INTER-COMMUNION?

Many people are uneasy at the Church's discipline on Intercommunion. Vatican II's Decree on Ecumenism said that there are two principles upon which worship in common should be based: 'that of the unity of the Church which ought to be expressed, and that of sharing in the means of grace'. Services of prayer express a common brotherhood in 'one Lord, one faith, one baptism'.

The celebration of the Eucharist, however, is so totally identified with church unity, which it realises and expresses, that it 'cannot be regarded as a means to be used to lead to full ecclesial communion'.

In answer to this unease, one might cite the Unity Secretariat's document of 1972 on Intercommunion, which makes the point that 'though it is a spiritual food whose effect is to unite the Christian to Jesus Christ, the Eucharist is far from being simply a means of satisfying exclusively personal aspirations, however lofty these may be'. To use a banal illustration: I cannot simply invite a citizen of another country, by saluting my flag and singing my national anthem, to become thereby a citizen of my country. This doesn't mean that he's not welcome in my country, or that my fellow citizens do not highly respect him. But sharing full citizenship involves a whole set of procedures and commitments (and indeed renunciations) without which behaving 'ritually' as a citizen is deprived of true significance.

The example is, of course, inadequate, since baptised Christians can never be like citizens of different states to one another. But it does say something about belonging and commitment, which can never be merely notional or 'spiritual'.

BREAKAWAYS IN THE CHURCH: SOME MAIN EXAMPLES

AD

100–200 Groups of Jewish Christians (e.g. the EBIONITES) break away on the grounds that the Law of Moses should bind Christians; and also on a reduced doctrine of the person of Christ, that he was Son of God only from the moment of his baptism, or from his birth; but not from eternity, and by nature.

172 MONTANISTS expected a speedy outpouring of the Holy Spirit on the Church. Following Montanus, who preached in Phrygia, in modern Turkey, they thought the Church was too lax in its discipline, particularly on those who had rejected Christ under pressure of persecution.

319 Arius, a priest in Alexandria, denies the full divinity of Christ. ARIANISM spreads rapidly, and was a major force against Catholicism for at least two centuries.

725 ICONOCLASM. Groups of Christians believed that images of Christ and the saints were in reality idolatry, and began to 'smash the icons' (hence 'Iconoclasm'). In 787 a General Council in Nicaea decreed that icons were legitimate, since God had become man in Christ, and thus human forms could be portrayed in images.

1054 The EASTERN ORTHODOX Churches, rejecting the jurisdiction of the Pope, and the Latin clause of the Creed which stated that the Holy Spirit proceeded from God the Father AND the Son (filioque), became more and more estranged from western Christianity.

1184 The WALDENSIANS (followers of Valdes, a rich merchant of Lyons), were excommunicated by the Council of Verona (1184) in particular for preaching 'freelance', outside of the jurisdiction of the Church; and for claiming that the Eucharist celebrated by an unworthy minister is invalid.

Thomas More, Lord Chancellor under Henry VIII, then executed by the King for refusing to recognise any other than the Pope as supreme head on earth of the Church of England.

1380   JOHN WYCLIF (called 'The Morning Star of the Reformation') preaches that the visible 'material' Church has its only authority from the invisible 'spiritual' Church in the heart of each believer.

1521   MARTIN LUTHER, an Augustinian friar excommunicated by decree from the Pope. Luther denied the Catholic Eucharist doctrine of Transubstantiation and the Sacrifice of the Mass; and believed that each Christian was 'justified by faith alone', personally, quite apart from the authority of the Church and its sacramental system. Foundation of the LUTHERAN CHURCH, and the launch of the Protestant Reformation.

1531   The English clergy were forced to recognise King Henry VIII as Head of the Church in England. Henry had wished the Pope to annul his marriage with Catherine of Aragon, to set him free to marry his new love, Anne Boleyn. But the Pope refused, and in 1534 the English Parliament passed the series of Acts severing links with Rome. The Church now broken away from Rome became known as THE CHURCH OF ENGLAND, or THE ANGLICAN CHURCH.

1533   JOHN CALVIN, a French lawyer, breaks with the Catholic Church after a religious experience in which he believed that he had received a mission to restore the Church to its original purity. In 1536, he accepted an invitation to go to Geneva to establish a Christian state based upon the Bible. Calvin had a strong doctrine of predestination, believing that God predestined some souls to go to heaven, others to hell. THE PRESBYTERIAN, CONGREGATIONALIST (now combined into THE UNITED REFORMED CHURCH), and the DUTCH REFORMED CHURCH take their inspiration from Calvin's concept of Reformed Christianity.

1612   The first BAPTIST church was founded in London under the leadership of Thomas Helwys, soon spreading rapidly in the new American colonies. Baptists believed that only 'born again' or committed Christians could be baptised; hence infant baptism was invalid, since the infant could not make a conscious act of commitment to Christ.

1738   JOHN WESLEY, an Anglican clergyman, experiences conversion, and becomes a phenomenally successful outdoor preacher, especially to the new poor of the industrial revolution. Wesley founded a group of like-minded lay preachers; but ran into trouble with the Church of England when he ordained a Bishop without official authority in the USA. The group of Christians following Wesley were called 'METHODISTS', a nickname given to his followers while Wesley was at Oxford.

1870   The First Vatican Council defines the infallibility and universal jurisdiction of the Pope (see Ch. 23). A group of Catholics break away from Rome, being unable to accept this doctrine. They joined the Church of Utrecht (divided from Rome in 1774) and small groups of Slavic origin, to form the OLD CATHOLIC CHURCH.

1900   A group of American Protestant Christians believe that they can receive the same gifts of the Holy Spirit as the first Christians received, particularly healing gifts and speaking with tongues (see *Acts 2:1–4*). First the American

'Holiness Churches', and later the Assemblies of God and denominations such as the International Church of the Foursquare Gospel are founded, and are called PENTECOSTALS.

1948   The mainline Protestant denominations form the 'WORLD COUNCIL OF CHURCHES', to work internationally for unity among all those Churches 'which accept our Lord Jesus Christ as God and Saviour'. Most of the Eastern Orthodox Churches are now full members, and the Catholic Church, while not being a full member, has permanently established liaison with the WCC.

1962   Pope John XXIII summons THE SECOND VATICAN COUNCIL, which has as one of its chief aims to re-establish that unity lost in various ways down the Christian centuries. While not compromising the truth as the Church sees it, the Council admitted that the Catholic Church must take its share of the blame for disunity.

PRAYER

Even as recently as the 1950s Catholics were not allowed to join publicly with others in saying the 'Our Father'. We have moved a long way. Now the Church is actively engaged in dialogue with other Christian denominations – and this involves much prayer.

Prayer is not just individuals speaking to God. The whole body of the Church in this world prays and praises, petitions and adores – individually and together.

Prayer is the most powerful tool with which to effect what Christ himself prayed for. Let us pray with his words:

PRAYER

Holy Father, keep them in your name, those you have given to me, that they be one as we are. Sanctify them in truth; your word is truth. As you sent me into the world, so I have sent them into the world (John 17:11 and 17–18).

LIGHT FROM THE COUNCIL

'The restoration of unity among all Christians is one of the principal concerns of the Second Vatican Council. Christ the Lord founded one Church and one Church only. However, many Christian communions present themselves as the true inheritors of Jesus Christ; all indeed profess to be followers of the Lord but they differ in mind and go their different ways, as if Christ himself were divided. Certainly, such division openly contradicts the will of Christ, scandalises the world, and damages that most holy cause, the preaching of the Gospel to every creature.

'The Lord of Ages nevertheless wisely and patiently follows out the plan of his grace on our behalf, sinners that we are. In recent times he has begun to bestow more generously upon divided Christians remorse over their divisions and longing for unity.

'Everywhere large numbers have felt the impulse of this grace, and among our separated brothers and sisters also there increases from day to day a movement, fostered by the grace of the Holy Spirit, for the restoration of unity among all Christians. Taking part in this movement, which is called ecumenical, are those who invoke the Triune God and confess Jesus as Lord and Saviour. They do this not merely as individuals, but also as members of the corporate groups in which they have heard the Gospel, and which each regards as his or her Church, and indeed, God's. And yet almost everyone, though in different ways, longs for the one visible Church of God, a Church truly universal and sent forth to the whole world that the world may be converted to the Gospel and so be saved.

'*The Sacred Council gladly notes all this.*'

QUESTIONS

1. What projects could the Churches in your area work on together to show Christian concern for the world?
2. What is your vision for ecumenism?

Jewish tradition has meticulously handed down the scriptures and the writings of the Rabbis through the centuries.

38-Dialogue with Judaism

**The Jews share a common ancestry with Christians.
Christ was Son of David as well as Son of God.
Anti-Semitism is strongly condemned by the Church.
Present-day Jews are not guilty of the death of Christ.**

'IS BEING a Jew a matter of race or of religion?'

The early Christians would most certainly have called themselves Jews, and never intended to be anything else. Racially, they were Jews. But much more, they shared the faith of Moses and went daily to the Temple to pray (*Acts 2:46*). They aimed to convert the whole of Israel to the idea that Jesus of Nazareth, the Son of David, King of Judah, was also the Son of God risen from the dead.

They also intended the 'Gentiles', non-Jews, to become Christians. But in their view, these newly converted Christians would then become Jews,

members of the covenant people of God, now assembled in the name of the Messiah, Jesus Christ.

It all went wrong. After the destruction of the Temple in AD 70, Christians and Jews had no common place of worship. Christians were excluded from the synagogues.

Within a very short time 'Jew' and 'Christian' became two alien groups at loggerheads with each other. This was the very first schism in the history of the Church.

As Pius XI put it in an encyclical 'We are all spiritually Semites'. This being the case, the more we talk to each other, the better.

ROOTS OF JUDAISM

When we speak about the 'Jewish background of Jesus' (not only Jesus, but his disciples and those amongst whom he worked were Jews) we have to remember that Jesus appeared about half way through the development of Judaism, that is, about half way between the call of Abraham and the present day.

STILL GROWING

So the Taanakh (this is the correct Hebrew term – Christians say 'Old Testament', but Jews prefer to say 'the Hebrew Scriptures') contains roots of Judaism, but only roots, and only some of the roots. Just as Catholics read Scripture through the eyes of the Church, Jews read it through the eyes of their own traditions, of which the main collection is the Talmud (completed in the 5th century), but which are still alive and growing, reflected in the writings of the leading rabbis of each generation.

Reading the Hebrew Scriptures alone gives only a distortion of Judaism. For instance, life after death is not clearly indicated in the Hebrew Scriptures; nevertheless, it has been a fundamental belief of many Jews for two thousand years. Then, the Hebrew Scriptures say 'an eye for an eye'; yet Jewish tradition has never understood this literally, but always taken it to mean that one who injures another person may pay compensation equal in value (not in kind) to the damage caused.

Misconceptions about Judaism arise not only from the Hebrew Scriptures but perhaps even more from uneducated reading of the New Testament, which was produced after the time of Jesus when early Christians were trying to distance themselves from Judaism. Jews are rightly indignant at hearing their religion contrasted with Christianity as a 'religion of law' rather than a 'religion of love'. Jesus' stress on the commandment in Leviticus 19:18 'You

The reading of scripture is a sacred task.

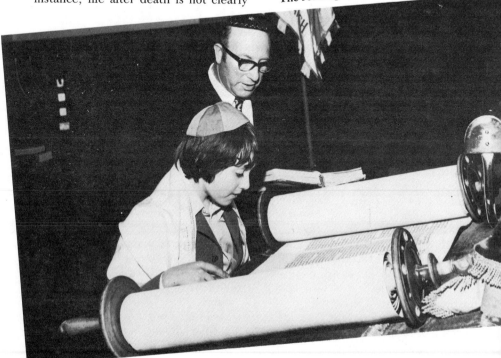

shall love your neighbour as yourself' is paralleled by sayings attributed to many rabbis, including his older contemporary, Hillel.

Rabbinic Judaism carries no 'burden of the law', nor even a guilt-burden of 'Original Sin', but serves God with love and joy, in gratitude for His commandments. Indeed, one of the results of modern scholarship on the opening centuries of the Christian era is to show how similar the concerns and attitudes of Jews and Christians were in this period. This was in spite of the major difference that Christians found the story and doings of Jesus important and Jews did not.

What roots did Judaism put down after the Hebrew Scriptures? Most important, because it constituted the common bond of worship and taught ordinary people about God and His Torah, was the liturgy, the thrice daily prayer and the regular readings of Torah defined and regulated under Gamaliel II in second-century Palestine. Prominent amongst the ideas it enshrines are the sovereignty of God over all mankind, God's grace in granting the Jews His Torah the election of Israel, and the coming of Redemption which will establish God's kingdom on earth and bring universal peace. Great stress is laid on the praise of God and on gratitude to Him for His loving compassion.

The rabbis saw the 'laws' of Torah as the application of its values in everyday life. The Mishnah forms the centrepiece of the two Talmuds, the Babylonian and the 'Palestinian' or Jerusalem Talmud. It was compiled under the saintly Rabbi Judah in Galilee at the beginning of the third century, and sets the framework of Jewish 'law' for all major aspects of life, from prayer to festival, to marriage and divorce, to civil law and even Temple matters; for Judaism knows no division between sacred and secular realms, between what is God's and what is Caesar's, but regards all life as one, to be lived under God's rule in accordance with Torah.

CREATIVITY

Jewish spiritual creativity continued unabated in the Middle Ages, despite constant persecution, oppression and minority status. There were innumerable saints and martyrs, great Bible commentators – Rashi, philosophers – Moses Maimonides, mystics – Moses de Leon of the Zohar and poets – Judah Halevi, as well as interpreters of the law.

The present century has seen a new flowering of the Jewish religious genius in response to new challenges, new sorrows (the Holocaust) and new joys (Israel). More than anything else, the isolation imposed upon Jews since Christians came into power in the days of Constantine (AD 313) has largely ended, at least in western countries.

The Catholic Church, since Vatican II in 1962, has helped this process by encouraging a new attitude towards Jews and Judaism. But there will only be openness and true dialogue when both Catholics and Jews learn to look each at the other in the other's own terms, not seeing them in the terms of an image plucked from ancient Scripture. Too often in the past we have 'borne false witness' against each other.

The last Ecumenical Council before Vatican II to discuss the Jews was held in Basle in 1434. It decreed that Jews were to be excluded from public office, banned from taking university degrees, obliged to wear a distinctive garb, to live in a special quarter, to listen to Christian sermons but to have no concourse with Christians.

Vatican II emphasised the spiritual bonds linking the Church to Judaism, confirmed the permanence of God's covenant with Israel and the spiritual values of post-biblical Judaism. It called for mutual esteem and respect and scholarly studies. It condemned earlier anti-Semitism and urged Christians to get to know Judaism as Jews themselves explain it.

It took the shock of the extermination of six million Jews in Nazi Europe to awaken the Christian conscience and bring about this unequivocal reversal of a long anti-Jewish teaching and practice. Renewal movements within the Church also played their part. The reform of the liturgy, the return to the Bible, a new ecclesiology and the search for ecumenism focused attention on the Jewish roots of Christianity and on the Jewish People living alongside the Church in faithfulness to the Sinai Covenant.

INITIATIVES

Documents have to be implemented at every level of Church life if they are to change attitudes, lead to repentance and evoke a new spiritual vitality.

Christians and Jews have been meeting regularly in groups during the past twenty years. There is, for example, a Vatican–Jewish Liaison Committee which brings together Jewish and Christian scholars and pastors to explore issues both theological and practical.

THE NEW TESTAMENT AND THE JEWS

An examination of some Christian textbooks revealed a false image of Jews and Judaism, but some new material has made progress in understanding Jesus, in his Jewish background. The parallels between the Gospel and the Jewish tradition have become clearer and the historical situation which gave rise to the conflict between the emerging Church and the Synagogue is seen as the cause of the anti-Jewish passages in the New Testament. As Jews saw this renewal in the Church they too have begun to take a new look at Jesus of Nazareth. Interesting Jewish studies about Jesus in his first century environment have emerged.

The implications of the holocaust for Christian life and theology have only just begun to be seriously explored and there is still too little awareness of the consequences of this traumatic event on the Jewish community.

The Passover, recalling the miraculous escape from Egypt, is perhaps the most important event in the Jewish calendar.

Diplomatic encounter. Britain's Chief Rabbi Immanuel Jakobovits meets Archbishop Barbarito, the Pope's special envoy ('Nuncio') to Britain.

LIGHT FROM THE COUNCIL

It was at the express wish of Pope John XXIII that the Council concerned itself with improving relationships between the Church and Jews. He had been deeply affected by the sufferings endured by Jews and he was also vividly aware that Christians and Jews share the same Old Testament heritage. He was reminding them of this when he greeted a delegation of American Jews in October 1960, with the words 'I am Joseph, your brother'. It was a gesture which caught the headlines, with its evocation of the Genesis story of reconciliation between brothers after a lengthy estrangement.

The document which eventually emerged is The Declaration on the Relation of the Church to Non-Christian Religions. In the sections of it which deal with the Jews it remembers, in the spirit of Pope John's encounter with the Jewish delegation, 'the spiritual ties which link Christians and Jews' and it goes on: 'The Church of Christ acknowledges that in God's plan of salvation the beginning of her faith and election is to be found in the patriarchs, Moses and the prophets. She

TO MAKE REPARATION

The Council turned its attention to the problem of anti-Semitism, of which many Christians had been guilty over the centuries. Cardinal Ritter, of St Louis, Missouri, said at the Council: '. . . we Christians have been guilty of error and injustice towards the Jews. In many ways we have assumed that God . . . had abandoned this people. Christians, and even ecclesiastical documents, have charged the Jewish people with the sufferings and death of Christ . . . We who are gathered here in this Ecumenical Council have today been given the opportunity to root out such errors and injustices and to make reparation.'

The Declaration states that, in spite of the fact that 'the Jews for the most part did not accept the Gospel' and that 'many of them opposed the spreading of it', they yet 'remain very close to God, for the sake of the patriarchs, since God does not take back the gifts he bestowed or the choice he made.' Indeed, the Church looks forward in hope to that day, 'known to God alone', when Jew and Gentile 'will call on God with one voice'.

The Declaration, further, is adamant that 'neither all Jews indiscriminately at that time, nor Jews today, can be charged with the crimes committed during his passion' and that 'the Jews should not be spoken of as rejected or accursed as if this followed from Holy Scripture'. It warns catechists and preachers to avoid teaching 'anything which is not in accord with the truth of the Gospel message of the spirit of Christ'.

While the Church 'reproves every form of persecution, against whomsoever it may be directed', she has a special word of reproof for the persecution of the Jews. Because of 'her common heritage with the Jews' and out of 'Christian charity', the Church 'deplores all hatreds, displays of anti-Semitism levelled at any time or from any source against the Jews'.

A DAUGHTER OF ISRAEL

It was a meeting of minds across four centuries which helped Edith Stein to her declaration 'This is the Truth' and to the path that led to her baptism in the Catholic Church. The woman whose autobiography she read who so impressed and moved her was St Teresa of Avila. In

professes that all Christ's faithful, who as believers are sons and daughters of Abraham, are included in the same patriarch's call and that the salvation of the Church is mysteriously prefigured in the exodus of God's chosen people from the land of bondage.

'On this account the Church cannot forget that she received the revelation of the Old Testament by way of that people with whom God in his inexpressible mercy established the ancient covenant. Nor can she forget that she draws nourishment from that good olive tree onto which the wild olive branches of the Gentiles have been grafted. The Church believes that Christ, who is our peace, has through his cross reconciled Jews and Gentiles and made them one in himself.'

The Declaration recommends that Christians engage in 'biblical and theological enquiry' and 'friendly discussions' with Jews in order to 'encourage and further mutual understanding and appreciation', a process which was given added impetus by the Guidelines which were issued nine years later.

1933, eleven years after her 'conversion' Edith entered the Carmel of Cologne where at her profession she took the name Teresa Benedicta of the Cross.

Born of a Jewish family in Germany in 1891, Edith was a self-confessed atheist until the age of 21. A brilliant student, she became a doctor of philosophy in 1916. In Carmel she continued her study and writing. In January 1939 Sr Teresa Benedicta was sent to the Carmel of Echt in Holland. It was a recognition of the danger of being a Jew in Germany. But the Nazi tide of hatred for the Jews swept also into the occupied countries. On 2nd August Edith Stein and her sister Rosa were arrested and taken away. Deported to Auschwitz they were among the four million victims of the death camp.

On 1st May 1987 in Cologne Cathedral Pope John Paul II beatified Sr Teresa Benedicta. 'She died in the camp as a daughter of Israel', the Pope said. And he quoted her last known words to her sister as they boarded the cattle trucks 'Come, let us go for the sake of our people'.

'HIS BLOOD BE ON US AND ON OUR CHILDREN!'

Perhaps no verse in the whole of the New Testament has been the excuse for so much anti-Semitism as this text from the Passion Narrative of Matthew (27:25). The scene is the trial of Jesus before Pilate. After trying vainly to release Jesus, and to substitute the villain Barabbas for him, Pilate washes his hands and says to the Jews, 'I am innocent of this man's blood. It is your concern' (27:24).

It is then that the Jews reply, 'his blood be on us and on our children'. This phrase is clear in its Hebrew meaning. The Jews are saying that they are guilty of the death of Jesus, and that this guilt will pass on to their children. This text, sadly, has been used too frequently to impute to the Jewish race the charge of being murderers of God's Son.

However, we must remember the context in which it was written. Matthew's Gospel was written for Jewish Christians, towards the close of the first century AD. It is therefore Jews writing about fellow-Jews. It is a dispute within the family, rather like the Catholic/ Protestant debate between Christians. It is not anti-Semitic.

Fresh in the memory of the author was the Fall of Jerusalem in AD 70. After a desperate Jewish revolt against the hated Roman authority, the Roman legions entered Jerusalem, desecrated the Temple, and carried the rebellious Jews to Rome for the gladiatorial games, bearing aloft in procession the seven-branch candlestick looted from the Temple.

To the Jewish Christian community, all this seemed to be a clear punishment of God's people for rejecting the Son of God and putting him to death. As so often with the prophets, 'the people' had sinned, and God's judgement had come, as with the Fall of Samaria in 721 BC (2 Kings 17:7).

But Matthew's Gospel, in line with the Jewish tradition, does not intend these words to be taken to mean that the Jews have been punished for all eternity, as is sometimes interpreted by Christians. It was to put this record straight that the Second Vatican Council made one of its most famous statements, sounding the doctrinal death-knell of anti-Semitism:

'Even though the Jewish authorities and those who followed their lead pressed for the death of Christ (John 19:6), neither all Jews indiscriminately at that time, nor Jews today, can be charged with the crimes committed during his passion' (Declaration on the Relation of the Church to Non-Christian religions, para 4).

QUESTIONS
1. How can the realisation that Jesus lived and died a Jew enrich our Christian faith?
2. What traces of anti-Semitism, if any, do you find still in the Church and society today?

The Pope prays with leaders of other faiths for peace and unity at Assisi.

39-Other Faiths

The Church proclaims Christ as Son of God.
But rejects nothing good in all faiths.
God speaks to all people who seek him in sincerity.
Our task as Christians is to try to overcome conflict.

BELIEVERS OF THE WORLD, UNITE

In our age there is a worldwide yearning for a drawing together of the different religions of mankind. Believers of many nations and cultures are seeking to put aside the religious antagonisms of the past, and to come together in mutual respect, understanding and spiritual fellowship. They want to work together for the good of the human race and of the endangered planet that is home for all of us.

In our encounter with non-Christian religions and believers, as in all things, the first law is love. Vatican II recalls:

'We cannot call on God as the Father of all, if we refuse to behave as brothers and sisters to other human beings who are created in the image of God'.

Inter-faith dialogue can have as its object not only mutual respect and practical collaboration for humanitarian ends, but also deeper searching and understanding at the religious and moral level. We all share the basic quest and questioning of the human spirit.

'Human beings look to the various religions for answers to those profoundly enigmatic questions concerning the condition of humankind, which today as at all times move the depths of the human heart. What is man? What is the meaning and purpose of our life? What is goodness and what is sin? Whence does sorrow take its rise, and whither is it leading? What is the path for attaining true happiness? What is the truth about death, and about judgement and retribution after death?' (Vatican II, Nostra Aetate 4).

In inter-religious encounter the participants seek not to attack the beliefs of others, but to be mutually enriched.

'The Catholic Church rejects nothing in those religions which is true and holy. With sincere respect she takes account of those ways of acting and living, those commandments and teachings which, though they differ in many respects from what she herself holds and teaches, nevertheless often reflect a ray of that Truth which enlightens all human beings' (Vatican II, Nostra Aetate 2).

ASSISI, AN INTER-FAITH MILESTONE

When Pope John Paul II asked religious leaders from around the world to join him at Assisi on 27th October 1987 to pray for peace, he invited not only Christians of many Churches but also representatives of the non-Christian religions. At that historic meeting the different faiths prayed in the same place – not in a common prayer but in their different ways – for world peace and for human welfare.

Assisi was a milestone in the pilgrimage of believing mankind. In the city of St Francis the voices of the world were raised in prayer to God and in aspiration towards the Holy: the voices of Baha'is, Buddhists, Christians, Hindus, Jains, Jews, Muslims, Sikhs, Zoroastrians, and of the traditional religions in Africa and America.

BEDROCK

This new spirit of inter-religious charity and fraternal outreach to non-Christians has not changed, and cannot change, the bedrock of our Christian faith in Christ. We believe that Jesus Christ is the eternal and only-begotten Son of God, through whom all things were made; that he is the one incarnation of God in human history; that he is the definitive messenger of divine revelation; that he is the only Saviour of the world, and the one mediator between God and men.

From his Spirit and through his Mystical Body, the Church, all grace and salvation and all spiritual and temporal blessings flow to humankind. He has given his commission to his followers to spread his Gospel and his salvation to all nations.

And yet . . . Only a minority of the human race are baptised members of the visible Church, or personally profess faith in Christ. What about the other truth of Scripture, 'God wants everyone to be saved and to reach full knowledge of the truth' (1 Tim 2:4)? For the great non-Christian majority of our

human family, what is the path of attaining the salvation brought by Christ, who gave himself as a ransom for all, and who enlightens everyone that comes into this world?

DIM HORIZONS OF THEOLOGY

Little wonder that theology can only glimpse an answer to that question, as in a mirror dimly. The mysterious secret of God's compassion and love for all his children is veiled. Every individual, everywhere, is linked to God's salvific will; it is Catholic teaching that no-one is debarred from the offer of grace and salvation.

Developing the Church's understanding of redemption through Christ, theologians have acknowledged that the grace-encounter leading to salvation comes also to non-Christians – not independently of Christ, but through him. Thus they have, as it were, a private link to Christ's grace, they may be considered to be 'anonymous Christians'. While for Christians the 'ordinary means' of salvation are available, for non-Christians 'extraordinary means' are possible. In this view, non-Christian religions can be seen, at best, as a preparation for the Gospel.

Will Christian theology widen its horizons still further, and come to acknowledge that non-Christians who embrace God's will are saved not merely by exceptional means, in isolation from their own religious culture and devotion? May these religions have, in God's providential design, a corporate function; to provide for their followers the place of encounter with divine grace and salvation?

NOTES ON OTHER FAITHS
Islam

- from 'Sa-la-ma', to be at peace, to surrender oneself to God.
- Islam is seen as the culmination of monotheistic revelation and submission to God. Allah is the One and Only True God, the Eternal, Infinite.
- Revelation is contained in the Qur'an. It is claimed to have come from Muhammad (570–632), the Prophet, through the angel Gabriel. Muhammad was only a messenger. The message is that humankind is created to worship God and to observe His Law. Man is born free from sin and is not responsible for the sins of others. God is merciful; is near to His people. No one can intercede between God and humankind.
- Jesus is a Prophet, but not Redeemer, and not God. Muslims believe in the Virgin Birth, but the Crucifixion is denied. The Ascension is accepted; according to some, Jesus will come back at the end of the world as another intercessor, with Muhammad.
- Both faith and action are essential to salvation. Muslims believe in judgement, with heaven and hell, and in angels.

- The five major practices (pillars) are:
1. Frequent profession of faith. There is no god but God; Muhammad is the apostle of God.
2. Prayer five times a day.
3. Almsgiving.
4. Fasting, very strict during Ramadan – a month-long time of purification.
5. If possible, pilgrimage to Mecca once in a lifetime.
- The Muslim population in the UK is about 1,500,000 with more than 500 mosques.

Hinduism

- the religion of the vast majority of the people of India.
- its roots go back more than 5,000 years.
- some characteristics: no founder, no creed, no church or hierarchy, but there is a priesthood and varied and complex rituals; a huge amount of sacred writings, diversely regarded by individual Hindus; no compulsory congregational worship; however, singing of hymns at devotional gatherings.
- some ideas and concepts usually associated with Hinduism are: Karma (Fate), and rebirth, gods as well as nature are manifestations, but temporary, of the Ultimate Reality; the importance of the Guru; family rituals; pilgrimages; the sacredness of the cow; sacredness of all life. There are 500,000 Hindus in Britain.

Buddhism

- its founder, Siddharta Gautama, lived in North-east India, between 560 and 480 BC.
- Buddhism does not recognise an absolute personal deity, but does not deny Ultimate Reality.
- all existences have three characteristics:
1. **Impermanence**: everything is

subjected to the law of cause and effect.

2. **Non-ego**: Buddhism did not deny the existence of ego or soul, but there is no permanent ego (self).

3. **Suffering**: disharmony with environment.

● Buddha set forth four basic truths:

1. no existence without suffering

2. suffering is caused by egotistic desire

3. if desire is eliminated, suffering ceases

4. there is a way: the Noble eight-fold path of right – view, mental attitude, speech, action, means of livelihood, effort, mindfulness, contemplation.

● the supreme goal of Buddhist endeavour is Nirvana, the release from the limitations of existence.

● Buddhists undertake to observe five moral rules: to avoid – taking life, stealing, indulgence in sensuality, lying, intoxication.

● Buddha founded a monastic Order (the Sangha) still thriving today.

● Worship is basically individual: gifts and services to Buddha, the Dharma (teaching) and the Sangha (monks); chants, meditation. There is no priesthood.

Sikhism

● originated in the Punjab, NW India, in the 15th century as a devotional movement led by Guru Nanak (1469–1539).

● **Sikhs believe:**
in one God
that God has spoken to us through prophets (gurus).
in judgement but this is a continuous process.
The future of the soul depends on the actions performed in this world. At death, the soul may be reborn, or it may remain in the presence of God.

● **Sikhs strongly uphold:**
the brotherhood of humankind; they must show kindness to all

Sacred centre of the Sikh religion, the Golden Temple at Amritsa, India.

human beings, particularly the poor.
the dignity of work; honesty and diligence.

- **Sikhs are required:**
  to pray daily, morning and evening; if possible in a temple.
  to wear long hair (covered by a turban); a comb, short trousers (sign of modesty); a sword and a steel bracelet.
- One becomes a Sikh by initiation. Special ceremonies, always involving the use of the Sacred Book, the Adi Granth, take place at birth, for a wedding, at death.
- The most famous place of worship is the Golden Temple at Amritsar,

The Blue Mosque in Istanbul, Turkey. Moslems modelled their places of worship on the Christian churches of the period.

in the Punjab. Local temples are called Gurdwaras.
- In the UK there are close to 400,000 Sikhs and more than 100 Gurdwaras.

HOW IT HAPPENED TO ME

I was going to evening Mass. My neighbour, Mrs Bhogal was going to the Gurdwara (Sikh Temple). She said, 'Come with me to the Temple.' I excused myself, she turned left, I turned right. And whilst Mrs Bhogal was bowing to the Holy Book of the Sikhs, making her offering, receiving in her palm the prasad, holy bread, and sitting cross legged in meditation as hymns were sung, I attended the Holy Sacrifice instituted by Jesus who shed his blood for all. And God, who has no favourites, was present in the Temple and in the Church, listening to both of us, loving each one of us.

VOICE OF THE PEOPLE

It was in 1982 that Bishop Mahon, Bishop in West London, asked me to work full time as an Interfaith worker in Southall. When I asked him to define my brief more clearly, he said, 'It takes time to share a cup of tea with somebody'.

Of course I knew a lot – or thought I did – about Interfaith Dialogue. I had spent 15 years in 'mission' in Bangkok schools. As 'O' Level RE examiner, I had marked on aspects of five world religions. I was unaware that the Bishop, and through him the Church, had launched me on a journey of faith.

Pope John Paul II said 'All Christians must be committed to dialogue with the believers of other religions, so that mutual understanding and collaboration may grow, so that moral values may be strengthened, so that God may be praised in all creation. Ways must be developed to make this dialogue a reality everywhere.'

I set about reading the Gospel in a new light. It is impossible to approach the faith of others sincerely without questioning and deepening your own faith.

SCRIPTURE AND OTHER FAITHS

The Scriptures condemn idolatry, the making of an image and worshipping that image as God. The prophets reject 'false gods' made by men's hands. But, on the other hand, the Scriptures recognise that the true God Yahweh reveals himself to people other than the descendants of Abraham. Beneath and through even idolatrous and false elements God was making himself known.

In the New Testament, St Paul recognises the presence of God among those who are not people of the covenant. 'For instance', he says to the Romans (2:14) 'pagans who never heard of the Law but are led by reason to do what the Law commands, may not actually "possess" the law, but they can be said to "be" the Law. They can point to the substance of the Law engraved on their hearts . . .'

And their worship can be in the right direction too. In Athens, Paul paid a visit to the debating place, the Areopagus, and said to the Athenians 'I noticed, as I strolled round admiring your sacred monuments, that you had an altar inscribed: To An Unknown God. Well, the God whom I proclaim is in fact the one whom you already worship without knowing it' (Acts 17:23).

LIGHT FROM THE COUNCIL

'The Church, therefore, urges her sons to enter with prudence and charity into discussion and collaboration with members of other religions. Let Christians, while witnessing to their own faith and way of life, acknowledge, preserve and encourage the spiritual and moral truths found among non-Christians, also their social life and culture'.

Catholics have been restricted in praying with other denominations and faiths. Since Vatican II much of this has changed, but there is still hesitation and doubt about prayer with non-Christians.

Ways of prayer in these faiths vary and so does acceptance of Jesus Christ. But Christian and other faith members can come together in meditation and contemplation of the One.

The value of knowledge and adaptation of ways of prayer can be seen in the development in the West by the Benedictine Monk John Main. He learnt meditation in Asia from a non-Christian guru and translated this into Christian meditation.

PRAYER

O Lord! Throw me not on myself: of my will I cannot speak nor observe silence.
Throw me not on my own strength; of myself I cannot pray nor give myself to thee!
Nor can I follow life nor even death!
Nor by my own power can I a beggar be or a king!
Throw me not on myself, for by myself I cannot gain my soul nor the knowledge of thyself.
Throw me not on myself, for I am unable to cross the sea of change . . .
I cannot, O Lord!

Guru Nanak

QUESTIONS

1. Why should the believers of the world unite?
2. How do you think Christians can prepare for and participate in inter-faith encounters?

40-Fighting for Justice

The Church does all possible to promote human rights.
Self-defence is justified.
Liberation is not just spiritual.
But the goal of the Kingdom is beyond this world.

JESUS CHRIST said that there would always be 'wars and rumours of wars' (*Matt 24:6*). In the two thousand years from his day to ours, this prediction has been amply fulfilled. In the twentieth century, war has become even more horrific. With new weapons, using ever more effective technology, we have instruments of death which could destroy our planet.

People who declare war will always justify their conduct. They are not monsters of destruction, they will claim. Rather, they are exercising their rights. For instance, they will claim, if they do not fight, they will be occupied by an enemy, and lose their freedom. They would rather die free, than live oppressed.

This problem is not new to Christianity, even if the problem is so much greater today. The question as to whether I should defend myself comes to all of us, in various situations; physical assault, verbal abuse, home, work, school. Should I take it, or hit back?

In St John's account of Christ's ordeal before the high priest at his trial, Our Lord is questioned about His teaching. One of the guards slapped His face because he thought that Jesus was being insolent. Jesus says immediately, 'If there is some offence in what I said, point it out; but if not, why do you strike me?'

He was acting in self-defence by pointing to the wrong that was being done to Him. Yet, elsewhere in the same story, He chooses to remain silent. This is evidence that self-defence is complicated.

The Sermon on the Mount, especially 'Blessed are you when people abuse you'; or 'But I say this to you: offer no resistance to evil' (*Matt 5:11,39*), could give the impression that Christians should just let the strong have their way. But this could be no more than cowardice. The whole question is subtle.

The following principles on self-defence seem to be implicit in the teaching of the New Testament and the great Christian writers:

a) if nothing else but individual interests are at stake and the Christian has done nothing wrong, there may well be times when all must be ready to follow Christ as St Peter wrote 'Christ left us an example . . . He did nothing' (*1 Pet 2:21*). And He was rewarded with crucifixion.

b) I may be required to defend my own life because God has given it to me as a gift. It might also happen that my good name is tied up with the reputation of Christianity itself. I would then have the responsibility of defending myself. St Thomas More, for example, used his razor-sharp mind on English Law to defend himself and the Church against an overbearing King (Henry VIII).

c) When the innocent and helpless are involved, the strong Christian has a duty to defend them. Physical force may be needed but it must never be excessive – a principle also recognised by English Law.

d) Civil authority must be able to use enough force to restrain those who disrupt society. This right is recognised by Ss Peter and Paul (*1 Pet 2:13–17*).

Cloud of death, the atomic bomb, overshadows the human race.

The tomb in Highgate, London, of Karl Marx, secular prophet of our time.

IS SELF-DEFENCE JUSTIFIED FOR A NATION?

As long as Christians were a persecuted minority the question of national self-defence did not arise. Once the Roman Empire became Christian the Church had to face a new situation. Many historians claim that Christians were pacifist until they were in power. Whether or not this is true, it was later in Christianity that the principles of the just war emerged. These were:

- There must be a just cause.
- War may only be declared by competent authority.
- There must be a right intention, that is, not merely a desire to triumph.
- War must be a last resort.
- There must be a probability of success.
- No war should be begun for trivial reasons.

Once war has begun there must be non-combatant immunity. There must not be use of terror by indiscriminate killing of civilians e.g. during bombing.

The prohibition on indiscriminate killing makes it clear that any weapon which can destroy a city cannot be morally used. However, there are smaller, more sophisticated weapons now available which some claim are legitimate because they can be aimed solely at military targets, and have a limited effect. But others maintain this is illusory because the most serious effect is radioactive fall-out which cannot be contained.

Some moralists maintain that the threat to use nuclear weapons is itself immoral. There are others who argue that nuclear deterrence has given peace in Europe for over forty years. And the arguments continue. In June 1982 Pope John Paul II told the United Nations 'In current conditions "deterrence" based on balance, certainly not as an end in itself, but as a stage on the way towards a progressive disarmament, can still be judged morally acceptable'. The only final answer to those complex and worrying questions must be the growth of trust between the nations who recognise everyone as God's children.

THE CLASS WAR

In the nineteenth and twentieth centuries, with the growth of an industrial economy, many people have felt exploited by the system. Karl Marx predicted a 'class war', in which the forces of the 'proletariat' (the working classes), would finally overthrow their oppressors, the factory bosses. Today, half the world is ruled by governments who claim to follow Karl Marx's philosophy. What is the Christian response to this?

CAN CHRISTIANS BE MARXISTS?

'Marxist' has become a smear-word, often used to discredit any and everyone passionately concerned about social justice. This is especially true in areas like Latin America. And sometimes the critics' motives have little to do with Christianity but a great deal to do with defending their own wealth, privileges and power.

Marx's starting point was the wretched state of the industrial working classes in 19th-century Britain. He traced this to the evils of unbridled capitalism. According to him the capitalist system led to a smaller and smaller number of people who owned the means of production growing richer, while the large numbers of workers grew poorer. This was because workers were not paid the full worth of what they produced. The owners took part of the price, often a very large part.

This led to a society of exploiters and exploited in which both sides were unhappy human beings. The exploiters because they were getting rewards to which they knew they were not entitled and came to judge their own personal value by what they owned; the exploited because they were not getting the proper reward to which they were due and despised themselves for being totally dependent on their employers. The solution, he thought, lay in abolishing all private property.

Many people, including Christians, have found this description and explanation convincing and think there are still parts of the world where it remains true. Others think it contains some truth, but that Marx underestimated the chances of cleaning up the worst features of the system, failed to recognise that it could have benefits and advantages for everyone, and was quite wrong to think that abolishing private property was the only answer. Either way it is a matter of practical judgement. Christians can believe Marx was right or wrong without betraying their faith.

The same cannot be said about Marx's general vision of mankind's history and purpose on earth. There, any Christian is bound to part company with him. That is so even though Karl Marx was born a Jew and baptised a Christian, and his theories echo ideas from both religions.

In fact he has his own version of salvation. The evils of capitalism take the place of Original Sin; liberation comes through a chosen people – the proletariat (wage-earners), after a battle between good and evil – the class struggle – the classless society will emerge, a sort of 'kingdom' of peace and justice where everyone will enjoy their full human dignity. But there the resemblance ends.

Marx has no place for God or the soul or the after-life, and he regards all religion as an illusion which stops us facing up to reality.

Marx Holds . . .

- that mankind's nature, behaviour and purpose are dictated by blind impersonal forces, and that nothing exists outside this visible, material world.
- that all our religious, philosophical and moral ideas spring from the way society is organised. Change 'the structures of society' and our ideas change too.
- that our personality is entirely shaped by our relationships with others and what they expect of us.
- that we can only achieve full human

dignity in a lasting state of peace and justice when the oppressed have overthrown their oppressors by hatred and violence.

● Marx's ideas tend to regard the individual person as expendable and to increase the oppression and worthlessness which he wished to fight.

Christianity Believes . . .

● that human beings come from a loving personal God, are put on earth to know him, love him and serve him in freedom in this life and to be happy with him in the next.

● that our social conditions affect us, but not totally. We have a natural ability to recognise truth and to tell right from wrong in the most important matters, and the word of God teaches us still more. We can know truth and good despite the worst possible social conditions and despite the prevailing opinions of others.

● that these things affect us, but that we each have an inner core of unique, personal identity, our spirit or soul, made in the image of God, which in the last resort and with God's grace, decides our character,

our behaviour and our aims in life.

● that we already possess a unique, priceless personal dignity; that Christ's kingdom of justice and peace only comes through learning to love each other, even our persecutors, and that it reaches fulfilment only in heaven.

● Christianity insists that every human being has a dignity and inborn human rights which set limits to any social programme, however well-intentioned.

Christians and Marxists share some things in common: resistance to oppression, a passion for peace, justice and full human dignity for all. Sometimes, in particular circumstances, they may even join forces. But at bottom their beliefs are worlds apart.

NB. It is important to emphasise that the Catholic Church condemns extreme forms of capitalism just as much as extreme Marxism. While defending the right to private property, the Church does not give 'carte blanche' to every form of wealth creation; particularly when this relies solely on the 'free market' without reference to social consequences.

LIGHT FROM THE COUNCIL

'In the midst of huge numbers deprived of the absolute necessities of life there are others who live in riches and squander their wealth; and this happens in less developed areas as well. Luxury and misery exist side by side. While a few individuals enjoy an almost unlimited opportunity to choose for themselves, the vast majority have no chance whatever of exercising personal initiative and responsibility, and quite often have to live in conditions unworthy of human beings.'

PLACE FOR PRAYER

Father, you have given all peoples one common origin and your will is to gather them as one family in yourself. Fill the hearts of all people with the fire of your love and the desire to ensure justice for their brothers and sisters. By sharing the good things you give us may we secure justice and equality for every human being, an end to all division, and a human society built on love and peace!'

QUESTIONS

1. Should the Church be involved in politics? Argue the case for and against.
2. How do you think the Church can show 'a preferential option for the

poor?' You might like to deal with this
   a) Internationally/nationally
   b) In your parish/community
   c) As a family/individual.

TURN THE OTHER CHEEK?

One of the most challenging sayings of Christ is recorded in Matthew 5:38,39. 'You have learnt how it was said: Eye for eye and tooth for tooth. But I say this to you: offer the wicked man no resistance. On the contrary, if anyone hits you on the right cheek, offer him the other as well . . .' is Jesus saying that it is forbidden to defend our rights? Clearly, he did not mean literally that we should 'turn the other cheek'; since he himself at his trial, being struck by one of the high priest's guards, answered him back '. . . Why did you strike me?' (*John* 18:23).

'Turn the other cheek' is an exhortation rather than a hard-and-fast law. The old law 'an eye for an eye and a tooth for a tooth' was intended as a limit on seeking revenge. Jesus goes further than equal vengeance. The Christian should work for reconciliation, even at the cost of his own pride.

Archbishop Desmond Tutu. Fighter for brotherhood and against apartheid, the system of compulsory separation of races in South Africa.

41-Work and Leisure
Work is sharing in God's Creative Plan.
Recreation is sharing in God's Sabbath joy.
Unemployment is a curse, but so is greed.

Work for many is a daily drudgery.

THERE ARE two heresies about work. The first is to imagine that our value as human beings is to be assessed in terms of our productivity. We admire 'workaholics', people who constantly produce.

The second heresy is to imagine that work is related almost exclusively to economics: its value is to be assessed in terms of financial profit, to ourselves or to others.

For the Christian, work (paid or unpaid) is sharing in the creative activity of God, building his Kingdom. In this sense, an unemployed person will also be working.

That is why stopping work is also important. Not only do we build up our resources physically and mentally for another round. God gave us the 'sabbath', time for re-creation, to admire our handiwork, and to thank him for giving us the courage, perseverance, and creative talent to see the job through.

WORK: CURSE OR BLESSING?

Work can be a pain. Getting up early, the rush-hour journey, the monotony, and the tension of working with people who are unpleasant or unco-operative or both.

It is hardly surprising that centuries ago theologians concluded that work was God's way of punishing mankind for Original Sin. They used scriptural support for their view. Genesis tells us that after the man and the woman in the garden had disobeyed him, God told man that only with suffering would he get food from the soil. 'With sweat on your brow shall you eat your bread' (*Gen 3:16–19*).

While that view of work fits some human experience, it is not always so. Many people derive pleasure from their work, the companionship that often goes with it, and the knowledge that what they do is of benefit to others. Such people experience the blessings of work

which God originally intended (*Gen 1:28*).

What is the Christian to make of these contrasts?

THE BIBLE

The Bible presents both God and Jesus as workers. God is described as resting on the seventh day after all the work he had been doing (*Gen 2:2*). Jesus worked as a carpenter (*Mark 6:1–6*) and in his public ministry so that he could say toward the end of his earthly life 'I have glorified you on earth and finished the work you gave me to do' (*John 17:4*).

Jesus chose working men for his twelve disciples, mostly fishermen. Many of his parables about salvation and the Kingdom were built around the common working experience of his hearers.

The disciples of Jesus were fishermen.

At the Last Supper (*John 13:4–15*), Jesus gave a powerful example of the way his followers should regard their work. He washed the disciples' feet. This was a menial but necessary task, and usually reserved for the lowliest servant, yet Jesus chose it.

That incident can teach us two

lessons. About humility: no task is below our dignity if we see it in terms of Christian service. About the value of work: it does not depend on what is done, and certainly not on what is paid for it, but on the person who does it.

Jesus' example points to another feature of our work – that it is necessarily a social activity, with or for others. To work is to co-operate with others, to depend upon them and they upon us.

In his encyclical on human work, Pope John Paul II drew attention to the fact that work is the foundation of family life; the family is both a community made possible by work and a 'domestic school' in which we learn how to work (Laborem Exercens 43).

The Pope also stresses that human work is creative. We co-operate with God in the continuing act of creation, which is both the past event described in Genesis and a present process in which we are God's agents.

Vatican II in its document 'The Church in the Modern World' and Pope John Paul have linked the pains associated with work with our redemption. John Paul suggests that through the way we accept the unpleasant aspects of our work we can find a small part of the Cross of Christ.

It is important to be clear about what the Pope is not saying. We cannot earn redemption. That is a free gift from God. It is not suggested that we should simply put up with bad working conditions or unjust treatment. Wherever possible we should strive to remove the cause of the problem, especially where it arises from greed, selfishness or mismanagement.

WHAT IS THE POINT?

Christian tradition has seen work as a duty for all those capable of it for three reasons: to support ourselves and those who depend upon us; to be in a position to help others less fortunate; and to develop the talents God has given us. In the parable of the talents, Jesus described how the fearful servant, the one who simply buried the talents he received, making no effort to increase it, was banished by his master (Matt 25:14–30).

St Paul made the point forcibly in his letter to the Church at Thessalonika: 'If anyone will not work, let him not eat' (2 Thess 3:10). His criticism was directed not against those who could not work but those who refused work of which they were capable.

WORK AND EMPLOYMENT

But we should be clear that work and employment are not necessarily the same thing. Much real and valuable work is done in the home or in a voluntary capacity with no question of payment.

It is dangerous to equate the right to work with a right to employment. Only an all-powerful state could guarantee such a right, and that would mean, giving over to the state the right to direct our labour wherever the authorities thought fit, without references to our wishes or abilities. That might be acceptable in a national emergency but not otherwise in a free society.

For some their right to work must mean a right to paid work. People who have no other means of supporting themselves have a right to earn a living. In times of high and persistent unemployment throughout the industrialised world, such people should have first claim to paid work. To demand or even to accept paid work, without any real need for an income, could well be to deprive others of the means of livelihood and support for their families and dependants.

In present circumstances, with no real prospect of any return to full employment, the distinction between employment and work becomes highly important. One way of expressing Christian love is to help the unemployed preserve or recover the dignity they may feel they have lost. Although human sinfulness can still render a curse, it is in reality one of our greatest blessings, and a creative experience.

If Christians can give a lead in recognising the importance and the dignity of work done without pay or employment, we can render others a real service. That would not eradicate the problem and we must not use it as an excuse to do nothing about unemployment, but it could help people to cope with it.

PRAYER AND WORK

Once the sisters in one of St Teresa of Avila's convents were complaining that there was so much work about the house that they had no time to pray. St Teresa remarked firmly: 'God moves among the pots and pans as well.'

It seems to be difficult for people to allow prayer to be part of daily happenings. Time should certainly be set aside for God in prayer each day, but St Paul's command was 'Pray at all times'. Something beyond the special prayer time is essential.

Specifically here, we should be considering what part prayer has in two ingredients of our daily living – work and leisure.

When working, you are supposed to be working. So prayer has to be introduced and become a habit by taking it as a natural part of life. This part needs sanctification as much as any other, and needs to recognise God's presence. Each individual should find a personal way. For some work is not very mind-consuming. It may be manual or repetitive. Then some of the mind and most of the heart can be God-centred without interfering with the work. Others are deeply involved in mind-using occupations and skills – planning, figures, legal work and so on. They may have to introduce God before and after work, on the way to work, an ejaculatory prayer and so on. These can be very short, a 'glance at God' or a 'Hello'.

In leisure, equally important to a balanced life, much depends upon how time is being spent. When involved in many leisure pursuits, God can be almost tangibly present in the scenery, in painting, in music, personal contact with a friend. At other times we can be so taken up in a particular sport, family party at home or any other activity that God is forgotten. Here again, we must do what we can and remember that Jesus relaxed with his friends.

MEDITATION

'Whatever you do, in word or deed, do everything in the name of the Lord Jesus, giving thanks to God the Father through him' (*Col 3:17*).

Unemployed

It's eight o'clock and I've slept in,
I'll have to let them know.
I've got no time for breakfast, love,
I'll really have to go.

On the bus and into town
Run through the teeming rain
I got to work at nine o'clock
To get sent home again.

I'm sorry John we've got no work
We'll have to let you go.
Home again by half past ten
I've never felt so low.

I've not been on the dole before,
I don't know what to do.
It's hard to hold your head up
As you stand there in that queue.

After all the questions
They never offered work.
The safest job on Merseyside's
An unemployment clerk!
John Churchill, of Hayton, Liverpool.
(When this poem was written, John was unemployed, but has since fortunately found a job.)

Sunday Rest

A housewife used to say, as she put the clothes on the washing line on Sunday, 'Six days shalt thou labour; and on the seventh do all the odd jobs.'

She had a problem. It was fine for those who worked a five day week, and could relax on Saturday and Sunday, to keep the Sabbath. For a busy shop-keeper like herself, the only time for housework was Sunday afternoon.

So much for the commandment 'Six days you shall labour and do all your work, but the seventh day is a sabbath for Yahweh your God. You shall do no work that day . . .' (*Deut 5:13–14*). For increasing numbers of people, with both partners working full stretch to pay the mortgage, a day of rest is becoming a dead letter.

More's the pity. In the Law of Moses, three thousand years ago, the Sabbath was introduced to protect the slave and poor worker from being exploited. God commanded that, at least on one day a week, everyone, rich or poor, must rest, even the donkey; because God himself rested on the Sabbath Day.

Christians changed the Sabbath (Saturday) to the Sunday, the 'Lord's Day', because on that day Jesus rose from the dead. On the 'eighth day', a Sunday, God began the new work of our redemption. But the idea remained the same. Peasants were exempt from work (servile work) on Sunday; their landlord could not exploit them for all seven days.

Conditions have changed. For many people who work in an office or school all week, hard physical work is good exercise, and a hobby. It is not 'servile work'. For them, to sit at the desk and negotiate on the telephone would be the equivalent of servile work. It could even be that putting the washing out on the line might, for some, be relaxation.

That is why the new Code of Canon Law does not use the expression 'servile work' (see Ch. 24).

But it does make clear that there are two obligations involved. The first is to keep Sunday holy by worshipping God, celebrating the supreme act of worship, the Eucharist. The second is to keep Sunday holy by 'due relaxation of mind and body'.

Both these obligations apply to holy-days. Even a mid-week holyday of obligation, when we have to go to work, can be a good excuse for a celebration as well as going to Mass.

A useful discussion point: how can we help to make Sunday a true holyday?

Some take their leisure pursuits much more seriously than their daily work, even dreaming of making their hobby a career.

LIGHT FROM THE COUNCIL

The Constitution on the Church in the Modern World (No. 34) says: 'Man was created in God's image and was commanded to conquer the earth with all it contains and to rule the world in justice and holiness . . . When men and women provide for themselves and their families in such a way as to be of service to the community as well, they can rightly look upon their work as a prolongation of the work of the Creator, a service to their fellow men and women and their personal contribution to the fulfilment in history of the divine plan.'

QUESTIONS

1. How would you help an unemployed person?
2. In our computer-based society, where unemployment or short-time working are semi-permanent states, how can people be helped to use their enforced leisure fruitfully and pleasurably?

How are you getting on? The church has always been
involved in the education of children.

42-Education

All have a right to be educated.
Parents have the prime duty of educating their children.
Education is lifelong.
The Church has a mission to educate the whole person.

All the world's a stage,
And all the men and women merely
  players.
They have their exits and their
  entrances;
And one man in his time plays many
  parts.

So says Jaques in William Shakespeare's 'As You Like It'. Shakespeare
speaks of seven ages in the life of a
person; and, at every age, we are
learning:

The Infant . . .

The first school we attend is our home.
There are no books to read, except the
love and care written on the faces of our
parents. A child deprived of parental
love has missed the most important

stage of his or her education.

Religion is caught, not taught. It is the
prayers taught at home, the examples of
forgiveness, the taking (not the sending)
of the child to church, the faith which is
communicated in an unseen way which
is really effective.

This is not to say that, if faith is not
given by one's parents, a decision cannot be made to follow Christ in later life.
After all, as we have said, most of the
earliest Christians were adult converts.
But even when we come to believe
when we become adult, it is often because of hidden factors which lead us to
'catch' religion; and, in particular, the
influence and example of other Christians, who become in a way our 'parents'
in the spiritual life.

LIGHT FROM THE COUNCIL

One of the sixteen documents of Vatican II is the Declaration on Christian Education and it has the following to say (No. 3) on the role of parents in education:

'As it is the parents who have given life to their children, on them lies the gravest obligation of educating their family. They must therefore be recognised as being primarily and principally responsible for their education. The role of parents in education is of such importance that it is almost impossible to provide an adequate substitute. It is therefore the duty of parents to create a family atmosphere inspired by love and devotion to God and their fellow-men which will promote an integrated, personal and social education of their children.

The family is therefore the principal school of the social virtues which are necessary to every society. It is therefore above all in the Christian family, inspired by grace and the responsibility of the sacrament of matrimony, that children should be taught to know and worship God and to love their neighbour, in accordance with the faith which they have received in earliest infancy in the sacrament of Baptism.

In it, also, they will have their first experience of a well-balanced human society and of the Church. Finally, it is through the family that they are gradually initiated into association with their fellow men and women in civil life and as members of the people of God. Parents should, therefore, appreciate how important a role the truly Christian family plays in the life and progress of the whole people of God.'

The Schoolboy . . .

The memorable day of children's first Holy Communion reflects the essence of Catholic education: a sacramental celebration of the community – children, parents, teachers and priest.

Preparation for the event reflects the strong partnership between parents and teachers. They share a common tradition, values and goals. They reinforce each other in the education of the children. The Catholic primary school is often located near the Church and plays a central part in the life of the parish. The vast majority of teachers are Catholic. One teacher has the same class for the whole year and is able to exert a considerable influence. The practice of the faith is to the forefront in the life of the school and is visibly present to all visitors.

These factors have helped to contribute to the high regard given to Catholic primary education. This is so much the case that many families who are not Catholic want their children admitted to Catholic schools.

The same rosy picture is not always associated with Catholic secondary education. Force of circumstances has meant that up to half the teaching staff in a secondary school may not be Catholic, such is the difficulty in obtaining qualified subject specialists. Parents, quite rightly, expect the school to provide not only a positive religious education and ethos but a high standard of secular education. The staff may not all be Catholic, but, if selection procedures have been properly applied, the majority of teachers in the school will be positive towards developing the distinctive character of the school.

The secondary school is larger than the primary with more complex organisational structures. Parents often feel less at ease visiting the secondary school. They are often less at ease with their children as they grow through adolescence. The pliant child of the primary school is replaced by the questioning rebellious child of the secondary school. This may be reflected in the teenage reaction to the teaching of faith. The challenge for the school is to respond to the changing needs of pupils as they move towards a more mature outlook.

Not all children who are Catholics are

able to attend Catholic schools. Some countries even forbid any church-based schooling (e.g. Communist countries). Sometimes, children grow up fully committed Christians within the context of a State or Private education system, their faith being strengthened by the demands of being with pupils of other persuasions. Also, in this ecumenical age, there are also Christian schools, where children of different denominations learn together. But in general and where circumstances are right, the Catholic Church builds her own schools, where the values of the Kingdom can be taught and lived, in preparation for life in the world. In this case, the Catholic School becomes the extension of the Catholic Home.

The Lover . . . The Soldier . . . The Justice

We tend generally to think that our education ends at school, unless we are part of a privileged minority able to follow a university course, or some other institution of Higher Education. In recent years, indeed, there has been a great emphasis upon 'continuing education' through evening classes and correspondence courses, which benefit many who had no chance to go to university after leaving school.

However, we would be wrong to think that the most important influences in adult life come necessarily from the institutions of learning we might attend. It is marriage, if we choose that, our vocation, our job, and our profession, which are themselves the prime way of our being educated as adults. Just as when we were infants, our learning is a discovery of ourselves and others through human relationships; so it is when we leave school'.

The Church is involved as much as possible in all adult forms of education. There are Catholic Teacher Training Colleges, even Catholic Universities in some parts of the world. No area of life is 'no-go' for the church. The Gospel itself demands that we try to permeate every part of life with Christ.

But again, the Church shares in adult education most of all by being the Church rather than by any specific institution which might be set up. By becoming members of a parish community, by exercising the responsibilities of being a parent, by trying to bear witness to Christian values at work, in ups and downs, joys and sorrows, the Spirit of Christ is in each of us. This sharing of the daily dying and rising with Christ is itself truly 'adult education'.

The Sixth Age . . . The Last Scene

Medical science has ensured that most of us live a great deal longer than in previous centuries. In addition, lack of

Eyes shut tight now, children. It is time for prayer. Religious education is not only lessons, but spiritual formation.

employment means that people are
being encouraged to retire earlier.
Many of us, therefore, can look forward
to perhaps twenty or thirty years of
'retirement' or 'semi-retirement'.

Vital to the happiness of an old person
is not to be abandoned by younger
members of the family. 'Honour your
father and your mother' applies to
uncles and aunts as well. This last stage
is not necessarily as negative as the
melancholy Jaques in Shakespeare's 'As
You Like It' puts it. When strength
and health fail, when the pace of life
slows, the presence of God can make up
for the loss of everything else that has
made life worth living previously. The
old person is becoming prepared for the
goal of education in Christian terms, the
vision of God after death.

QUESTIONS
1. 'The chief source of education in
   wholeness is the family, where in a
   loving atmosphere children more
   easily learn real values; as they grow
   up their minds are cultivated almost
   unconsciously'. How can we foster
   family life?
2. Is better education achieved in schools
   by central control with regard to
   standards and curriculum, or is this
   more safely left to Head Teachers?
   What part do parent-Governors play in
   improving educational standards?
3. 'Christians should live in close contact
   with their contemporaries and strive to
   enter fully into their outlook and
   thought'. How far do Catholic schools
   help to aggravate differences between
   sections of people?

Rowanne Pasco, on location in Jerusalem for TVAM.

43-Mass Media

All have a right to know the truth.
The Church has a mission to proclaim the Good News through the media.

IT HAS been estimated that if the last 50,000 years of mankind's existence were divided into lifetimes of approximately 62 years each, there have been about eight hundred such lifetimes. Six hundred and fifty of those were spent in caves.

Only in the last seventy has it been possible to communicate securely from one lifetime to the next by means of writing. Only during the last six lifetimes did substantial numbers of people see a printed word. In the lifetime before this, universal compulsory education was introduced into Britain: Lord Northcliffe bought the *Daily Mail* and a new era of popular journalism was born. Most modern means of communication were developed during that same lifetime.

The first 'electric theatre' was opened as part of a tented circus in Los Angeles in 1902. The first cinema in London dates from 1905. Marconi transmitted the first wireless signal from Cornwall to Newfoundland in 1901 but almost twenty years elapsed before any public broadcasts were made. A hand-cranked foil cylinder phonograph – the forerunner of the present record player – was first developed towards the end of the last century. The telephone was patented in 1876.

Only in the present, the 800th lifetime, was the first practical demonstration of television made by John Logie Baird in 1926.

PROBLEM AND OPPORTUNITY

The pace of change has taken the Church by surprise. Within a single lifetime an old order has died and a new world has been born. It is growing up to a large extent without God and without the Gospel. The Church, already for centuries on the defensive, had lost ground in the Industrial Revolution and finds it hard now to mount an effective pastoral response in the new Information Age.

British society today largely ignores the mainstream Churches. Catholics constitute the largest body of regular worshippers, but less than one person in ten goes to any Church on Sunday. The vast majority of our fellow-citizens no longer worship in any church. But this does not spell the death of religion. The human spirit remains restless and there are echoes of God in unexpected places. Here is a problem and an opportunity. The Church can still satisfy some of the hunger for God if it learns the language of contemporary society and speaks to present needs. If people today are not in church, they still read newspapers, visit cinemas and theatres, listen to radio and watch television. Mass media are the nervous system of modern society. They are the means by which we speak and listen to each other. They bring us images of the world around us. The Christian has to take part in this ceaseless conversation.

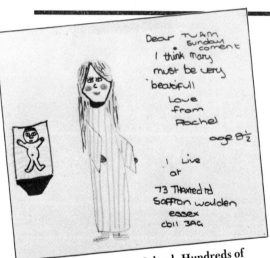

A new type of Sunday School. Hundreds of children each week send their drawings in to TVAM.

Batman captured at last. Millions worldwide watch the exploits of the fantasy superman on his daring missions.

POTENTIAL FOR GOOD

Many people criticise mass media. They allege sensationalism, distortion, bias, over-emphasis on sex and violence. There is lively controversy over whether media reflect society or intensify its corruption. Much discussion ignores or takes for granted the immense enrichment that the media bring to our lives.

Never in history has such richness and diversity been available to every household in the country and so cheaply. Radio and the printed word combine with television to bring into our homes the greatest works of human genius and the current picture of the world.

Obviously there are silly, pernicious and brutalising programmes as well. Some of the tabloid newspapers in Britain rank among the most trivial and nasty in the world. The media can harm as well as help. We can be exposed to unhealthy and corrupting influences. There is constant need for discrimination on the part of the audience and reader and for a positive response to producers of programmes and editors of newspapers. Passive silence signifies assent.

MASS MEDIA AND THE CATHOLIC CHURCH

The Second Vatican Council is confident and enthusiastic about what the mass media can do for the world. In its document on social communications, it says that the media are there for the good of everyone helping to bring people closer together and to understand each other by sharing knowledge and fears. They are seen to offer a 'great round table' for humanity and 'like salt and light add savour to the world'.

The mass media are also presented as crucial to carrying out Christ's command to teach all nations. If the Church fails to use the media in this way she is accused of refusing to obey God and of 'burying the talent' given by Him.

The media has a threefold role – helping the Church reveal herself to the world, encouraging dialogue in the Church and making current opinion clear to members of the Church. In many cases the media are the only communication between the Church and the world. In England, for example, where so few go to church, the only time the majority of people can be in contact with religious teaching or news is through radio, television or newspapers. The media can also help Catholics to have a stronger experience of belonging to the universal Church.

How, for instance, do Catholics, even those who do attend church, know what the Pope is saying? It is mostly through Catholic newspapers. As the Pope travels more and more and as, partly because of this, interest increases in Catholic affairs, the national press, radio and television also report the Pope's words though not always without bias or omission.

One of the greatest and most widely seen communications of forgiveness was surely the photograph of Pope John Paul II sitting closely and looking with compassion on the man who had tried to kill him.

Looking at other possibilities for good offered by the media the Council suggests they could help overcome illiteracy, spread art and culture, further equality and help people to relax by 'lightening burdens and filling leisure'.

Among the very few negative comments that the Council makes is a warning that viewers, listeners and readers should be discriminating about the media and not allow it to waste time or damage their faith or dignity. Parents are reminded of their responsibility to keep dangerous material out of their homes and priests are asked to help people to make the best use of the media.

Clergy or lay people taking part in programmes must do so professionally and well because people have become used to high standards.

Most programmes and articles contain a message whether the recipients realise it or not. They are often created with a motive. So many values and standards are constantly being preached. Objective programmes or articles do not exist. The camera, tape recorder or typewriter is in the hands of one person. They only reveal as much as they decide, and this is not always the whole truth.

When Pope John Paul went to Poland for the first time in 1980 he celebrated Mass with some two million people at Auschwitz. Polish television cameramen were instructed to keep their cameras on a small side entrance to the camp which only relatively few people were using.

Information and freedom of opinion are important for the running of society but as the Second Vatican Council points out this must be 'true and complete', not always easy when even the most responsible reporters involved have so little time to discover what has happened and to assess it.

The Catholic press is seen by the Council to have a particularly important role to play in uniting the Catholic community. Members of the Church are invited to read Catholic papers and Catholic publications in order to be informed, and grow in their faith and discernment. Catholic publications are urged to be a 'glass reflecting the world and a light to show it the way'.

Those working in all branches of the media are judged by the Council to have a great responsibility and be able 'to drive man along a good or evil path'.

Where today are we allowing the media to take us?

QUESTIONS
What can Christians contribute to public entertainment and the media?
How could we use these to present Gospel values?
What difficulties do you envisage?
Is censorship an answer?

PRAYER
Lord God, may we effectively use all the means of social communication. May standards improve in the media to present – not perversion and evil – but good and enlightenment to all your people, through Jesus Christ Our Lord. Amen.

LIGHT FROM THE WORD
'WHAT YOU HEAR IN WHISPERS, PROCLAIM FROM THE HOUSETOPS' (*Matt 10:27*). Jesus told his disciples many things in secret, because only his close followers could understand them. But, after his resurrection, and especially during these times of mass media communication, it is the Christian's vocation to share with everyone our relationship with God, which is in many aspects secret and mysterious.

Go forth, Christian soul. A 'Requiem' Mass, the celebration of the Eucharist for the eternal rest of one who has died.

44-Life and Death

**All human beings have a fundamental right to life.
Taking innocent human life directly is always wrong.
That is why the Church condemns abortion and the direct killing of
the elderly, the dying and the handicapped.**

THE HIPPOCRATIC OATH was drawn up probably in the 5th century BC in Greece. It was affirmed by each doctor on entry to the medical profession. In 1947 the newly-formed World Medical Association produced a modern restatement. In medical schools today the affirmation of the oath is a matter of local custom.

Part of the 5th century oath reads: 'I will follow that system or regimen which, according to my ability and judgement, I consider for the benefit of my patients, and abstain from whatever is deleterious and mischievous. I will give no deadly medicine to anyone if asked, nor suggest any such counsel; and in like manner I will not give to a woman a pessary to produce abortion.

With purity and with holiness I will pass my life and practise my art. Into whatever house I enter, I will go into them for the benefit of the sick, and will abstain from every voluntary act of mischief and corruption; and, further, from the seduction of females or males, of freemen or slaves. Whatever, in connection with my professional practice, or not in connection with it, I see or hear, in the life of men, which ought not to be spoken of abroad, I will not divulge, as reckoning that all such should be kept secret. While I continue to keep this oath unviolated, may it be granted to me to enjoy life and the practice of the art, respected by all men, in all times. But should I trespass and violate this Oath, may the reverse be my lot.'

VOICE OF THE PEOPLE

Some years ago I took my elderly father to see his first great-grandson two days after he had been born. Dad was absolutely fascinated by all the perfect details of the baby – his fingers and toes, his eyes and nose, his ears and nails. He sat speechless, enjoying the sight of a new-born baby.

Some years later I went to Lourdes as chaplain. The two outstanding members of the party were Tom and Susan, both 19, both suffering from cerebral palsy. Neither was able to do anything for themselves.

They were the life and soul of the pilgrimage. The helpers vied with each other to care for them. They told me that they had not come to Lourdes to be cured. They wanted to help other people to understand that disabled people have real emotions and feelings and expectations. They had a splendid 'quality of life' – though different from other people.

Recently I was present at the deathbed of an 80-year-old lady. Around her were her daughter, the Sisters and staff who looked after her in the home, some of her fellow residents, the doctor and myself. As her daughter leaned over to kiss her, and I gave her a final blessing, she died in great tranquillity, to go and meet her Maker.

These experiences have taught me much about the sanctity of life and the need to respect people at all stages in their lives and whatever their condition.

Sadly in this country and other modern civilised nations there has been a sudden and serious decrease in respect for life.

PRINCIPLES

The Church has always taught that the taking of innocent human life directly is wrong, based upon the commandment 'Thou shalt not kill'.

Traditionally, the church has accepted the principle of self-defence and of the 'just war' (see Ch. 41) on the basis that we are able to defend our own life, even at the cost of the life of someone else who is attacking us. Some moral theologians have also argued that the state has the right to put criminals to death, e.g. for the crime of murder. But the taking of innocent human life has always been held to be absolutely wrong.

It is because human beings are made 'in the image of God', that the absolute right to life exists. Traditionally animals have not been seen as having the same rights, because they are not fully human; but, in recent years, the consciences of human beings have been more and more exercised about 'animal rights', and at least the principle of the love of God's creatures should make cruelty to animals repugnant.

The Church, and medical authorities until recent years, have taught that life begins at conception with the fertilisation of the ovum by the sperm. This is now being seriously questioned to meet the demands of experimental scientists. Nevertheless Robert Edwards and Patrick Steptoe, pioneers in test-tube baby techniques, agree with this traditional teaching when they say 'the conceptus even in the pre-implantation stage is a microscopic human being – one in its very earliest stages of development' (A Mother of Life, 1981).

For this reason, the Church teaches that the abortion of an unborn foetus is always wrong.

SUICIDE

If direct killing of the innocent is always gravely wrong, as we have already argued, then it follows that to kill oneself is wrong. Throughout 'Faith Alive' we have emphasised that the commandment 'Love your neighbour as yourself' implies what is often forgotten, namely that we must love ourselves as well as our neighbour. To take our own life is

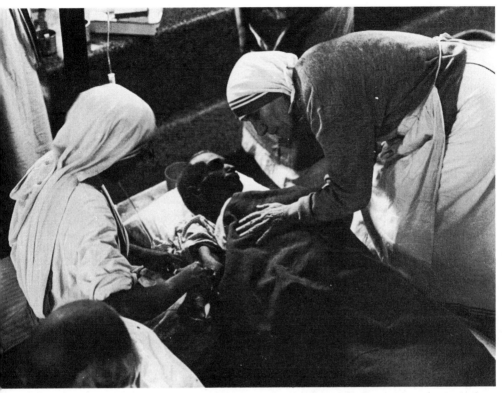

**Our most vulnerable moment is when we are dying.
May we have all the spiritual help we need.**

the ultimate act of hating ourselves, of saying 'no' to the existence that God our loving heavenly Father has given us.

Of course, we all realise that a person who commits suicide is very often in a state of unbearable depression and despair. Over the centuries, the Church has modified her discipline regarding the burial of those who have taken their own life. In the Middle Ages, Christian burial was forbidden for suicides; but in the Catholic Church today, this is never refused, on the principle that the poor person was not fully responsible for his or her terrible act.

A story goes about a famous priest, the Curé d'Ars, who was hearing a confession from a mother who was distraught about her son who had just committed suicide by throwing himself from a bridge into a river. 'Do not worry, my dear', said the holy man, 'Your son

repented between the bridge and the river'.

Although we have every sympathy for those who are driven to commit suicide, it is quite untrue to imagine that nothing can be done to help a person who is tempted to this terrible act. Worldwide organisations of volunteers such as the Samaritans, who answer calls from those in despair, testify to the possibility of instilling hope in those who have come to imagine that their life is no longer of any worth.

The best antidote for a person who is tempted to suicide is Christian faith and hope. In the midst of despair, when life seems meaningless, a Christian can see his or her life as of infinite worth. 'You are of much more value than many sparrows', said Jesus. Christ loved each one of us so much that he died in agony for us saying, 'Father, into your hands I commend my spirit'). A person who believes this, and thus believes that God has a plan for each and every one of us, can never think finally that life is worthless. And, when tempted to despair, will go to confession to find help from the Church, will go to the doctor to find specialist help in the medical and psychological field, and will find befrienders such as the Samaritans.

But why should we not take the apparently easy way out of our troubles? After all, do not Christians believe that the next life will be much better than the present valley of sorrows? This is where the Christian doctrine of the Lordship of God over our lives is important. God is the author of life, and God determines when that life is taken away. This thought is relevant when we consider what is called 'euthanasia'. Suicide is the ultimate way of burying our talent, since our life is the greatest gift of all to us from God.

Euthanasia

Euthanasia (Greek for 'easy death') is closely related to the problem of suicide, because very often the argument is heard that a person who wishes to die, because of age, or great suffering, or from handicap, should be allowed to have that wish fulfilled, by being painlessly killed. In such a case, therefore, a person would be committing suicide by means of a medical agent such as a doctor.

The same moral argument applies as with suicide, whether indeed such 'mercy killing' is with the full consent of the patient, or (as no doubt would often be the case in practice) by means of a little helpful persuasion from relatives or professional consultants. The Christian view is clear, that God is the author of life, and God likewise determines when and under what circumstances our life on this earth is to be terminated.

The question again arises as to the value of life. It is often argued that a terminally ill patient, or one who is old and incontinent, has no longer any reason for living. The growth in the lobby for euthanasia arises not only from the technology explosion, with methods of death being so much more efficient. It arises from a false belief that life can somehow be judged in terms of its quality; and, if that quality is not apparent, then we human beings have the right to terminate it.

The Christian answer is that life cannot be quantified, or be subject to quality control, because we are made in God's image. As human beings, by virtue of our creation, we have a share in the infinite God, whether we are rich or poor, successful or failures, healthy or handicapped. A terminally ill patient in these terms has just as much right, and indeed duty, to live as long as God wills, as does the doctor treating the patient, or the relatives.

St Paul told the Galatians, 'Let us never slacken in doing good; for if we do not give up, we shall have our harvest in due time' (Gal 6:9). This applies again to everyone, to the apparently useless and rejected in our society too. The 'harvest' of our lives is not how much money we make, or how much impact we make on society, but rather the harvest of good deeds. Those nursing the terminally ill testify to how they themselves are helped by the very people they are nursing. Parents of handicapped children testify that they draw closer to God through sharing in the life of one who needs them utterly.

Again, the Church rejects 'mercy killing' for what it is, a crime against humanity. But this does not mean that doctors must strive to preserve life at all costs. To allow a person to die with dignity is not only allowed morally, but may sometimes be the only moral decision. 'Extraordinary means' of preserving life such as life-support systems, and complicated and painful operations which do not have any real hope of restoring to health, may, and sometimes should, be dispensed with.

One of the greatest challenges to our society in the last quarter of the

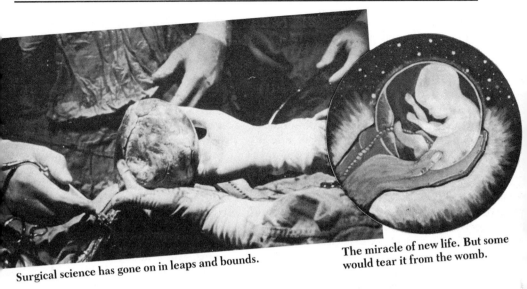

Surgical science has gone on in leaps and bounds.

The miracle of new life. But some would tear it from the womb.

twentieth century is this whole question of 'playing God'. And one important part of a Christian vocation is to testify to the value of human life in these agonising situations.

The Doctor's Dilemma

The vocation of a Catholic doctor or nurse in today's world presents many challenges, even crises of conscience.

Test-tube Babies?

In current medical practice the aim is to try and obtain as many eggs as possible, to fertilise these, and then to select and implant three into the womb. What happens to surplus embryos or abnormal embryos? They are either frozen, experimented upon, or flushed down the sink. Frozen embryos may, or may not, be used at a later date. The whole process is not acceptable.

Dr Anne McLaren, one of the Warnock committee, wrote: 'In a society that tolerates so many thousand abortions per year, and does not offer the abortus baptism or Christian burial, it would seem inconsistent for the pre-14 day human embryo to be given absolute protection'. In truth, experimentation

Non-human life is also a miracle.

on human embryos will be used to develop more effective methods of fertility control including abortion.

None of us has the right to have a child, for children are not material possessions, but gifts from God. We must recognise that infertility causes deep distress, and we should be concerned to alleviate this, but not at any cost.

Abortion is the deliberate killing of the unborn baby or foetus. Abortion is not a question of a woman's rights, or a man's rights, but a question of human rights. Because something is legal does not make it right; abortion is against the natural law of God. The Church respects the sanctity and dignity of every human being irrespective of age, race, colour, creed, weakness or imperfection.

Almost three million abortions have been performed in Britain since abortion was legalised in 1967, and the majority were carried out on fit young women, and the majority of the babies aborted were normal. (6 out of 162,000 abortions in 1983 were performed in an emergency to save the life of, or prevent grave permanent injury to, the mother.) The largest Maternity Hospital in the English-speaking world critically analysed their maternal deaths for 25 years, and found that none of these could have been prevented by aborting the babies. Respect for life is now so eroded in our society that abortion is sometimes demanded where the sex of the child is not what the parents wanted.

We must support any woman with a problem pregnancy, during the pregnancy and afterwards. We must concern ourselves with helping the handicapped to lead as independent a life as possible. We should have compassion for those who have recourse to abortion – they are victims of our selfish society and need help. We must be well informed and speak out when we can.

We are not obliged to use extraordinary methods of keeping handicapped babies alive. However, we are obliged to use ordinary methods of treatment. A newborn child has a right to all normal care, that is feeding, warmth and love. It is not acceptable to starve a child, or to sedate a child so that he or she is unable to feed.

The presence of several abnormalities in one child may produce ethical problems. Sometimes Down's syndrome is associated with other abnormalities of the heart or bowel. A recent law case involved a baby with Down's syndrome and a blockage of the bowel. The initial reaction of the family was to refuse consent for surgery. The local authority took legal responsibility so that surgery could be carried out. The baby was treated successfully and was later reunited with her family.

Modern treatment methods may produce their own problems. Life support machines are used regularly in the case of the newborn. Very occasionally it becomes apparent that there is no hope of a cure and that a child is dependent on the ventilator. At this stage a decision has to be made about the wisdom of continuing with this treatment. Such decisions need to be taken by the parents with the appropriate professional advice.

Neonatal care is changing very fast, the problems involved are changing as well. The staff of neonatal units need to be prepared to deal with ethical problems. They need the support of their chaplains in helping babies and parents during a vital time in the family's life.

A GREAT SHOCK

The birth of an abnormal child comes as a great shock. In a sense the parents are bereaved, they mourn the loss of the perfect child they expected. Not only the child has a handicap but the family will have extra stresses and problems relating to the care of the child.

The community can help these families. Visiting and sharing their stresses is important. Later the parents themselves need a break. Looking after a handicapped child can be very tiring – so what about looking after their child for a night or a weekend? Brothers and sisters too may need an opportunity to go out with their parents without the handicapped child. Here too the caring community can help. The health service can provide the medical care, but this is not enough. The handicapped and the families need acceptance, support and care from the community as well.

The physically or mentally handicapped person has the same rights, duties and aspirations as all of us, but has probably learnt to modify his or her hopes in accordance with limitations.

If we do not accept ourselves as we are and if we are unable to love ourselves as we are and lack self-respect, then we

Death, where is your victory? The beauty in death of a saint,
Bernadette, the girl who saw the visions of the Lady at Lourdes.

will be unable to love and serve others as God commanded. If we feel we are of no use to ourselves and to others then life becomes meaningless. It is too often forgotten that a person must feel worthy of love and respect before he or she can be outgoing.

We are one Mystical Body in Christ. Part of the problem is the attitude of those who are able-bodied towards those with obvious handicap. They may ignore or over-protect the disabled.

Although legalisation and social attitudes have improved, there is still a great feeling of not wanting to be bothered with handicapped people, possibly making the excuse that there is no time or that one does not know what to do. The disabled long to be treated as normal members of the community in the parish, at home and at work, no more and no less.

It is the job of the able-bodied and the handicapped to work together to change attitudes so that all are looked on as Children of God, with something to give and something to receive. As Christians we are rightly exhorted to learn to give but also we must learn to receive, either physical assistance or spiritual example from others.

There is a need for humility but also we should have a rightful pride in what we have achieved. Those who appear to have been given more of God's spiritual, mental or material gifts have a duty to share them with others, especially those who are disadvantaged. But it is together that we need to strive to establish social relationships and enlarge the opportunities for disabled people.

'Mercy killing' implies that someone who is in one's power and does not deserve pity will be killed. The two words cannot go together, it is impossible to have mercy on someone and to kill them, for the only one who benefits is the person who survives.

If we reject the chronic sick by killing them there is no point to medicine because its purpose is the alleviation of suffering by diagnosis and treatment.

Mankind can kill but cannot give life. That we leave to God. Physicians try their best to alleviate suffering and prevent death.

When death is inevitable, drugs may be used to control pain which, in some cases, as a secondary effect, may accelerate death but doctors do not, and never should, accelerate death to relieve suffering.

QUESTION

Think about one or more of the issues outlined in this chapter. How would you face such a problem yourself?

PLACE FOR PRAYER

Make up your own prayer for someone, either doctor, patient, or relative, who has a moral dilemma such as dealt with here.

LIGHT FROM THE COUNCIL

'All offences against life itself, such as murder, genocide, abortion, euthanasia and wilful suicide . . . all these and the like are criminal; they poison civilisation; and they debase the perpetrators more than the victims and militate against the honour of the creator' (Church in the Modern World, para 276). Note that the Council condemns crimes 'against human dignity', such as inhuman living conditions, in the same paragraph. It is no good to defend life while making life not worth living. (See Chapters 3 and 14.)

'From the moment of its conception, life must be guarded with the greatest care, while abortion and infanticide are unspeakable crimes' (Church in the Modern World, para 51).

Into the Jaws of Hell. A Mediaeval nightmare.

45-The Final Journey

In death, we experience the frailty of life.
But in Christ, death is a final offering of our life to the Father.

'DYING HE DESTROYED OUR DEATH'

The one certainty in life is that each one of us will die. Throughout the centuries philosophers have sought to give some meaning to the experience of death. The existentialists who emphasised human freedom and a person's right to determine his/her own destiny have shown that death is something specifically human. Even if it is true that plants and animals die, only for men and women is death a conscious experience. For human beings it is not just something which happens at the moment of biological extinction. It is a reality which we face daily.

LIMITED

Death is the horizon which colours every choice we make. It is a constant reminder to us that life is radically limited. All our choices have to be made within this perspective which threatens and undermines the lasting value of all achievements. Perhaps the most painful awareness of this ultimate limit is in our relationships. Every genuine love experience carries with it the dimension of the eternal. And yet even the most beautiful experience of loving another is constantly threatened by the knowledge that death will mean the loss of the beloved.

On the one hand, death is positive. It brings life with all its choices, actions and values to a completion. Death in this sense is the fulfilment of human freedom. Sometimes this completion is revealed in a dramatic way, for example, in laying down one's life for some great value or for another person. Jesus pointed to this dimension when he said, 'Greater love has no man than this, that he lay down his life for his friends' (*John 15:13*).

On the other hand, death represents an insuperable limit. Death means ultimate destruction, something which we cannot escape, which places a great question mark over life and its value.

On the one hand, the scientific reason for death is rather simple. Every finite being is so made that it is destined to perish. This is the law of biological life. But such an answer hardly resolves the deepest questions about death that lie in the human heart: Why must I die? Why am I afraid to die?

REVELATION

For Christians, the answers to these questions are given by God's revelation. The Scriptures assert that the deepest response to these questions lies in the connection between sin and death. The book of Genesis explains how death became the punishment for sin. St Paul takes up this theme in Romans: 'As sin came into the world through one man and death through sin, so death spread to men because of sin' (*Rom 5:12*).

In explaining Paul's ideas, theologians have suggested that he is not thinking primarily of biological death. Even if man had not sinned, he would have died biologically, but this biological death would have been a natural transition to life with God in heaven. But because man sinned, death means being cut off from everything that can fulfil the person.

SORROW AND HOPE

'Belonging to Christ, companionship with him even in death, is the good news for all who search for an answer to the apparent meaninglessness of death.'

Fear of death is the fear of the loss of everything dear. It is ultimately the dread of the loss of God, who is the ultimate source of life and man's only true destiny.

The Christian, however, has another

In death, we share the experience of the One who said 'It is fulfilled' (John 19:30).

story to tell, of God's entrance into the human situation of sin and death. The Old Testament called life beyond the grave Sheol, a shadowy existence in which there was no vitality, no praise of God; the dead were mere dust. Sheol was often described as solitude, aloneness, the pit from which the dead never return to life. The extraordinary Good News of the New Testament is that God's only son entered into this experience of death and Sheol for us. In Gethsemane he knew the dread of death. On the cross he knew our sense of abandonment when he cried out 'My God, my God why have you forsaken me'. Lying in the tomb on Holy Saturday he was a lifeless corpse.

Scripture teaches us that human death as we know it came about because of disobedience, because we human beings wanted to make ourselves God. Jesus reversed this disobedience even to the point of the cross. He was so open to the Father's love that he allowed himself to become a corpse until the Father breathed new life into him in the resurrection.

We Christians cannot avoid death but we do have a story to tell of how God came to us in our death and overcame it from within.

The Gospel tells us that because of Christ's death, we will never more be alone.

CARING FOR THE DYING

A time comes in an advanced progressive and incurable illness when further attempts to cure become inappropriate. The role of those caring for the patient then changes, and continuing care concentrates on ensuring that the remainder of the patient's life is free from physical and mental distress.

The first duty of the doctor and nurses is to gain the patient's confidence and trust by providing appropriate treatment to alleviate physical suffering. This does not include extraordinary or excessive measures which are quite inappropriate for a patient who is dying. It does require medications, therapies and nursing procedures which when correctly applied will relieve physical suffering, while avoiding diminution of mental alertness.

Other causes of suffering must then be considered – social, emotional, spiritual. A dying patient is still a living person and we should help them to 'live' until they die and to use the remaining precious weeks to good purpose.

It is easy for dying patients to become isolated and lonely. They are weak, dependent, vulnerable and in need of that security which can only be demonstrated by love and kindness.

The most valuable thing we can give is our time. This provides them with the opportunity to express their fears and anxieties, and these may well be dispersed by unhurried and repeated conversation. They may have particular worries concerning their families, financial or legal difficulties; emotional or spiritual problems, and these may need the involvement of the appropriate expert, especially the Chaplain.

As the patient's life disintegrates there may be a parallel disintegration of the family. Even before death the anguish of grief will be evident and the total care of the dying includes care of the family with bereavement support. Grief is the price to be paid for loving someone, and there is no short cut through it. It is, however, a particular aspect of suffering for which a firm religious faith will give great solace.

THE HELP OF THE CHURCH

One of the most important prayers of the Church is that pronounced over the Christian at the approach of death:

'*Go forth, Christian soul, from this world,*
in the name of God the almighty Father, who created you,
in the name of Jesus Christ, Son of the living God, who suffered for you,
in the name of the Holy Spirit, who was poured out upon you,
go forth, faithful Christian.
May you live in peace this day,
may your home be with God in Zion,
with Mary, the virgin mother of God,

With Joseph, and all the angels and saints.'

The life of the Christian begins and ends, as does all our public and private prayer, in the name of the Father and of the Son, and of the Holy Spirit. We are baptised in the name of the Blessed Trinity, and commended to God in the same name when our pilgrimage of faith is ended and shadows are about to give way to vision.

The Church exhorts us to pray regularly for the grace of a happy death. Many prayers reflect this aspect of salvation. The last words of the 'Our Father' ('deliver us from evil') and the 'Hail Mary' ('pray for us, sinners, now and at the hour of our death') are a reminder of it. In the liturgical prayer of the Church it is mentioned in Night Prayer ('May the Lord grant us a quiet night and a perfect end'). At Mass, the conclusion of the Penitential Rite prays for the forgiveness of our faults and for perseverance in God's grace: 'May almighty God have mercy on us, forgive us our sins, and lead us to everlasting life. Amen.'

BEREAVEMENT – SHOULD A CHRISTIAN BE SAD?

Sometimes Christians feel guilty if they mourn the loss of a loved one. This is a pity. It is both human and Christian to be sad when we lose someone dear to us, even if we realise that they are in a better place, and free from suffering. The shortest verse in the Bible is 'Jesus wept' (*John 11:35*); when he mourned at the news that Lazarus his friend had died. St Paul does not tell the Thessalonian Christians that they should not 'grieve' over those who have died; but rather that they should not grieve about them, 'like the people who have no hope' (*1 Thess 4:13*).

In the midst of our grief, we have hope. That is the 'Christian difference'.

Beyond specific references and prayers, however, the celebration of the Eucharist is itself our great pledge of eternal life. Already St Ignatius of Antioch at the beginning of the second century referred to the Eucharist as 'the medicine of immortality'; St Thomas Aquinas calls it 'the pledge of future glory'. The link between Eucharist and eternal life is underlined by the obligation on Christians to receive the Eucharist when they are in danger of death. This reception of 'viaticum' (provisions for a journey) 'is the completion and crown of the Christian life on this earth, signifying that the Christian follows the Lord to eternal glory and the banquet of the heavenly kingdom' (Rite of Viaticum).

The minister says, 'Jesus Christ is the food of our journey; he calls us to the heavenly table'. When the dying Christian has received the Body and Blood of the Lord the minister adds: 'May the Lord Jesus Christ protect you and lead you to eternal life. Amen.'

PLACE FOR PRAYER

In facing terminal illness, prayer can be wonderfully helpful. This works both for the dying person and for the relatives and friends. It can bring great strength. In knowledge of the situation, shared through prayer, the approach of death can be faced, recognised and even accepted . . . Instead of empty phrases about 'How well you look today', there can be genuine truthful expression of the real feeling, the real state of affairs.

Sometimes the dying, when they know the prognosis, want to reminisce, share sorrows or regrets, make their peace with everyone, settle outstanding debts.

Through weakness, the dying person may only be able, without speaking, to 'hold the rosary entwined in his fingers following an Our Father or Hail Mary'.

Many hours may be spent at a bedside in a mixture of hope, fear, sorrow, despair. To be able to pray during this time is most supportive when it is not possible to help in any other way, except by sitting and waiting.

Before and after death, before and during the funeral, grief can and should be expressed in prayer, singly or with others. Mingled with this is the hope of resurrection and the need to comfort and be comforted. Finally, bereavement which will come to everyone can be an empty, lonely and often guilt-ridden period. Prayer does not end but eases the pain. It calms, enlightens, deepens faith and trust, and leads to the bereaved person's own resurrection in a new life in the world.

Prayer

'The one whom you love is ill.' (*John 11:3*)
'Father let this chalice pass, but not my will but yours be done.' (*Luke 22:42*)
'Into your hands I commend my spirit.' (*Luke 23:46*)
'I am the resurrection and the life. He that believes in me, though he die, yet he shall live.' (*John 11:25*)

LIGHT FROM THE COUNCIL

'It is in regard to death that the human condition is most shrouded in doubt. People are tormented not only by pain and by the gradual breaking-up of their bodies but also, even more, by the dread of forever ceasing to be. But a deep instinct rightly leads them to shrink from and to reject the utter ruin and total loss of their personalities. Because they bear in themselves the seeds of eternity which cannot be reduced to mere matter, they rebel against death. All the aids made available by technology, however useful they may be, cannot set their anguished minds at rest. They may prolong their lifespan; but this does not satisfy their heartfelt longing, one which can never be stifled, for a life to come.

'While the mind is at a loss before the mystery of death, the Church, taught by divine Revelation, declares that God has created men and women in view of a blessed destiny that lies beyond the limits of their sad state on earth. Moreover, the Christian faith teaches that bodily death, from which humankind would have been immune were it not for sin, will be overcome when that wholeness lost through sin will be restored by the almighty and merciful Saviour. For God has called men and women, and still calls them, to cleave with all their being to him in sharing for ever a life that is divine and free from decay. Christ won this victory when he rose to life, for by his death he freed men and women from death. Faith, therefore, with its solidly based teaching, provides men and women with an answer to their anxious questions about their future lot. At the same time, it makes it possible for them to be united in Christ with their loved ones who have already died, and gives hope that these have found true life with God' (Church in the Modern World, No. 18).

QUESTIONS

1. Gilbert Harding, the famous broadcaster of the 1950s, was asked whether he was afraid of death. 'No, I am a Christian', he replied, 'I am not frightened of death. But I am frightened of dying.' Do you agree with him?
2. How would you try to comfort a friend you knew was dying?

VOICE OF THE PEOPLE

'One of my most moving experiences as a priest was visiting an old lady, whom I had known as a 'regular' at the church where I was curate. I anointed her, and gave her Holy Communion, in preparation for her Final Journey. She knew clearly that she was soon to leave this world to go to the Father. After I had completed all the ceremonies, she took my hand, and drew me down to kiss her. It was a beautiful farewell, full of joy and hope, and yet of human sadness. That memory has been an inspiration to me, and a strengthening of my own faith.'

46-The Other Side

Here we have no lasting city.
We believe in the Resurrection of the body.
We believe in the life everlasting.
We believe that Christ will judge the world.

I BELIEVE IN THE RESURRECTION FROM THE DEAD AND LIFE EVERLASTING

What will heaven be like? The picture of harps and clouds and winged angels, which forms the basis of so many robust jokes, is entirely without foundation in the early documents of the Church and the Scriptures.

One of the sets of imagery which St Paul uses is that of the Roman triumphal procession. In his early First Letter to the Thessalonians he speaks of a final coming of the Lord, when, at a signal given by the trumpet of God, both living and dead will be taken up into the clouds 'to meet the Lord in the air' (1 Thess 4:16–17). This is a little more developed soon afterwards: the procession ends with the presentation of the kingdom by Christ to the Father, when he has abolished every ruling force and power and has made his enemies his footstool (1 Cor 15:23–26).

The same sort of imagery is used in the Synoptic Gospels to sketch Christ's liberation of the Church or of his chosen ones at the Day of the Lord. But what is meant by all this is not easy to say. Another perspective is given by Jesus' statement in John (John 16:33) 'I *have* conquered the world,' and Paul's 'He *has* stripped the sovereignties and the ruling forces and paraded them in public, behind him in his triumphal procession' (Col 2:15).

A different model for the final state of things is given elsewhere in both John and Paul. For John 'eternal life is this: to know you, the only true God, and Jesus Christ whom you have sent' (John 17:3). So eternal life would consist in knowledge, not of intellectual propositions, but of a person (or persons). God has the profoundest and most fascinating and lovable personality that could even be imagined. It is the discovery of this personality which is the unparalleled and indescribable thrill of eternal life.

Paul puts it slightly differently but in the same mould: we are somehow absorbed into the sphere of the divine, taking on the attributes which properly belong only to the Godhead: 'What is sown is perishable but what is raised is glorious; what is sown is weak but what is raised is powerful; what is sown is a natural body and what is raised is a spiritual body' (1 Cor 15:42–44). The risen person takes on the imperishability, the glory and the power which are all primarily properties of God. And these three aspects of the transformation are summed up in the transfer from the natural plane to the spiritual, that of the Spirit of God.

These are no more than hints and pointers, but Paul warns us against attempting to probe too far into this matter: 'Someone may ask: How are dead people raised, and what sort of body do they have when they come? How foolish!' (1 Cor 15:35). The golden thread which shows the way throughout is that Christ is the first fruits of all who have fallen asleep, so that just as in Adam all die, so in Christ all will be brought to life. Whatever the quality of his risen life, it is ours to share.

THE RESURRECTION OF THE BODY

Most people, indeed most civilisations, believe in some kind of shadowy existence after death, the survival of what we

Lest we forget. Making crosses from poppies, the symbol of those who died in the campaigns in Flanders and France during the First World War, 1914–1918.

call the 'soul' or the 'personality'. Spiritualism is still very much alive, even in a scientific age.

But Christian Faith professes much more than simply the survival of the soul after death. First, we believe in the Resurrection of the body, that is of the whole person. The discovery of the empty tomb, and the appearance of the risen Christ to his amazed disciples, is a sign that in Jesus the whole of nature, material and spiritual, will be redeemed.

Second, belief in the Resurrection of the body is a statement that it is not just a question of our rising individually from the dead, but together as the whole human race, in what is called the 'General Resurrection'. Our final salvation will be not only individual, but together in perfect unity with Christ and the whole of the human race united in him. St Paul tells the Thessalonians to 'encourage one another' with this faith (1 Thess 4:18).

On this earth, then, we do not only learn to be related to God, on a one-to-one basis. We learn to be related to each other as human beings; because Christian faith tells us that we will be related to each other in eternity also!

There is a strange consequence of the doctrine of the General Resurrection: that is, a period of what Paul calls 'falling asleep' in the Lord before the final event of history, when we shall rise together body and soul. If we die before Christ returns, we wait for him to come. In that condition, we see God; but it still is a period of waiting before the final fulfilment of the Resurrection.

HEAVEN, HELL AND JUDGEMENT

These are often taboo subjects, even among Christians. The idea that God will in the end act like a judge, and condemn souls to hell fire, seems hardly to be the kind of God anyone of us would want to believe in.

But God does not fit easily into any image we make up for him; even the image of a decent fellow who will always let bygones be bygones in the end.

Heaven, hell and judgement remind us first of all that this existence gives us all desperately important choices. It matters whether we decide to follow Christ or not; and it matters eternally. God said to his people just as they were about to enter the Promised Land, 'Look, today I am offering you life or death, blessing or curse. Choose life, then . . .' (Deut 30:19).

Second, the doctrine of heaven, hell and judgement reminds us that our choice for God is not once and for all. It is a daily decision. And it is not sufficient for us to say that we follow Christ. We must do his will. In the parable of the sheep and the goats (Matt 25:31–46), the 'goats' are sent off to hell because they did not feed the hungry, clothe the naked, and visit the prisoners. They are surprised; just as the 'sheep' are surprised, because in feeding the hungry, they did not realise that they were helping Christ. The King answers, 'in so far as you did this to one of the least of these brothers of mine, you did it to me' (Matt 25:40).

Third, the doctrine of heaven, hell and judgement is a doctrine of hope. We know that no one will go to hell unless, in a sense, they have decided that that is what they want. A person who truly wants to love God and to be with God forever will be given the grace and help to fulfil that best of all desires.

We have considered what heaven is like, and how difficult it is to picture it. Similarly with hell, the Scriptures give us picture language. But the idea of the flames of hell is most likely an image rather than the reality. Hell is basically, and most frighteningly, love lost.

We do not know for sure how many people, if any, will undergo that terrible fate. It is up to us to pray that none will. What we do know, from the Church's teaching, is that many millions have gone and will go to heaven, to rejoice in the eternal vision of God.

'My dear friends, we are already God's children, but what we shall be in the future has not yet been revealed. We are well aware that when he appears we shall be like him, because we shall see him as he really is' (*1 John 3:2*).

PURGATORY

The idea of the holiness of God, however limited, requires that we should be purified before entering His presence.

This is the basis of the Church's doctrine of Purgatory. It is found indirectly in Scripture and developed from the earliest centuries. The Jews prayed for those fallen in battle, in expiation for the idolatrous charms they were wearing (*2 Macc 12:42–46*). Our Lord says that the sin against the Holy Spirit shall not be forgiven 'either in this world or the next' (*Matt 12:32*). St Gregory the Great concludes from this that other sins can be remitted in the world to come. St Paul speaks of the Christian teacher being judged by his fruits 'and though he is saved himself, it will be as one who has gone through fire' (*1 Cor 3:15*).

There is a saying: '*Lex orandi, lex credendi*' (the belief of the Church is rooted in the way the Church prays). So the doctrine of Purgatory was explained in Tradition from the very early practice of praying for the dead, and believing that such prayers could help them. The doctrine became linked to the notion of the treasury of the Church, whose prayer and good deeds assisted the dead as well as the living. And with the recognition that even after forgiveness, sin left traces or scars upon the soul, and that there was need for satisfaction which might not be completed on earth.

There was much speculation about the nature of the 'cleansing fire' of Purgatory, and some understood the imagery in too literal a sense. One of the greatest explanations of the doctrine is the dramatic poem *The Dream of Gerontius*, written by Cardinal Newman and later set to music by Edward Elgar. Gerontius, the old man, dreams he is on his deathbed and in a vision of the tremendous holiness of God he recognises his utter unworthiness and pleads to be purified in Purgatory, which is a state both loving and painful to him, both dreaded and longed for.

INDULGENCES

The first principle of 'indulgences' is that the members of the body of Christ can help each other. From the earliest days of the Church, Christians who were doing public penance for sins committed after baptism were helped by the prayers of the martyrs, and sometimes had their penance reduced by those prayers. By the same token, we can ask other members of the body of Christ, who have run the race of life and won, to help us in our daily struggle.

The second principle of 'indulgences' is that a Christian, after being forgiven by the grace of Christ in baptism, needs daily to be 'sanctified', the process by which that forgiveness is applied in daily growth. 'Indulgence' simply means 'forgiveness', where the life of the whole communion of the saints is made available to us.

We must be careful not to misunderstand indulgences. Pre-Vatican II, people used to speak of '500 days, indulgence', a language which dates back to public penance, where 500 days' public penance might have been given, and then dispensed with by an indulgence. It is fruitless to try to 'quantify' indulgence to this extent. Rather, indulgences are used to realise more fully our communion with the whole body of Christ, living and dead.

CHINESE LEGEND

A Chinese legend tells of a man who dreamed of heaven and hell. In the first dream he found himself in a huge hall where many people were gathered around great tables laden with food. Their problem was that the chopsticks they had been given were so long that it was impossible to use them to lift the

I saw the holy city, the new Jerusalem . . . (Revelation 21:2).

food to their mouths. The people were becoming angry, pushing and fighting in their efforts to reach the food.

In the second dream the man found himself in a hall exactly the same, with tables of steaming hot food. But in this dream each person was using the giant chopsticks to lift the food to the mouth of the person sitting opposite. In this way all were satisfied.

HEAVEN IN OUR MIDST

Christians pass over to the new reality by baptism. 'You have died', Paul says, 'and your life is hidden with Christ in God'. They already *are* in eternal life. It is not merely a question of looking forward to it after death. The decisive transition has taken place. Physical death no longer has the finality it once had. The Christian's true life is not extinguished by it. The continuity between now, when we live by faith and signs, and after death, where we hope to live by

sight and in fullness, is real. We lack adequate means of representing to ourselves what eternal life is like. For this reason we find it vague and unreal. And it is not much help to speculate about it. We simply know that it is a fulfilment and a crowning of all we have striven for and all we have longed for; that no effort of ours towards good is lost, nothing we have loved is forgotten.

We are speaking, in a way, of that 'beyond in our midst' which the liturgy celebrates. In the Mass we pray that we may be kept free from sin and protected from all anxiety 'as we wait in joyful hope for the coming of our Saviour, Jesus Christ'. It is those who 'hunger and thirst for righteousness' who will be filled, those who long passionately for the day when peace and justice will spread throughout the earth.

The liturgy must foster our sense of the discrepancy between the way things are and the way God wants them to be. It must challenge us to live up to its wonderful vision of a life where people give not just a sign but the reality of peace to one another, where all are truly brothers and sisters in Christ, sharing the same bread and cup and becoming one body.

But there is always hope. Liturgy is the action of Christ and the Christian community. Its possibilities are limitless.

Now to him who by the power at work within us is able to do far more abundantly than all that we ask or think, to him be glory in the Church and in Christ Jesus, to all generations, for ever and ever. Amen (*Eph 3:20–21*).

QUESTIONS

1. 'All the way to heaven is heaven and all the way to hell is hell.' What do you understand by this comment of St Catherine of Sienna?
2. What guidelines would you propose for telling children and young people about heaven and hell?
3. 'Some people are afraid to live and others are afraid to die.' What has Christian faith to offer both these groups?
4. 'Then I saw a new heaven and a new earth . . . I saw the holy city and the new Jerusalem coming down from God out of heaven as beautiful as a bride all dressed for her husband' (*Rev 21:1–2*). What does 'Faith Alive' teach you about the meaning of this verse?

THE BOTTOM LINE
ANAKEPHALAIOSASTHAI: to bring together as head.

We end with the longest word in the New Testament, found in one text only, Ephesians 1:9–10. 'God has let us know the mystery of his purpose, according to his good pleasure which he determined beforehand in Christ, for him to act upon when the times had run their course, THAT HE WOULD BRING EVERYTHING TOGETHER UNDER CHRIST, AS HEAD, everything in the heavens and everything on earth.'
Paul had to invent a new Greek word to say what he wanted to say. His great vision was, at the end of time, to see everything 'heading up' in Christ.

CATHOLIC PRAYERS
IN COMMON USE

THE OUR FATHER

Our Father, who art in heaven,
Hallowed be Thy Name,
Thy Kingdom Come,
Thy will be done,
On earth as it is in heaven.
Give us this day our daily bread,
And forgive us our trespasses,
As we forgive those who trespass
against us,
And lead us not into temptation,
But deliver us from evil.

For Thine is the kingdom, and the
power, and the glory, for ever and
ever. Amen.

(This ending is not in the original Prayer taught
by Christ; but it has been added by ancient
tradition, is used by many Christians today, and
is included in the Catholic Vatican II liturgy
almost immediately after the Our Father, as part
of the Communion.

For an explanation of this prayer taught by Our
Lord Jesus Christ himself, see pages 19 and 136
of this book.)

THE HAIL MARY

Hail Mary, full of grace,
The Lord is with Thee,
Blessed art thou among women,
And blessed is the fruit of Thy womb,
Jesus,
Holy Mary, Mother of God,
Pray for us sinners,
Now, and at the hour of our death.
Amen.

(For an explanation of this prayer, see page 144 of
this book.)

THE GLORY BE

Glory be to the Father,
And to the Son,
And to the Holy Spirit,
As it was in the beginning,
Is now and ever shall be,
World without end. Amen.

(For an explanation of this prayer, see page 152 of
this book.)

THE ROSARY

This is an ancient prayer of devotion, using the
repetition of the Our Father, the Hail Mary, and
the Glory Be to the Father, as a means of
meditating on the mysteries of the Gospel. It will
be useful to find a set of Rosary beads, which
serve as a means of counting the prayers, not as a
'vain repetition' which our Lord condemned, but
rather as an aid to concentration; Mary, as it
were, takes us around the 'rose-garden' (hence
Rosary) of the Good News of her Son's life, death,
and Resurrection:

THE JOYFUL MYSTERIES
1. *The Annunciation.*
   (Our Father once, Hail Mary ten times,
   Glory Be once, after each of the fifteen
   mysteries.)
2. *The Visitation.*
3. *The Birth of Christ*
4. *The Presentation*
5. *The Finding in the Temple*

THE SORROWFUL MYSTERIES
1. *The Agony in the Garden*
2. *The Scourging at the Pillar*
3. *The Crowning with Thorns*
4. *The Carrying of the Cross*
5. *The Crucifixion*

THE GLORIOUS MYSTERIES
1. *The Resurrection*
2. *The Ascension*
3. *The Descent of the Spirit*
4. *The Assumption*
5. *The Coronation of Mary*

At the end of the Rosary, we say this prayer:
O God, whose only-begotten Son by his
life, death, and Resurrection, has
purchased for us the rewards of
eternal life. Grant we beseech Thee,
that meditating upon these mysteries
in the Most Holy Rosary of the
Blessed Virgin Mary, we may both
imitate what they contain, and
obtain what they promise. Through
the same Christ our Lord. Amen.

N.B. Before beginning to use this wonderful
meditation, it would perhaps be helpful to find a
priest or lay person who can set you on the road
to praying the Rosary. Many Christians have
found this prayer a great strength, so easy is it to
use, no books being required.

THE ANGELUS

This prayer is said at 6 a.m., 12 midday, and at 6 p.m. by many people, in order to remember the stupendous fact that God became man in Jesus, and that Mary said 'yes' in faith to the Angel (hence 'angelus' in Latin). Perhaps you might begin by just reciting it each midday:

The angel of the Lord declared unto Mary:
And she conceived by the Holy Spirit.
Hail Mary, etc. . . . .

Behold the handmaid of the Lord.
Be it done unto me according to Thy Word.
Hail Mary, etc.

And the Word was made flesh,
And dwelt among us.
Hail Mary, etc.

Pray for us, O holy mother of God;
That we may be made worthy of the promises of Christ.

Pour forth, we beseech Thee O Lord, Thy grace into our hearts; that we to whom the Incarnation of Christ Thy Son was made known by the message of an angel, may by his Passion and Cross be brought to the glory of his Resurrection. Through the same Christ our Lord. Amen.

There are many other Catholic prayers, some of which you will find in Faith Alive, and some you will find as you look through various prayer books. But the above represent the 'basics'.

THE CREED

(For the theology underlining the Creed, see especially page 80.)

We believe in One God the Father Almighty
Maker of Heaven and Earth,
of all that is, seen and unseen.

We believe in one Lord, Jesus Christ,
the only Son of God,
eternally begotten of the Father,
God from God, Light from Light,
true God from true God,

begotten, not made,
of one Being with the Father.
Through him all things were made.

For us men and for our salvation
he came down from heaven:
by the power of the Holy Spirit
he became incarnate from the Virgin Mary, and was made man.
For our sake he was crucified under Pontius Pilate;
he suffered death and was buried.

On the third day he rose again
in accordance with the Scriptures;
he ascended into heaven
and is seated at the right hand of the Father.
He will come again in glory to judge the living and the dead,
and his kingdom will have no end.

We believe in the Holy Spirit, the Lord, the giver of life,
who proceeds from the Father and the Son.
With the Father and the Son he is worshipped and glorified.
He has spoken through the Prophets.
We believe in one holy catholic and apostolic Church.
We acknowledge one baptism for the forgiveness of sins.
We look for the resurrection of the dead,
and the life of the world to come.
Amen.

(The above is the Nicene Creed, expressing the faith of the Council of Nicea, cf. page 22. The translation is that in current use in the Catholic liturgy in England, Wales, Scotland, Ireland, and South Africa.)

PRAYER FOR THOSE WHO HAVE DIED

Eternal rest grant to (him, her, them), O Lord.
And let perpetual light shine upon (him, her, them).
May (he, she, they) rest in peace.
Amen.

APPENDIX

THE RITE OF CHRISTIAN INITIATION OF ADULTS (RCIA)

The schema for this book 'Faith Alive' is based upon the process of the instruction and initiation of those who wish to become members of the church.

The Vatican (the central organisation of the Catholic Church in Rome) has recently issued a new Rite of Christian Initiation of Adults (English official edition published by Chapman, 1987), which revives the ancient practice of the formation of initiates by stages.

STAGE ONE; EVANGELISATION
(FAITH ALIVE, chaps 1–6)

At this stage, the person wishing to become a member of the church makes preliminary enquiries as to whether he or she accepts the Good News of Christ. When the enquirer is able to make an act of faith in the Gospel, the service of Enrollment takes place, and the period of formal instruction commences.

STAGE TWO; THE CATECHUMENATE
(FAITH ALIVE, chaps 7–36)

At this stage, the new 'catechumen', the person now committed to learning about life in the church, is introduced into doctrine, morals, spirituality, and above all into the community life of God's people, as a preparation for full initiation. At a suitable time, the candidate is 'elected', and a final period of spiritual preparation ends with the wonderful liturgy of baptism and welcoming into full communion by receiving the Body and Blood of Christ in the Eucharist.

STAGE THREE; POST-BAPTISMAL CATECHESIS
(FAITH ALIVE, chaps 37–46)

The Church does not wish the learning process begun during the catechumenate to finish after the candidate is made a full member of the church. In fact, in the early days of the church, it was only after initiation that the central mysteries of the Christian faith were disclosed to the candidate, these doctrines being kept secret from all those except full members of the church. That is why this period is sometimes called 'mystogogical catechesis', because it was instruction about mysteries undisclosed to unbelievers. In Faith Alive, however, we have simply used this period of post-baptismal catechesis in order to reflect more about the mission and ministry of the church, and the Christian's role in it.

N.B. For teachers, catechists, and group leaders, it will be most useful to look more closely at the RCIA, in order to relate the material in 'Faith Alive' to the whole process of Christian Initiation.

CONTRIBUTORS

In most chapters of 'Faith Alive' there are contributions from Fr Austin Flannery ('Light from the Council') and Fr Michael Hollings (Prayer sections).

Other contributors are:
Fr Ninian Arbuckle OFM (chapter 8)
Wendy Mary Beckett (chapter 25)
Sir John Betjemen (chapter 16)
Fr Steve Bevan SVD (chapter 17)
Rabbi Lionel Blue (chapter 15)
Sr Cecily Boulding (chapters 6, 21, 23)
Fr Frederick Broomfield (chapter 36)
Prof F. F. Bruce (chapter 17)
Bishop George Cary (chapter 20)
Dennis Chiles (chapter 41)
Fr Tony Churchill (chapter 12)
Dr Francis Clark (chapters 16, 28, 39)
Fr Hubert Condron (chapter 33)
Mgr Michael Connelly (chapter 44)
Dr John Coulson (chapter 23)
Tom Coyle (chapter 28)
Fr Gabriel Daly OSA (chapter 22)
Fr Robin Duckworth (chapter 31)
Michael Emms (chapter 42)
Dr Rachel Evans (chapter 44)
Fr Sean Fagan SM (chapter 13)
Br Daniel Faivre (chapter 39)
Fr W. Fearon (chapter 40)
Julian Filochowski CAFOD (chapter 14)
Dr Anna Flynn (chapter 32)
Dr John Goodwill (chapter 44)
Dr James Hanratty (chapter 45)
John Harriot (chapter 40)
James Hastings (chapter 18)
Sr Martina Hayden OP (chapter 35)
Sr Perpetua Healy (chapter 10)
Peter Hebblethwaite (chapter 23)
Dr Ian Jessiman (chapter 32)
Mgr James Joyce (chapter 24)
Fr Ignatius Kelly (chapter 26)

Mr John Kelly FRCOG (chapter 44)
Fr Dermot Lane (chapter 3)
Fr Tom Lane CM (chapter 21)
Fr Rene Laurentin (chapter 18)
Mgr George Leonard (chapter 3)
Br Damien Lundy (chapter 2)
Rabbi Magonet (chapter 8)
Fr Thomas Marsh (chapter 16)
Fr Edward Matthews (chapters 8, 29)
Dr Enda McDonagh DD (chapter 12)
Fr James McManus CSsR (chapter 16)
Prof Peter Millard (chapter 44)
Canon Edward Mitchison (chapter 29)
Mgr Martin Molyneux (chapter 15)
Bishop Donal Murray (chapter 11)
Gertrude Mueller Nelson (chapter 10)
Gloria and Laurie Nobbs (chapter 30)
Fr Gerald O'Collins SJ (chapter 20)
Fr Sean O'Collins (chapters 4, 32, 37)
Bishop C. Murphy O'Connor (chapter 37)
Fr Christopher O'Donnell (chapter 32)
Fr Paul O'Leary (chapter 11)
Fr John O'Toole (chapter 16)
Fr Robert Ombres OP (chapter 14)
Vicky and Sandra Pajak (chapter 30)
Sr Maria Parcher (chapter 13)
Fr Michael Prior (chapters 15, 19)
Fr Pius Smart OFMCAP (chapter 29)
Fr Michael Smith (chapters 17, 23)
Mgr Peter Smith (chapter 30)
Rabbi Norman Solomon (chapter 38)
Cardinal Suenens (chapter 6)
Bishop Frank Thomas (chapter 27)
Fr Hugh Thwaites (chapter 19)
Fr Simon Tugwell (chapter 19)
Fr Henry Wansborough (chapters 5, 9, 20, 25, 30, 32, 34)
Archbishop D. Warlock (chapter 37)
Anne White (chapter 12)
Fr David Williamson (chapter 11)
Fr Edward Yarnold SJ (chapter 36)

Picture Credits

Barnaby's Picture Library
Pages 3, 4, 14 left, 55, 57, 58, 68, 69, 71, 73, 75, 79, 82, 104 left, 104 right, 105, 112, 117, 122, 134, 149, 150, 154/155, 167, 175, 180, 185, 207, 215, 216, 218, 224 top, 228 right, 232, 236, 239, 259.

The Bodleian Library
Pages 54, 253, 262

Carlos Reyes
Pages 2, 8, 9, 12 left, 12 right, 13 top left, 14 top right, 14 bottom right, 19, 61, 62, 65, 85, 147, 160, 165, 169, 174, 177, 183, 203, 221, 245, 249 top right.

Sonia Halliday Photographs
Pages 18, 22, 37, 41, 48/49, 76, 88 left, 88 right, 90, 93, 130, 188/189, 224 bottom, 233, 249 top left, 249 bottom, 254.

The Universe
Pages 7, 11, 15, 24, 26, 33 top, 33 bottom, 42, 47, 80, 96 bottom, 98, 108, 110, 119, 123, 126, 129, 137, 144, 156, 157, 199, 201, 205, 209, 219, 228 left, 237, 247.

The Keystone Collection
Pages 113, 139, 195, 196 bottom, 197, 213, 231.

Associated Press
Pages 14 centre right, 161, 190.

TVAM
Pages 241, 242 left, 242 right.

CIRIC
Pages 13 bottom left, 13 right, 135.

St Paul's Cathedral
Page 21

Kathleen Fedouloff
Page 31

Century Hutchinson
Pages 39, 40

John Rylands Library
Page 50

The National Gallery
Page 52

Society of St Vincent de Paul
Page 67

McCrimmon Publishing
Pages 89, 164

Camera Press
Page 96 top

Penguin Publications
Page 109

Burns and Oates
Page 120

Clip Art
Page 131

Catholic Truth Society
Page 132

Geoffry Chapman
Page 148

Topix
Page 172

Tate Gallery
Page 196 top

Collins
Page 210

INDEX OF GENERAL SUBJECTS